My Life in Pieces saturates the reader with hope and provides a roadmap of healing through the shadow of death. The author brilliantly articulates Alice's journey from hell into a triumphant explosion of victory. Monsters are real, but LOVE is stronger. Must-read for counselors, therapists, and anyone unraveling Dissociative Identity Disorder (DID). As a therapist, I have read a lot of DID. material, but none that weaves the pieces of dissociation and healing together like this!

Amybeth Levie Berner, MA, LPC

You are about to embark on a journey that will take you deep into a place of darkness, the darkness that seeps from the hearts of evil men. I was sitting on the edge of my seat rooting for Alice, a young girl faced with unspeakable terror and abuse at the hands of her own father. My heart pounded with fear and anguish for the child whose innocence was shattered at such an early age. Yet through the trauma, she had hope, faith, and courage to stand strong and survive. I was captivated by the eerily accurate details of satanic rituals and abuse. The account of Alice's life though fictionalized, is so accurate in detail and emotion that I felt as if I were going through her tragedies and triumphs with her. This is a must-read book for anyone who wants to open their minds to the truth of things that go on in the darkness, and the power and resilience of the human spirit that stands strong with faith in God.

Susan M., Ritual Abuse Survivor

I read *My Life in Pieces* in one sitting hoping the cost of Alice breaking her silence would result in freedom and wholeness. Her journey is a powerful testimonial that a life shattered in the most inconceivable and depraved manner can be transformed and restored through faith in God. I picture her perseverance to uniquely restore her traumatic fragments as a collage of grace. Alice's courage reminded me, a therapist, of the sacredness and power of listening and bearing witness to someone's darkest moments through compassionate, daring faith.

L. Ruiz, LAC

As I began the journey of reading through *My Life in Pieces*, I wasn't sure what to expect. The invitation to hear Alice's story captured my attention and interest immediately. The depths at which trauma can affect a human being isn't often articulated well. However, *My Life in Pieces* has beautifully captured the rippling effect our histories can have on our present. The author captures and expresses Alice's story of both exceptional devastation and revitalization in the most masterful way. I found myself unable to stop reading this inspiring story of triumph. As a counselor, I often find myself disappointed by the description of Dissociative Identity Disorder (DID) in television, movies, and reading material. However, the description of Alice's mind being fragmented into several pieces, but each piece still being Alice, gave me great hope that some who need it will pick up and read *My Life in Pieces* and better gain an understanding of DID.

Ian Thomas Douglas, MS, PLPC

Thank you so much for writing this book and for telling Alice's story. I thought I was reading my own life story. It amazes me that Alice and I grew up near one another. As a survivor of Satanic Ritual Abuse (SRA) I could relate to her experiences at the hands of such evil people but the thing I related to the most is the freedom Alice found in Christ. After many years of pastoral ministry, and then as the wife of a district superintendent of our denomination, it was my privilege to lead ministries to the pastor's wives of our state. At the same time, there were many years of counseling with two Spirit-filled counselors to unwind the programing and devastation that SRA brought to my life and that of my family. It was worth every step of the journey with my Lord and Savior. It is my prayer that this book will encourage others like Alice and me to seek out help, and most of all, to come into a relationship with the One who will set them free, the One who makes all things new. His name is Jesus.

Mary Ann Colletti, Satanic Ritual Abuse Survivor

As a psychiatrist of over 35 years, I am thrilled that this book uses the true story of Alice to convey four profound truths that every person must consider very seriously.

First, we are all sinners in a fallen world, but we can also be sinned against. Alice suffered much sexual abuse by her father and by the satanic cult.

Second, there are no quick fixes to mental illness and trauma. It takes time, patience, and perseverance. God gives His grace one day at a time like the manna that fell from heaven in Exodus.

Third, no one can go on this journey alone. God, a loving God, is omnipotent, sovereign, and in control. He provided Himself and His grace to Alice. He also provided skilled and empathetic professionals for Alice, along with loving friends, and His Church. God gave His grace both to the Christian and non-Christian helpers in order for her to heal. I could easily identify with Alice and all her helpers. They all needed God's hope, not wishful thinking, to sustain them. Working with broken people over many years, I have certainly needed this hope. When I felt tired, frustrated, or even hopeless, God's love was deeper than my flesh and gave me hope to persevere.

Fourth, God was the loving force that guided Alice through her journey. God's love was deeper than the horrible deep pit in which she found herself. In Isaiah 60:22b NLT, the Lord promises, *"At the right time, I, the LORD, will make it happen."* God became Alice's rock, giving her hope as she struggled.

For all these reasons, *I highly recommend this book.* I pray that each reader is deeply touched by Alice's story.

Cheryl L. Sanfaçon, M.D.
Board Certified Psychiatrist,
American Board of Psychiatry and Neurology

I have studied many books on trauma. This journey into the life of Alice is extraordinary. It offers incredible insight to the contribution of therapy, spiritual formation, and devoted Godly friendships. Somehow the author has brought these elements together in a book that caused me to laugh, cry, rejoice, and mourn in every chapter. I could not put it down until I knew the story of this incredibly strong, beautiful person named Alice. I recommend this book to therapists, friends of those who are hurting, and everyone on a journey of discovering their true identity.

Dr. Robb Horner
Christian Psychologist

Alice's story is gripping, horrific, tragic, and triumphant. CJ Schaeffer transforms Alice from victim to victor in a passionate, poignant, and sensitive telling. She "tells it like it is," but her style is articulate, compassionate, and understanding, as only a caring friend would express it. Schaeffer's vivid description of abuse brings you inside the awful behavior of the monster who dominates the early chapters. Readers will share the profound ugliness of sin and the soaring freedom of God's grace and deliverance as they journey through Alice's challenges and accomplishments. This message of sin and forgiveness offers hope for all through Christ. Anyone who has ever traveled the roads of pain and problems will benefit from *My Life in Pieces*.

John Bernstein, Retired Pastor
Military Chaplain and Professional Book Reviewer

A modern-day Mary Magdalene, Alice fights a daily battle against multiple personalities and past trauma. Her story is told with blunt honesty, ends with triumph in Christ, and offers hope to all who suffer from similar childhood abuse and brokenness.

Emily Parke Chase, Counselor, MA;
Author of *Help! My Family's Messed Up!* (Kregel)
and *Standing Tall After Falling Short* (Moody)

As I read *My Life in Pieces*, I was thoroughly captivated by Alice's cutting-edge story. Her journey evoked multiple emotions: heaviness, sorrow, anger, joy, despair, hope, and freedom. I cheered for Alice as she continued to persevere and push through the depths of pain and fear. There were other moments of Alice's journey where I desired to personally rescue her from the Monster!

The author's expressive writing style created "word pictures" where I found myself beside Alice during her darkest times, her tender and joyful ones, as well as her powerful victories. Alice's journey is a tremendous tool for learning about DID and the types of trauma that cause this misunderstood disorder.

CJ Schaeffer threaded the beauty of spiritual truths that were a vital component to Alice's survival throughout her journey. The author eloquently wove various styles of therapy, counseling tools, and "messengers" revealing God's truth and character, which created the tapestry of healing and wholeness.

I knew Alice. *My Life in Pieces* captures her legacy of releasing healing, hope, freedom, salvation, and redemption to benefit anyone needing change and transformation.

Pam Reynolds, Children's Ministry Director, Intercessor

My Life in Pieces is a moving story of strength and courage. Alice's journey from unimaginable abuse to breakthrough and healing will greatly inspire you. As Alice moves from fear to faith, you will be encouraged to greater levels of hope. The pages follow her life through stages of self-revelation and faith in a God who is present. He brings the pieces of a broken life together which leads to true freedom despite the most unimaginable obstacles life can bring. This is a powerful read for anyone who needs to know that there is hope for the hopeless and God will make a way where there seems to be no way.

Rev. Carol Ball, Women's Ministries Director
Elim Fellowship, Lima, NY

None of us want to believe that such a dark, twisted world could exist for a young child. A world so torturous that the only way to survive will fragment him/her to their very core. CJ Schaeffer depicts such a world in a way that highlights the resiliency of the human mind to protect itself from being overwhelmed.

My Life in Pieces will help victims of such atrocities hold on just a little longer while giving them a voice to express their pain. It will bolster any reader's spirits, lend hope and strength to the weary, and supply a sense of peace and joy to the downtrodden. As a counselor/Life Coach, I am always looking for innovative approaches to help those who have endured trauma live full and healthy lives; this masterpiece will do just that.

Anna Paige Miller, Counselor/Life Coach

One woman's courageous journey...

My Life in PIECES

Shattered by Satanic Ritual Abuse
Splintered by Dissociative Identity Disorder
Redeemed and Restored

by CJ Schaeffer

To Barbara, my dear friend and fellow book lover! You knew Alice. I think you'll be surprised by her truth. Much Love, many Blessings, CJ Schaeffer AKA Connie for His glory ✝

Printed in the United States of America

My Life in Pieces: Shattered by Satanic Ritual Abuse, Splintered by Dissociative Identity Disorder, Redeemed and Restored

By CJ Schaeffer © 2020
www.cj-schaeffer.com

ISBN: 978-0-578-70218-6
Library of Congress Control Number: 2020912898
BIO018000   Biography/Autobiography>Religious

All Rights Reserved. No part of this publication may be reproduced or transmitted in any form without the written permission of the author.

Mimi Liberta, Cover Design
Kathryn Ross, Editor

Unless otherwise noted, all Scripture is taken from THE HOLY BIBLE NEW INTERNATIONAL VERSION®, NIV® Copyright © 1973, 1978, 1984, by International Bible Society. Used by permission of Zondervan. All rights reserved. New International Version®, NIV® Copyright © 1973, 1978, 1984, 2011 by Biblica.

Additional Scripture as noted is taken from the New King James Version®. Copyright © 1982 by Thomas Nelson. Used by permission. All rights reserved.

Addition Scripture as noted is taken from Holy Bible, New Living Translation, copyright © 1996, 2004, 2015 by Tyndale House Foundation. Used by permission of Tyndale House Publishers, Inc., Carol Stream, Illinois 60188. All rights reserved.

Dedication

I dedicate this book to my courageous friend, Alice. You asked me to write your story and so I have. You left an imprint on my heart and an indelible mark on the world. I will see you again.

This dedication extends to all who have been abused at the hands of those who knew what they were doing and did it anyway.

Further, I dedicate this book to all who seek healing and wholeness as a result of being abused emotionally, verbally, physically, or sexually—may you find full restoration and renewal in the One who loves you. The One who created you.

Table of Contents

Acknowledgements — 1
Note to Reader — 6

PART 1: THE EARLY YEARS

Prologue — 8
Chapter 1   Monsters are Real — 9
Chapter 2   Childhood, the Beginning — 12
Chapter 3   Hillford Church and Cemetery — 16
Chapter 4   Trouble Brewing — 19
Chapter 5   Into the Darkness — 23
Chapter 6   Descent into Hell — 26
Chapter 7   More Tales from Hell — 30
Chapter 8   The Horrors of High School — 33
Chapter 9   I Killed My Oma — 38
Chapter 10 The Secret Society of the Serpent — 41
Chapter 11 The Innocents — 44
Chapter 12 Escape — 50

PART 2: TOO MANY ME'S

Chapter 13 Knowledge Quest — 55
Chapter 14 Behind the Books — 60
Chapter 15 Behind the Curtain — 64
Chapter 16 The Decision — 68
Chapter 17 Shattered — 73
Chapter 18 Living the Dream — 75
Chapter 19 Undone — 79
Chapter 20 Broken — 83
Chapter 21 Who Am I? — 86
Chapter 22 I Am Me — 91
Chapter 23 Therapy — 95
Chapter 24 The Storm Inside — 98

Chapter 25	Courage	100
Chapter 26	Beginning Again	103
Chapter 27	The Power of Three	106
Chapter 28	To Go or Not to Go	109
Chapter 29	Road Trip	112
Chapter 30	The Closet	115
Chapter 31	The Straw	118
Chapter 32	Hope	122
Chapter 33	Persevere	137
Chapter 34	Faith	140
Chapter 35	Friendship	143
Chapter 36	Revelation	147
Chapter 37	Highs and Lows	152
Chapter 38	Lost and Found	155
Chapter 39	All of Me	159
Chapter 40	Interlude	164
Chapter 41	Gains and Losses	170
Chapter 42	New Friends	176
Chapter 43	Freedom	179
Chapter 44	Inner Healing	185
Chapter 45	Unfinished Business	190
Chapter 46	Forgiveness	194
Chapter 47	Gratitude	201

PART 3: THE FINAL BATTLE

Chapter 48	The Diagnosis	205
Chapter 49	The Lasts	207
Chapter 50	Random Thoughts	211
Chapter 51	Life Sentence	216
Chapter 52	If You Choose, God Will Use	219
Chapter 53	Tantrums	222
Chapter 54	Winning	225
Chapter 55	Almost Home	229
Chapter 56	Reflections	234
Chapter 57	Epilogue	238
Chapter 58	In Alice's Own Words	240

PART 4: REFLECTIONS

Dr. G. Wallace, Ph.D., Alice's Psychologist	246
Susan, Alice's Art Therapist	257
Pastor Jack Charles, Alice's Pastor	260

Katie, Close Family Friend	263
Penny, Alice's Caregiver	266
Grace, Alice's Best Friend	275

PART 5: APPENDIX

Group Discussion Questions	283
Resource Guide	287

Acknowledgements

First and foremost, this book could not have been written without the leading, guiding, and protection of the Holy Spirit, the true Author. I am honored to have been the chosen vessel to hold the pen. Jesus, you took the wheel!

Deepest appreciation goes to my prayer team—the faithful band of warriors who consistently stood in the gap, lifting me and my requests to the throne room. You will never know how your timely words watered my soul and encouraged me to keep going to the finish line. I am deeply blessed to have been surrounded by such a great cloud of witnesses. May the generosity of your spiritual investment find its way back to you in unexpected ways. In appreciation of your investment, your names have been embedded into the narrative.

To all the beta readers—I owe you a debt of gratitude for your enthusiasm to read the manuscript in its raw and original state. Your intensive critiques, keen insights, and meaningful feedback was an invaluable asset to the writing process.

Thank you to Dr. Wallace, Alice's psychologist—your writing has informed and educated us on DID and showed us a glimpse of what it was like to counsel a courageous human being named Alice. She loved and respected you and appreciated the dignity and gentleness you showed her. She valued your wise, compassionate counsel and so have I! I was grateful for your recommendation to read *The Stranger in the Mirror,* by Marlene Steinberg, M.D. and Maxine Schnall, so I could further understand the hidden epidemic of dissociation.

To Susan, Alice's art therapist—if a picture is indeed worth a thousand words, consider these thanks framed in gold. I appreciate

Acknowledgements

that you entrusted me with Alice's art books which gave another level of insight and understanding into the complexity of her life. It was difficult to narrow down which pieces to include as there were so many creative and brilliant choices. Some were graphic and difficult to view, but necessary to see what words couldn't express. Susan, your gifts and talents helped Alice, and assuredly many others like her, by giving her an outlet to heal from the pain of abuse through artistic expression.

Dear Katie—you and your family have always been a delightful and loving addition to Alice's home. The laughter of your children was a welcome sound to her ears, on both the good days and bad. You faithfully shared the love of Christ through Scriptures, prayers, and good heart talks. Thank you for writing a chapter as a tribute to Alice and the many adventures you and Penny took with her. You were such a valuable part of her caregiving team and helped make her days more bearable with your sweet spirit.

Pastor Jack—your servant's heart was evident during your many visits to Alice. You demonstrated what true spiritual leadership looks like by accepting and embracing Alice for who she was without judgment. She loved you for that and so do I. Thank you for contributing a chapter and showing us what it's like to minister to someone who's broken. It's what Jesus, the Good Shepherd, did and you tend your sheep well.

To Thelma—our love of reading is what cemented our friendship from the beginning. Your unfailing support through this multi-layered process of writing a book was a treasured gift. The real gift though is you. You know me and love me despite my imperfections. Your gentle reminders to look back to see how far I've come was always just the right encouragement to keep me moving forward, albeit at times, at the speed of a turtle. Thank you for walking with me through the dark research and putting into words the inhumanity of torture bestowed upon Alice. God had you hold the candle to light the way. I appreciate that we were able to have lively discussions as each phase of Alice's emotional journey unfolded onto the written page. Like Alice, your imprint is deep within my heart and I am forever grateful. Remember, you offered to carry my luggage at all book signings! Love, Louise

Acknowledgements

Brenda—over a decade ago, you became a friend when you joined our newly formed book club, "Hooked on Books." We experienced God through our mutual passion of reading. Your God lens always offered a unique perspective to our group discussions. You were the perfect person to lay the foundation for the Reader's Guide. You had so many questions and I love that the first one was, "What happened to Oreo?" The readers will have the ability to ponder and discuss all the questions that surfaced during this emotionally wrenching, but ultimately redemptive journey. For all of that, I commend you.

Mimi Liberta—you are more than a beautiful, talented, and creative graphic designer, you are my friend. Your generosity of time in laying out the cover and editing Alice's artwork is a gift that honors her and one that I am extremely grateful for. I compliment you on your professionalism and for allowing me to endlessly tweak until, like Goldilocks, it was just right.

To my favorite anonymous shutterbug—one beautiful, crisp fall day, you grabbed your camera and with your imaginative eye, I became the beneficiary of professional photos. Your ability to capture life through the lens is an inspired gift and I am a thankful recipient.

My deepest gratitude goes to my editor Kathryn Ross. Our shared vision and common belief system confirmed that you were God's choice for this assignment. Your meticulous attention to detail and clarity in direction while maintaining Alice's voice was a blessing beyond description. I appreciated you patiently enduring the whirlwind journey with me while still doing real life. You truly are a word shepherdess and it's made me a better writer. The combination of your skills, Godly wisdom, and editorial polishing are true gifts. I believe Alice is applauding your efforts from above.

Thank you to the owners of the beautiful villa in Florida where Alice's story came to life. Your generosity in opening up your home and giving me two months of silence and solitude to write was a gift beyond measure. It was a wonderful opportunity to slow down the demands of everyday life and immerse myself in Alice's world and then write about it. The added bonus was introducing me to your

Acknowledgements

house of worship—the perfect way to refresh and renew my spirit every week.

Dearest Pam—you lovingly turned me into a basket case teaching me the finer techniques of basket weaving through the years. I treasure our friendship woven with strands of love, generosity, and faith. I extend heartfelt gratitude for laying the groundwork for the Resource Guide. May the beginning of healing be found there for many.

A big shout out of thanks goes to the Greater Philadelphia Christian Writers Conference, led by Marlene Bagnull. This is a gathering place that allows Christian creatives to grow. It launches new writers and makes good writers better. It was there that I experienced the thrill of pitching my book before agents, editors, and publishers. I met other dreamers and networked with published authors. I highly recommend all writers to attend this annual conference or one like it in your area. I was grateful to reflect on Marlene's *Writer's Statement of Faith* from time to time to remind myself why I need to stay motivated to write—because the world needs His answer. God bless you, Marlene, for your ministry to writers of every genre.

To Oreo, my constant and faithful furry companion—thank you for the unconditional love and comfort you give me every day, but especially throughout this writing journey. Your Mama gifted you to Penny to be sure you would be well-taken care of. Humans usually adopt dogs, but in this case, you have adopted me. If I had a tail, it would be wagging with the love I have for you.

Note to Self: You stood on John 5:30 NKJV, *"I can of myself, do nothing. As I hear, I judge; and my judgment is righteous, because I do not seek my own will, but the will of the Father who sent me."* These powerful words of Jesus reminded you that on your own, you can do no thing—nothing! It is ALL by the leading and guiding of the Holy Spirit. These truths, along with the word BELIEVE, kept you humble throughout the journey. You had to constantly remind yourself to believe BIG and dream BIG and leave the results in the Lord's hands. To this, you have tried to remain true.

To my daughter, whose very name means beloved. This project was more difficult than I ever could anticipate but was made easier

Acknowledgements

by your steadfast encouragement to keep going to the finish line. You knew how challenging it would be to organize all the pieces of Aunt Alice's story into a format that would inspire and transform lives. You knew the importance she placed on truth and as her truth came to light you were one of her greatest supporters—a friend, family member, and caregiver to the very end of her journey this side of Heaven. You knew the difficulty, but you also knew the hope that would shine through her story. Thank you for allowing me to interrupt you endlessly when I needed your opinion, edits, prayers, hugs, laughs, and common sense. My prayers were answered when you came into this world. You are a delight and I'm grateful we live together in this season. I love you Bee, more than you'll ever know.

Lastly, to my dear husband—you love me unconditionally, what a gift that is! You have traveled beside me, believing BIG with me. You are a man of few words and I more than make up for that. You have supported me in all the ways that count so that I could write. You are a Christ follower, a man of integrity, a true patriot, and Marine Corps veteran. Your motto has been *Semper Fi*, while mine has been *Simplify*! We've been through some challenging times and yet, here we are, trusting God, enjoying growing older together and laughing all the way! I love you to the sun and back!

Note to the Reader

Reader beware! Alice's story is horrific, shocking, and filled with heartache. Her epic tale involves real people and events that go to deep, dark places, hard to imagine within the realm of humanity. Alice's courageous and compelling journey of survival through Satanic Ritual Abuse (S.R.A.) and its debilitating effects is as gut-wrenching as it is memorable.

All events and conversations are represented as accurately as possible based on memories, personal journals, poetry, and academic papers (including original entries and composites), therapy artwork, and extensive one-on-one-interviews with Alice. Where trauma shadowed details, they have been re-constructed as the narrative required. All names and physical descriptions have been changed to protect the identity of the innocent and the guilty.

Throughout her story, Alice's life hangs on by a thread of faith in God. She survives with a powerful testimony and wants the reader to know that they can rise above all adversity holding fast to a thread of God's faithfulness in their life as well. Walk with her through family secrets, darkness, and triumphant endurance, thankful that this isn't your story. Or, maybe it is.

Publisher's Note: The publisher and author are not engaged in rendering professional services. If ministerial, therapeutic, psychological, or any other expert assistance is required, the services of a competent professional should be sought. The author and publisher specifically disclaim any and all liability arising directly or indirectly from the use or application of any information contained in this publication.

Part 1
THE EARLY YEARS

*"At the dreaded time when the sun goes down,
the beauty of the farm disappeared."*

Prologue

Are monsters real?

Definitely. Absolutely. Positively. Yes! A monster has many names: gremlin, goblin, ogre, phantom, specter, wraith, and bogeyman. I know one personally—my father. Perhaps that sounds a little dramatic, but I will introduce you to him and you can decide for yourself.

My name is Alice. Alice Iris Fisher. Everything I tell you about my journey is the way I remember it. Some details may be missing due to my shattered mind, my broken spirit, and my devastated soul. As horrific events unfolded in my young life, I could not bear them all, so I tucked away pieces of myself into locked compartments.

Years later, therapies revealed that my mind had fragmented into twenty-one different personalities. All Alice. All me. Each personality expressed different facets of me. Each one viewed life from a different perspective and served a specialized, individual purpose in order to survive childhood experiences too overwhelming for one human to bear. Shame floods me even now as I write out my story.

We can all relate to life's many disappointments, tragedies, and sorrows. We are all broken in some way. It's the human condition. We start out on solid ground and end up in unexpected places wondering how we got there.

Whether you feel hopeless, helpless, or are hurting in any way, I pray my story helps you see that God created you for a divine and holy purpose. The Bible tells us that God's plan for our lives is one filled with hope and a future. He creates a beautiful masterpiece from the shattered pieces of our lives with His gentle and patient hands. He banishes all the bogeymen and monsters that threaten our peace and wraps us in His loving arms. In Him there is light. We need not fear the dark.

In the following pages, I open my heart and soul in utmost transparency and share my story. I invite you along on my journey.

Monsters Are Real

For such people are false apostles, deceitful workers,
masquerading as apostles of Christ.
And no wonder, for Satan himself masquerades as an angel of light.
2 Corinthians 11:13-14

My father's given name was William. He used this name in every*day* life—with stress on the word *day*. He was a physically imposing man with a six-foot, two-inch-tall frame. You had to look up to this man—even if you didn't want to. I didn't want to. He weighed in at a solid 250 pounds. Working on our small, but productive farm naturally left him with hefty muscles, adding to his beefy, burly look. I likened him to one of our sturdy oak trees, hard and unforgiving.

Since his dark wavy hair matched his penetrating eyes, it was hard to say exactly what color they were. I never looked directly into them. If I had, he would've read every thought in my head—including the constant fear I tried to hide. Those eyes. Determined. Scary. Commanding. Just a quick glance at them caused me to quiver. His calloused hands, rough from field work, felt like sandpaper when he touched me. But that rarely happened in the daylight.

Yes. My father. William by day. Everyone liked him. He had a friendly demeanor and kind manner in speaking to strangers. He was known at the Hillford Church and Cemetery for his good deeds and generous giving. William had a way of getting along with all kinds of folks, which is why the church leaders asked him to be a deacon.

Deacons. Men of integrity. Men who value life. Men who keep the commandments. Men who treat people kindly—especially his own family members. Those church leaders should have asked me about his qualifications if they had wanted an *honest* opinion.

William by day. He married my mother, Josephine, when they were both twenty-one, straight out of college. He coveted Josie from the first time he set those piercing eyes on her in Economics 101. It may have been her soft curly brown chin length hair, her best feature,

CHAPTER 1 ~ Monsters Are Real

that attracted him. She resisted his advances for a while, but no one said "NO" to William.

Josie didn't realize until after she said, "I do," that she'd married someone completely opposite of the gentle, patient man who courted her. My mother always seemed frail, weighing a mere 110 pounds. If a hurricane came through our area, it would blow her out to sea, even though the sea was hundreds of miles away. Her tortoise-shell glasses hid the depth of her kind, gentle green eyes, but if you looked closely enough, you'd see fear hovered just at the edge.

After their brief honeymoon at Niagara Falls, New York, in the fall of 1953, they settled down on the Central Pennsylvania farm. This 200-acre parcel, named Shivering Acres, passed down from my father's father, Reynard Fisher. Family history whispered through the years said that Reynard gave my grandmother Ada syphilis with his philandering ways, leaving her confined to an insane asylum for sixteen years.

Ironically, Reynard preceded Ada in death by a tragic and bloody farm accident that involved a plow and a tractor. No one was ever supposed to talk about Granny and Grandpa Fisher. I asked about them once and was told to never ask again. Mystery shrouded my family's history. We were supposed to be grateful that we had a decent place to live in at Shivering Acres.

What a strange name for a farm. It's the shivering part of the name that's creepy. The name came from the sound the leaves made when the wind whistled through the hardwood trees that bordered the property. Oak, maple, and walnut trees created a thick, dense, dark canopy. The land in between the borders, gardens and fields, yielded hay, straw, and corn to feed our animal population. I had other reasons to agree with the name, *Shivering*, but that had nothing to do with the trees.

The farm animals numbered more than 1,165 to be exact. The chicken coops held 998 laying hens, minus two eaten by a fox. One-hundred-fifty steers grazed in the pasture just over the hill from the big red barn, along with two guinea fowl, fourteen outdoor cats, and one lovable dog, Pepper, who roamed around outside with a freedom I envied.

Just after my parents celebrated their first wedding anniversary, my brother William, Jr. made his appearance into this world. From day one, he'd been known as Billy and was the spitting image of our father except that his eyes were grayish-blue and gentle like Mom's.

CHAPTER 1 ~ Monsters Are Real

Trained at a young age to feed and water all the cattle, he worked hard. Even so, he got off easy. I collected the eggs every morning from the 998 hens and placed them in yellow wire baskets. I stored them in the wash house to be cleaned and sorted after school. The egg collection van came once a week for pick up, and the six crates had better be packed up and ready or else!

Sandra, my baby sister, had it the easiest of all of us. Sandy did nothing. She was supposed to feed the cats and dog, but she never did. She knew I would do it if she didn't. She had no love for anyone but herself and her stuffed animals. She never got into trouble, even when a problem was her fault. She was Daddy's Little Girl—a title she was proud to bear. She made sure she never got in trouble like me. Trouble can be tricky. Even when you do things right, trouble finds you. I know. It always found me.

Now you know a little bit about my family, and it sounds so normal. By day, we were a nice, normal, flag-waving family of five from Central Pennsylvania, who attended the Hillford Church and Cemetery faithfully every Sunday and most Wednesdays.

But at night, things changed.

At the dreaded time when the sun went down, the beauty of the farm disappeared. All those beautiful, leafy trees surrounding the property made eerie shadows reach over the house as the sun set. Everything felt closed in, oppressive, dark, claustrophobic. The darkness made me shiver.

William, the monster lurked.

William. My father. The Monster.

Childhood, the Beginning

Your eyes saw my unformed body; all the days ordained for me were written in your book before one of them came to be.
Psalm 139:16

I entered the world during the 1950's, on April 10, at Hillford General Hospital. I weighed seven pounds, seven ounces, and measured nineteen inches long. I'd like to think I was a child that my parents looked forward to having as part of their little family of three. That was probably true, until my father realized that a daughter had been born instead of a son. Farms need workers! No problem. He discovered, as I grew older, that a girl could work as hard as any boy, including my brother Billy who was four years older than me.

The first year or so of my life was rather uneventful. I ate, slept, and was content and laughed in this short peaceful season of my existence. Aunt Mollie Fromm, my father's sister, said I was a happy baby. She said I seemed to thrive and grow as any normal little girl. For some odd reason she added that I somehow broke my nose around age one, shortly after I learned to walk. She seemed uncomfortable sharing this with me.

But soon enough, life at Shivering Acres changed. I was about two and a half years old when "playtime" with my father's "live bunny" began. I woke up in my mother and father's bed. Mom was busy getting dressed or out of the room. Father put his finger to his lips and whispered, "Shhhh!" as he showed me his prized manhood. It started there—just showing—and progressed to "playtime with his bunny."

I hated that reference! I had a treasured stuffed brown bunny with pink bows around her ears. The bright white tag above her tail said her name was Hope. My maternal grandmother, Oma Elise, gave her to me when I was born. I clung to Hope, my constant friend and companion, especially after "playtime with father," and waited for a rescuer to whisk me away.

CHAPTER 2 ~ Childhood, the Beginning

After bedtime, when darkness and stillness invaded the house, I dreaded my father's idea of playtime. During the day, I feared a touch or a pinch when he thought no one was looking.

The abuse did not let up. I wet the bed most nights, a pattern that continued through high school. Billy wet the bed, too. Mom was frustrated. Soaked in urine, I stripped the sheets after she woke me. Then she grabbed my arm and marched me toward the laundry room with them. My father pushed my face into the wet smelly bundle and asked in disgust, "How do you like your new perfume?"

When I was five, my sister Sandy was born a month earlier than her due date in May. It wasn't her fault, but now I had to share my birthday month with her. I noticed the love and tender care given to my sister, especially from my father, while I was continually berated as stupid and worthless.

Even so, this tiny, helpless baby won me over. I enjoyed rocking, feeding, and holding her close and learned how to be a helper at an early age. The more useful I was, the less trouble I would have. I cherished my baby sister and allowed Hope, my precious bunny, to cuddle with her in the bassinet.

Father didn't like my interest in Sandy, so he assigned chores to keep me busy. I helped in the house with dishes, laundry, dusting, and even scrubbing floors on my hands and knees. Outside work included gathering the eggs, weeding the garden, and lugging firewood. I had no pretty dolls, tea sets, puzzles, or books. Only Hope.

While Sandy got bedtime stories read to her at night, I endured the horror of the Monster's rough hands all over my body in the dark. And he expected more. He forced me to touch him, using my mouth in private places.

Father had a set of unwritten rules not to be disregarded or forgotten.

Rule #1: *Don't tell anyone about "playtime" or you will not live to see another day, or your baby sister, ever again.*

The fear of such a threat helped me commit his rules to memory and I believed every word. After all, we had two loaded shotguns in the house for use against unexpected intruders—or so I was told. One propped in the kitchen corner, the other stationed in the master bedroom, they terrified me whenever I cleaned. I feared I might knock them over and be accidentally shot if they discharged. I

CHAPTER 2 ~ Childhood, the Beginning

panicked at the thought they might even be used to fulfill a breach of Rule #1.

I thought about telling my brother Billy the truth after a painful "playtime," but didn't, knowing he dealt with abuse too. He told me his black eye was from a fight at school, but I knew better. And, then there was the incident with the pitchfork through his arm after a steer broke through the pen. How could that be his fault? We both knew it was best to be quiet and act like everything was normal–whatever that was. Remember, Rule #1.

Beginning school at five years old should have been a welcome reprieve from my life at home with the Monster. It was not. The first time I boarded the school bus, tears ran down my cheeks. I waved good-bye to Mother, convinced I would never see her again, sent away for bad behavior. I refused to sit down on the cracked vinyl seats and stared out the back window until Mom blurred from view. Mr. Finch, the bus driver, yelled at me to sit down. When that didn't work, he pulled over and stopped the bus. I was horrified when he grabbed his wooden paddle and headed my way. My face turned red from humiliation and the laughter of the other kids. After one stinging whack, I sat down, ashamed and desolate, unable to see Mother.

I was very quiet in school, easily confused and often unable to follow directions. Though I knew the answers to questions, I refused to respond, which was interpreted as a learning problem. I hated school and all the boys who called me smelly and retard. I did smell. Father didn't allow me to wash-up before school even if I peed the bed. Every morning, the boys shouted, "Stinky, Stinky is your name!" I was devastated by the taunts, and sad that Hope, my comforter bunny, wasn't allowed at school. I grabbed her first when I ran through the door after an exhausting day of ridicule. Teachers and students confirmed everything my father said about me. I was stupid.

Miss Jean Avery, my first-grade teacher, seemed irritated with me day after day. I longed for her to say one kind thing to me like I heard her say to the other children: "Good job, Marianne, you are so creative." "Excellent work, Christie!" "Thank you, Ross, you are so helpful." Instead, she asked, "What is wrong with you, Alice?"

I knew I was worthless and stupid. Was there something else wrong, too?

CHAPTER 2 ~ Childhood, the Beginning

One day, two boys pushed me into the play oven and shut the door. I was stuck and couldn't get out. Alarmed, I felt as if I were trapped for hours, but it was probably only a few terrifying minutes. After recess, a little whistleblower told the teacher where to find me. Most children scream or cry, but not me. I was focused on Rule #2.

Rule #2 – *Never cry or you will get something to cry about.*

Mrs. Avery pulled me out of the oven as everyone laughed. I didn't laugh, I peed myself. The shame multiplied as the laughter got louder. I hated school now even more than I did in kindergarten! When I rode the bus home, my thoughts focused on one thing—that my clothes would dry before I arrived or punishment would follow.

The verbal, physical, and sexual abuse was relentless throughout my early childhood. The Monster unfairly assigned chores to me, more fit for a teenage boy than a frail first, second, or third grade girl. Living up to my father's expectations and demands was impossible. My penalty for failure: more labor or skipped meals. I lived in constant uncertainty. One scant glance from my father's dark eyes caused me to panic, lose control, and wet myself. Again.

If I peed myself during the day, I had to strip off my clothes and lie naked on the bed. The Monster smacked me hard with his sandpapery hands. He did things a father should not do until I screamed, "I'm sorry, I'm so bad."

Cry? No! (Rule #2) *No matter what, I will not cry.* Holding back tears, I curled my fingers around the sheets and screamed inside. As I grew older, I realized these were inappropriate sexual things, but Father told me it was well-deserved punishment because I was a horrible, rotten, stupid, worthless kid.

Why, oh, why couldn't I be like my sister who didn't pee the bed or smell? Sandy got rewarded with toys or books and did well at school. *Why? Why? Why?* I asked myself a million times over. *Why was I born so bad? What was wrong with me?*

Hillford Church and Cemetery

Being confident of this, that he who began a good work in you will carry it on to completion until the day of Christ Jesus.
Philippians 1:6

Odd. Why did our church, the Hillford Church and Cemetery, include the word cemetery in its name? Wasn't church for the living and cemeteries for the dead? The name of our church always gave me the creeps! But that was the least of my worries. The dead couldn't hurt me. It was the living who terrified me.

Built in the late 1800's, layers of grey blue stone made up the exterior wall of the church. A tall bell tower topped with a cross reached high into the sky. Two giant, bright red doors opened into the sanctuary. I couldn't open the heavy doors by myself, even though I was strong from carrying firewood. Father opened the doors. As we shuffled through, he whispered Rule #3.

Rule #3: *Smile and look happy.*

So, we pasted smiles on our faces and silenced our inside pain.

I loved the way the building smelled of varnish, old paper, candle wax, mustiness, and a hint of old lady perfume like my father's sister, Aunt Mollie, wore. I trusted these smells. Quite the opposite of the manure smell that hung in the air at home, outside and inside the house from work boots lined up in the laundry room. That faint manure odor clung to our clothes. Whenever father came close to me, I smelled it on his hands and felt nauseous in my stomach.

Sunday School took place in the hour before church service began. Father was a deacon and had meetings at that time. Mom signed Sandy into the Nursery then sat and prayed in the pew. *What did she pray about? Did she know what the Monster was doing to me at home? Did she care? Maybe she felt a sense of peace and calm in church, like I did. It was the one place I felt safe.*

All children from age five to eleven went into one big classroom. Kids twelve and older were down the hall in the Fellowship Room.

CHAPTER 3 ~ Hillford Church and Cemetery

I could hear the noise of laughter spilling out of that room. They were having fun. I wanted to be in THAT room.

Our room was quiet, even though there were thirteen of us gathered around the horseshoe shaped table sitting on hard yellow plastic chairs, too big for me. I was one of seven girls and Billy, one of five boys. I hoped this school would be better than the one I attended Monday through Friday.

I liked the way my teacher's name sounded: Miss Mary Miller. M.M.M. It flowed together so nicely. I repeated her name over and over again so I wouldn't forget—Miss Mary Miller. M. M. M. Even stupid kids like me can remember things if they say the words over and over. She wore a bright paisley ribbon to hold back her beautiful flowing blonde hair. *That ribbon would look perfect on Hope.*

Miss Mary Miller stood before an easel holding a four-foot square board covered in soft emerald-green fabric. *How would Hope look with emerald-green fur instead of drab brown?* After calling the class to attention, Miss Miller prayed and told a story about a man named Jesus. She placed colorful fabric figures on the board as the story unfolded. It surprised me to see how they stuck there like magic. I stared at the figure of Jesus. I never saw a man with long hair before and marveled at his face. His eyes looked straight at me. I didn't want to look away like I did with father. I wondered why he couldn't have kind eyes like the man on the emerald-green felt board.

One time, Miss Miller told a story about a woman who had a bleeding issue for a long time. Why hadn't anyone helped her before? Maybe she was a bad lady, too. Sometimes, after one of father's bedtime visits, I had bleeding issues, and no one helped me. To my surprise, Miss Miller said that this kind man helped this woman after she touched the bottom of his clothing. The bleeding stopped instantly. He must be a doctor of some kind. I have never been to the doctor, but a doctor for animals comes to the farm sometimes. I determined right then and there that whenever I was hurt and bleeding, I would ask this long-haired man named Jesus to help me. His gentle eyes would see my pain and make me better.

After that decision, I looked forward to attending Hillford Church and Cemetery each week and treasured my Sunday School hour. It was easy to be joyful and smile in church and Sunday School. I didn't have to worry about Rule #3. I eagerly looked forward to each story Miss Mary Miller shared with us. Even so, I hoped she

CHAPTER 3 ~ Hillford Church and Cemetery

wouldn't ask me to pray or read because I didn't do those things well at all.

Framed Bible scenes hung all around the classroom. Above the upright piano with the three golden pedals was a picture of a crowd of children gathered around a man with long hair. I recognized his face, with the kind, dark eyes, as Jesus, from the stories Miss Miller told. In the picture, his hands extended, gently and lovingly, to touch the cheeks of a little girl with brown hair, just like mine. Each boy and girl in the scene stretched their arms to Jesus desiring to be held or hugged. They all had different skin colors and clothing styles. I stared at that picture for a long time pretending I was that little girl Jesus touched in the loving way. I wanted to be loved by my father the way it looked like Jesus loved me in the picture. Every time I went to church, I looked at that captivating picture and pretended that someone gentle and kind loved me.

Filled with anxiety, I sat by father during the extra-long services each week. I never knew when to sit, stand, or kneel. If I hesitated in confusion I was met with a sharp pinch on my leg as a reminder of what I should or should not do. As a result, I left each church service with a string of black and blue marks down my leg.

The bellowing sound of the pipe organ soothed me. It made me happy and drowsy at the same time. My love for music began at this church, as did my love for the kind-eyed man named Jesus.

Trouble Brewing

*Fathers, do not embitter your children,
or they will become discouraged.*
Colossians 3:21

A hospital stay at the age of seven provided a brief respite from my troubles at home. After a tonsillectomy, I enjoyed a peaceful and restful time for a few days. The kind nurses fussed over me and brought chocolate ice cream whenever I asked for it. I ate more ice cream during recovery than I had in the entire year. Chocolate ice cream became my favorite flavor.

Nurse Kathy asked me if I was enjoying my vacation. I didn't know the meaning of the word. But, if vacation meant you didn't have to do chores or get beaten up, then yes, I was officially on vacation. And loving it!

No visitors came to see me, not even my Oma and Opa Herman whom I loved dearly. Their names meant grandmother and grandfather in German. I knew Oma and Opa would have visited me if mother or father had thought it important enough to tell them I was in the hospital.

I dreaded the day I was set to be released, afraid to go home. None of the hospital staff noticed all the bruises dotted over my body. Or, maybe they did and remained silent.

Other than the bout with tonsillitis, I was a pretty healthy kid. Thankfully so, because I had to go to school whether sick or well.

Rule #4: *Don't ever say you are sick. We can't afford a doctor so, deal with it!*

As I grew older, verbal, physical, and sexual cruelty not only continued, but increased. I couldn't do anything right according to the Monster. I shoveled the snow and threw it on the right side of the sidewalk. The taskmaster said, "No! I said on the left side!" It never mattered, left or right, both sides were wrong. In a short-lived moment of defiance, I once threw one shovelful of snow to the left

CHAPTER 4 ~ Trouble Brewing

and the next one to the right, until the job was completed. *I'll show him!* My plan covered all the requirements. But Father deemed me a "smarty pants." He kicked me a dozen times with his manure crusted work boots. I knew it was exactly twelve. I silently counted each painful blow.

Punishment was swift, no matter the infraction! My slave driver whipped me, slapped me, or pulled my hair out by the roots according to his whim on any given day. He locked me in the outhouse for hours, even on the coldest winter day. In that dimly lit prison cell, I breathed a prayer, "Jesus, help me not to cry!" Alone in the aftermath of a wrathful episode, I talked to myself and imagined my words were heard by the long-haired man who loved all the children in the Sunday School picture.

I tried to do everything the right way, but it was never good enough under the scrutiny of the Monster. I couldn't hold a pencil or a glass full of milk correctly. I was not able to snap the beans fast enough, husk the corn suitably, stack the wood logs in the precise pattern, or feed Pepper the dog the exact amount of food. Mother chose to look the other way, sometimes with tears in her eyes, when Father dispensed disciplinary action. Sandy ran to her room. Billy hid in the barn.

Beatings with a wooden paddle or birch switch were only the beginning. Part two was doled out in the bedroom, in darkness, and hurt worse than any paddle ever could. I can't remember a single day when I wasn't man-handled by my father, a patriarchal brute.

One day, my job was to mop the ancient, cracked linoleum floor until it gleamed. I finished just as Sandy strode in from the garden with her muddy rain boots. She tracked mud everywhere. My father stomped in behind her and cursed. Red-faced and angry, he demanded to know why there was mud all over the floor. I stuttered and tried to explain what had occurred. "How dare you blame Sandy! I told you to clean it! Clean it again, but this time, lick it up, every bit of muck!" Something fractured in me that day. Hate birthed deep within my soul. Beyond hate, I didn't know a word that could capture what I felt for the man called Father. My personal Monster.

On a spring day, I cleaned the hallway floor that led to the bathroom. Father declared it a "no walking" zone, even after it dried. But I had to pee. I tiptoed down the hallway thinking the Monster was outside. Halfway to the bathroom and relief, he sprung out from behind the bedroom door and scared me. I peed myself, and to my

CHAPTER 4 ~ Trouble Brewing

horror, he unzipped his pants and proceeded to pee all over the clean floor himself! He laughed, "There, now lick THAT up." When I didn't get it all cleaned up in the time allotted, he half-dragged me upstairs and did that thing that left me wounded. Every time.

My father delighted to inflict pain and always found a reason to justify his behavior. He didn't always do sexual things, but he did them often enough. Sometimes, he'd wait until we were outside and no one else was around. He assigned a lot of outside chores, so I walked about with heightened awareness of my surroundings. I tried to avoid him and found places on the property where I could disappear into the barn loft, hen house, spring house, or garage.

Fifty feet from the edge of the dense woods, tucked behind a giant oak tree, I cleared a hiding place for Hope and me. I felt safe in that peaceful spot. After my chores were completed, I hid there until darkness forced me to go inside or help Mom with dinner.

Rule #5: *Dinner on the table by six o'clock.*

If Billy and I arrived at the table a second past six, we didn't get to eat dinner. I felt bad when Billy didn't get to eat because I messed up on the time now and then. But Sandy always got dinner, even if it was after six.

My father never touched me in a gentle or loving way. He was a forceful man—harsh and coarse. We lived in fear of him. My sister, whom he never touched in an inappropriate way—as far as I know—was anxious around him. I tried to look out for her believing it was my duty, as an older sister, to protect her as best as I could. If she was at fault for something, I'd take her punishment. When father spoke, we were expected to listen and pay close attention to his every word. He didn't repeat anything. I was expected to hear it right the first time or painful consequences swiftly followed.

Rule #6: *Listen and hear it right the first time it's spoken.*

If I didn't want painful outcomes, I obeyed and never argued. My duty was to faithfully do what he said and never talk back.

Rule #7: *Never argue back.*

Father's rules were non-negotiable.

These rules applied to Mother as well. He never hit her that I know of, but blamed her whenever something didn't go his way. Verbal abuse would be unleashed in ear-shattering decibels. Many times, I saw the Monster pinch the tender skin under her arms, but Mother never broke Rule #2. Not under any circumstances did I ever hear her cry out or shed tears. Father reached for the loaded

CHAPTER 4 ~ Trouble Brewing

shotgun once following a heated argument about a grocery bill amount he thought was too high. Mom kept her cool and survived the day, though it came close to an irreversible end.

The scariest episode happened on the day Father and Billy cemented the breezeway between the house and garage. As they poured the floor area, Billy slipped and fell. Quicker than my next breath, father yanked Billy up and threw him against the wall. He crumpled down into a quiet heap on the floor. Billy looked dead. Terrified I would be next, I ran like the wind until I reached my secret place where I hid, trembling for hours behind my favorite oak tree. When I heard Mom call me home, I feared to leave my cozy, safe spot. I had never seen my father so livid. I wondered what horrific terror might be waiting for me. I have no memory of what happened after that except that Billy didn't die that day. I wanted to cry for my brother's pain, but like Mom, I couldn't break Rule #2. I knew if I did cry, I might be the one to die. *"Only babies cry, I must not give in. I won't give in. I will not cry! Kind-eyed Jesus, Where are you? Help me!"*

Into the Darkness

He has driven me away and made me walk in darkness rather than light.
Lamentations 3:2

Every year on our birthdays, Mom made sure to prepare a celebration dessert on our big day. One year, a lonely cupcake might surface for me, another time a delicious strawberry rhubarb pie. But for my eighth year, Oma Elise baked me two-layers of chocolatey goodness topped with whipped vanilla frosting, rainbow sprinkles and pink candles. When they arrived, Opa George burst through the door with a big smile and a half-gallon of chocolate ice cream. Oma carried the cake hidden in a white plastic container with a red handle. I had never seen such a fancy cake and felt special that it was for me. That was the last happy event I remember from that year.

In addition to the cake, Oma and Opa gifted me with four sets of ribbons for my bunny, Hope. Red, green, blue, and my favorite—the yellow polka dot set. All four pairs were wrapped in pink tissue paper that smelled like Oma's Jean Naté powder. After eight years, Hope's ears were getting a little worn from being rubbed so often, but she looked festive and refreshed in her new ribbons. Hope once whispered, after a punishment from the Monster, that she was *"scared for both of us."* Most people think bunnies don't talk, but mine whispered just loud enough for me to hear.

I loved when Oma and Opa visited, but it only happened a few times a year when they helped with canning at harvest and celebrated Christmas. I have a picture of me in a colorful hat with a bow standing with them at Easter, so they must have visited then, too. When Oma and Opa were around, Father acted like he did in church on Sundays. He turned from Monster into William and gave an Academy Award-winning performance of a fine, upstanding Christian family man.

Mom was forbidden to visit Oma and Opa without Father by her side. In fact, Sandy or Billy were required to accompany her to

CHAPTER 5 ~ Into the Darkness

the grocery store, so she wouldn't be alone. I never went. I wondered if I was too stupid to push a cart around the store or into the parking lot. Except for school and church, I rarely left Shivering Acres.

Did you know houses have secrets? A few weeks after my birthday, I noticed an odd upstairs window from the outside of the two-story white-framed portion of our farmhouse. I reviewed all the rooms of the house in my mind's eye and couldn't place where this window was located. I decided to wait for a chance to investigate and find the mysterious window room when no lurkers or watchers were around.

Our house was made up of two homes built side by side. The original structure was an old stone house. Years later, a wooden house addition was built against the outer stone walls. A locked, dwarf-sized door connected the two buildings. I never saw that door used. Even so, it was possible to enter the musty stone house through the formal living room in the wooden house. How strange. I wanted to ask about why the house was built in such an odd manner but didn't fancy inviting any more trouble than what came daily without invitation.

We stored the eggs in the stone half, called the "old house," because it was cooler there, especially in the summer heat. During winter's frigid temperatures, we ran a heater so the eggs wouldn't freeze.

Besides the egg baskets, crates, and scale, the rest of the old portion contained various kinds of junk, such as broken chairs, rusty cans, outdated newspapers, old tires—some with metal rims and some without—bushel baskets, tools, and other once useful or important items that had reached their expiration date. There was no treasure to be found in the old house. Only useless odds and ends.

A concealed black door in the shadowy back left corner of the house led to the ground cellar. It could be easily missed, unless you knew it was there. The narrow steps spiraled steeply downward. Sometimes, I was sent to fetch some lard stored there and had to be extra careful on the steps, battling spider webs as I descended, so as not to fall.

I hated being the one tasked to go down there! Why not Billy or Princess Sandy? The chilling dark and damp of the cellar added to the shivers at Shivering Acres. Six quick steps in complete darkness must be conquered before the short string attached to a low wattage bulb could dispel dark with light, and send the mice scuffling for

CHAPTER 5 ~ Into the Darkness

cover. In the corner, a coal bin overflowed with the promise of fuel for the house furnace and heat in winter. But, in the cold cellar, the black nuggets piled in the bin caught the light, glinting like a bin of disembodied eyes staring at me with a threat of accusation. I shuddered in the dingy light of Shivering Acres, again.

One day, I was sent on a mission to the cellar to grab a can of lard stored with a butchered steer and pig in our two meat-filled freezers. The gold tin lard cans lined up on the wooden planks like soldiers laid over workmen horses. The pretty containers once held yummy butter cookies gifted to us each Christmas by the local hardware store. I grabbed the closest can, pulled the light cord, and raced up the stairs, terrified by the dense darkness and any haunts that might lurk there, still undiscovered.

Descent into Hell

No, but the sacrifices of pagans are offered to demons, not to God, and I do not want you to be participants with demons.
1 Corinthians 10:20

Summer Solstice, on Monday, June 21st one year, began like any other day that muggy hot summer. Mondays meant laundry day and it was my job to hang the clothes on the four wash lines strung on wooden posts near the vegetable garden. Father walked by as I clipped the freshly laundered towels onto the line with wooden clothespins. I sensed his threatening presence and looked up. He stopped to stare at me, smiled, and nodded his head. I jerked my head and looked away.

How strange! My father only smiled on rare occasions, like when we went to church, when Oma and Opa visited, or when our veterinarian, the egg pick-up man, repairmen, or one of our neighbors stopped by. In those moments, William was out for all to see while the Monster hid from view.

That day, my mom seemed extra quiet and self-occupied. After a lunch of homemade apple jelly on white bread and grape juice, Mother said I could do whatever I wanted all afternoon. *Time alone with no chores? This was new. Did turning eight make the difference?* Billy suggested I take a nap. *A nap?* I never slept in the day. I remained on high alert, aware of the Monster's movements, so I could always manage to be somewhere else.

With Hope in tow, I headed to our secret spot in the woods. I pretended to have a tea party, just like the story about another Alice I discovered in Sandy's colorful picture book. Big leaves, dried, fallen, and curled brown, became make-believe cups. I used smooth stones for snickerdoodle cookies, like Oma Elise made. This peaceful childhood memory is the last of its kind that I recall.

CHAPTER 6 ~ Descent into Hell

After dinner, father thrust a glass in front of me just before bedtime and demanded I drink the purple contents. It looked like the grape juice we had at lunch but didn't taste like it. I didn't feel quite right after drinking it and wanted to ask what was in it. But, Rule #8 and Rule #9 were in play.

Rule #8: *Do what you're told.*

Rule #9: *Don't ask questions.*

I was ordered to go to bed, so I did.

For some time, I lay snuggling Hope close to me in an eerie silence. We held each other and listened for the creaky stairs, which meant the Monster was on the prowl, before I finally drifted off to sleep.

Once asleep, I entered a dream-like state. I was aware that someone carried me from my bedroom to a secret chamber dug out of the ground cellar behind a door I had never noticed before. I remembered hearing male voices murmuring around me in low, flat tones. The room seemed as big as our kitchen and dining room combined, which measured twenty by twenty feet. The heavy air in the open area filled with a smoky haze from lit candles placed in a perfect circle around the room. I saw tall, dark figures like shadows behind the candlelight and heard them hum low in unison. Dressed in black flowing robes, pointed hoods covered their faces with slits through which I could see piercing eyes. All faced the center of the room and stared at a stone slab. It resembled a bed with leather straps and buckles at the top and bottom. *Why would anyone need to be strapped while lying down on a bed?*

The person who carried me let me down out of his arms to sit next to a figure taller than me, but not as tall as the others. The figure leaned over and whispered, "You'll be okay, kid. Just remember all the rules." *Billy! I knew that voice!* It was my brother, Billy. Shocked at the revelation, I couldn't speak in response.

I felt woozy; my legs weak and wobbly. I was afraid I would pee myself. The voices grew louder and louder as the robed figures circled the stone. One of them grabbed my wrist, pulled me into the circle, and stated loudly, "Honorable and worthy Master, Amaru, we present the girl child." The one called Amaru, who appeared to be the one in charge, advanced to the stone bed and bowed to it like it was an altar, then turned his attention onto me. I looked up into the faceless hood instantly recognizing my father's penetrating eyes. My knees buckled beneath the weight of the nightmare. *Was it a*

CHAPTER 6 ~ Descent into Hell

nightmare? Was I dreaming? I tried to scream out loud but couldn't make a sound. My heart pounded in pure terror within. My mind rang with silent shrieks of horror. *Where was my mother? Why was my brother here? Who would hear me even if I could scream for help? What was the Monster going to do to me? Jesus—JESUS!*

Then, my father, who should have been my protector, stripped off my thin summer pajamas and underwear. I stood before him and the hooded figures defenseless and naked. The unfriendly atmosphere in the room chilled me to the bone. I shivered, trembling in uncontrollable fear, trying to swallow and catch my breath. *Don't cry! Don't cry!* I repeated to myself. I squeezed my eyes shut tight and tried to picture Jesus with His bright eyes and kind smile welcoming me into His embrace, but His face and eyes wouldn't focus. A dizzy lightheadedness washed over me from head to toe. I thought I would crumple to the floor like my sister's rag doll.

Suddenly, one of the taller hooded ones stepped forward holding a long birch branch stripped of its bark. With a flick of his wrist, he whipped me three times on my bottom and mumbled some words. The welts on my rear stung and rose as they swelled. My eyes watered. I didn't cry. *What did I do to deserve this punishment? I must be very, very bad.* Spanking was Part One of punishment in the Monster's house. *Was it Part One in this strange place, too?* I grew woozy again, wondering about what Part Two of my punishment would be, surrounded by the dark beings and their sinister humming.

My head cast down, I looked intently at my feet and tried to stand very still. The voices grew louder again. I looked up. In the middle of the stone altar, something dark and furry lay still. The smoke burned my eyes, but as I looked through the haze, I noticed the white tip on the tail contrasted against the black fur. In a rush of realization, I finally screamed, "No! No! No!"

On that cold block of stone lay Frisky, one of our cats. A long, sharp knife blade flashed in the air before being thrust down upon him. My stomach quivered. Bile rose in my throat. I felt sick. I looked away. The hooded man behind me grabbed my head on either side, forcing me to look. The Monster held Frisky up by his two front paws while his blood flowed downward into a silver cup like they have at church for communion. The Monster approached me and held the cup to my lips while hands forced my head down to the rim. I took the tiniest sip and gagged. Then the cup passed from figure

CHAPTER 6 ~ Descent into Hell

to figure until it reached the Monster, again; the figure called Amaru. He drank thirstily until the cup emptied.

The sun broke through the window of my room in the morning. I woke up in my bed. *What happened to me last night? Had it been a nightmare? Had I been dreaming?*

The sun had risen. Breakfast was ready in the kitchen. The day started the same as it always did. Mom looked the same. She sounded the same as she urged me, "Eat your breakfast, Alice. There is work to do." No one seemed to be affected by the events of the previous night. Everyone acted like it was just another Tuesday—the same old, same old. *But life would never—could never—be the same for me. Never again! Was it all a dream? A bad nightmare? What was real?*

I choked my corn flakes down and ran to the barn to feed the cats. Frisky didn't come when I called him. Frantically, I looked everywhere for him. I called and called, and he still didn't come. I flopped down on the ground and rocked back and forth feeling helpless. *I wish I had brought my bunny outside. My Hope.*

That's when I noticed how sharp my bottom stung.

More Tales from Hell

You shall not murder.
Exodus 20:13

I had learned a valuable lesson: Never allow Father to notice anything important or cherished. He'd destroy it.

After the Frisky incident, I developed a particular fondness for a white cat I named Tillie. I loved Tillie. When I pet her, she responded with loud, trilling purrs and pushed against me in want of more. I talked with Tillie like a friend and, on rare occasions, I whispered to her the secrets of my inner struggles. Cats can't yell or tell me how stupid or ugly I am.

One hot summer Tillie got pregnant and birthed four adorable kittens. Father noticed my affection for these wee, helpless ones. He decided he didn't want any more cats around, so he got rid of them. Tillie missed her babies and protested with loud, painful howls. Father determined the racket had to stop. He forced me to watch as he tied a weighty stone around Tillie's neck. I heard her gurgling as the Monster tossed her into the depths of the pond located at the farthest corner of the woods. He laughed and walked away. I swallowed hard and wondered if Jesus could see and could save her. I knew I couldn't.

Father often took his unexplained wrath out on my dog Pepper. For no reason at all, he yanked the metal chain Pepper was tied to outside, choking him. More than once I witnessed the Monster kicking Pepper until he cowered and limped away. When I was ten, Father killed Pepper. He bashed him over the head with a two by four, twisted his head and broke his neck. Billy and I were speechless eyewitnesses to the horror. On one level, I felt relief as I knew Pepper would never have to suffer again. *Would I one day face this same fate? Would Billy?*

CHAPTER 7 ~ More Tales from Hell

I missed my pets. They were the only friends I had. Sometimes, Father made the animals do things to me. I can't quite bring myself to write about those repulsive moments. I felt so empty inside—ashamed, and guilty—that I didn't somehow try to stop the Monster from his murderous rages.

Beyond all these things, I most feared that Father would destroy Hope, my treasured bunny. In my tenth or eleventh year, my fears were realized. I hid Hope between my mattresses before I left for school every day. Hiding places in our house were few. Secret places, yes. But not for bunnies and other important treasures.

One day, my teacher mailed a note to my parents, *"Alice is simply not paying attention in school. She frequently has her head on the desk and drifts off to sleep during a lesson. She doesn't respond when called upon and ignores the other children. I am afraid if I don't see immediate improvement, she will be assigned to special education classes and to an after-school program."* She signed the note, *Sincerely, Miss Eckhoff.*

The day after the note arrived, I went to my room to change into my work clothes; jeans, and a plaid flannel shirt. Shock coursed through my veins when I spotted Hope—or what was left of her—lying on my pillow in ragged pieces, gutted from her neck down the center of her body. Her head had been twisted off. Her button eyes pulled out. Her whiskers plucked. Stuffing was scattered all over my chenille bedspread. For an instant I stopped breathing, then gathered all the broken pieces of Hope together and gently tucked her in my pillowcase. Tears welled from deep within my broken heart, but I choked them back and slid, helpless, to the floor. I rocked back and forth. *Death surrounds me. When you're really, really bad this is what happens.*

Father either stole or destroyed everything I cherished. *Would he have done that if I wasn't such an awful person? Why didn't Sandy's or Billy's belongings get ruined?*

Even though I knew Father thought cards were evil, I enjoyed playing Solitaire when sleep evaded me. Oma Elise once taught me how to play on a visit to her house and said I could keep a deck of cards. When Father caught me playing with them, he grabbed me by the hair and forced me to toss the cards into the fireplace. I stood before the flames until nothing was left of them but ashes. He caustically declared, "Cards are from the devil." *How could playing cards be from the devil? The Monster hadn't given them to me.*

No television or radio graced our home. I didn't go anywhere except church other than rare visits to Oma and Opa's house. Father

CHAPTER 7 ~ More Tales from Hell

said there were too many bad influences out there in the world and a good parent didn't expose their children to them. *What a joke!* Unless father approved, we were not allowed to talk to anyone. That's why I never said much in school. I didn't know who I could or couldn't talk to, so I remained silent. My teachers interpreted the silence as rebellion or stubbornness, noting such on my report cards, along with my inability to think clearly, focus, or comprehend.

At age eleven, poor grades on my report card required a parent's signature. I asked Mom to sign it and hoped to avoid it getting into Father's hands. Mom glanced at it and quietly responded. "Your father will take care of it."

He took care of it, all right. He taught me a lesson about deficient report cards by hauling me to my bedroom where he ordered me to shed my clothes and do inappropriate things to him. I felt sick and wanted to throw up. In due course, I did, which sent him into a rage. He stuck my head into the vomit and rubbed the sickness all over my face. But I could not cry. Only babies cried. I had to be tough. After Father left, I peed myself in relief. His child-training techniques involved pain, torment, and trauma. There wasn't an ocean big enough to contain the loathing and disgust I harbored in my heart for him.

I never achieved a good report card in school—always on the borderline of failing. First grade was bearable, but every school year after that brought new torments and humiliations. The teachers pushed me through to the next grade and the next grade and the next grade, never able to address my inability to learn, or grasp that my deficiencies stemmed from profound problems at home. *But that's normal for bad kids like me, right?* My childhood blurred, one horrible day into another horrible night. And another. And another. In a continuous loop of fear, punishment, pain, and failure.

The Horrors of High School

With us is the Lord our God, to help us and to fight our battles.
2 Chronicles 32:8b

High school put me further behind my peer group, due to an inability to concentrate on school subjects. The lack of achievement in my academic life complicated my struggles at home.

I got in trouble for everything and believed I deserved it. One activity that comforted me, though, was eating. I needed a lot of comfort, which initiated a destructive eating pattern. I gorged myself until I became nauseous and gained weight with each passing week. I genuinely became everything I believed people saw me as: sick, stupid, ugly, and fat!

Junior high rebellion grew to a whole new level when I reached high school. I knew in my "knower" that the actions at home were wrong. I became acutely aware of the hypocrisy embedded within my family life and couldn't handle the double standard anymore. Home life consisted of a constant, throbbing anxiety and unrest compared with how Mother and Father presented us at church as though everything was peachy keen. It didn't make sense to me. I daydreamed of escape.

Even with the trials of school, it provided a safety zone and became the easiest part of my day when school was in session. No one there beat or *'depar'* me. *'Epar'* was a word related to Father's actions whenever the mood struck him. *Epar* was the first word I ever wrote backwards. I couldn't cope with spelling it the correct way, least of all saying the word out loud.

My grades continued in a downward spiral. The teachers and principal didn't know what to do with me. I refused to talk to the other students, and I only spoke to the teachers when the situation necessitated it. Violating Rule #1 might require a severe retribution: death! Who would risk that?

CHAPTER 8 ~ The Horrors of High School

The faculty finally concluded that I should be put in a special education class which I took as a nice way of saying, "You are a stupid, dumb retard." My written skills were grossly inadequate. I read on a first or second grade level. To graduate high school senior year, I worked with a tutor as part of my special education—a kind, but shy girl named Tricia. At test-taking time, she read the test questions, and I answered them orally. I classified Tricia as normal because she was nice to me for no reason. I secretly wished she could be my friend and pretended it to be true.

One teacher, Mr. Richards, thought my eyesight was an issue since I always selected to sit in the back of the room, even though seats were available up front. His frustration with me reached the red zone when, one day, he ordered me to make a choice: either move to the front of the class or leave. To his surprise, I chose to leave. There was no way I was going to sit up front and be watched or laughed at behind my back.

The next day, he commanded me to stay seated after class so he could speak to me. He guided me into the projection room at the back of the forum where our class met. He proceeded to share how he cared about me personally and wanted to help me be a better student. After a few minutes of this counterfeit lecture, he reached out and fondled my breasts. I scrambled out of there never to return to his class. A suspension notice arrived at the house which caused more trouble. I now had a valid reason to be scared at home *and* at school. Who could be trusted?

I stuttered when anyone in authority expected an answer from me and struggled with my writing pattern where everything turned out backwards. Not just the word *epar*. I truly believed myself to be a big, fat, ugly baby and feared I would never grow up. Confusion invaded my mind, and I found it harder and harder to think straight. It seemed, at times, like I was more than just one person. There was "Baby Alice" who peed the bed; "hardworking like a boy Alice"; "Mean Alice" who wanted her father dead; "I've got a secret Alice," "Church Alice" who wants to learn more about Jesus; and finally, "Disappearing Alice" sliding down the rabbit hole, lost in a world of chaos. These different personalities swirled through my mind, each one requiring specific attention.

Who is the real *Alice? Where do I find* her?

Even though school was a reprieve from my DDT—Daily Dose of Terror—doled out like a prescription for bad, ugly, fat teens like me—I despised it. During those painful years, I wrote down bits and pieces of my thoughts. Writing gave me something to do while the teachers droned on about this date in history, that dangling participle in grammar, and math problems about the train leaving the station at five forty-five . . . blah, blah, blah. *Who cares?*

Let Me Out!

I want out, out, out!
Out of this hot stinkin' room
that smells like the end of the week
out of this room where Mrs. Reed
says: "Do this, don't do that."
I'm sick of getting in trouble.
All I want is out of here Lord
5 minutes
300 seconds
It feels like years, decades until the bell…then hell.

Why doesn't she just shut up?
Nobody hears her
Rattling on about this or that
I don't even see her
I just see the secondhand crawling around the clock
And feel the minutes in my muscles
Tense,
Waiting…
Always waiting.
Do I miss something or other
waiting like this Lord? Do I?

A Day in Jail

It's Monday morning, time to get up and go to the jail house. Oh, what a thing to wake up to. Every morning I ask God to help me through another day. I try to understand and get my work done, but I just can't tolerate another day. I stand and stare at the sky waiting for my ride to come; the one I dread day after day. There are others taking the same ride and they laugh at me, call me names, and grab my change purse filled with lunch money. I pretended it didn't matter, but it's not true. Who wants to be the reject? My ride takes an average of twenty-

CHAPTER 8 ~ The Horrors of High School

four minutes. The driver lets me off at the jailhouse and I walk in. They lock me in for the rest of the day.

I report to my first cell, the one I dread the most. This is where they check to see if you made it to jail and if you are late. Either scenario would be grounds for a tongue lashing. Pretty soon, the bell rings, the signal to go to the next cell. In this lock up, they try to teach you how to read, write, spell, and everything else you are supposed to know about books. You are supposed to know how to do it so it will supposedly help you out the rest of your life. Yeah, right—supposedly!

You take tests and you either pass or fail. Then, the bell rings again and you shuffle to the next cell. In that one, they try to teach you all about the rest of the world outside of the jailhouse. They tell you about the laws and all, but we never get a chance to break them because we don't get a chance to see the outside world. If they wouldn't keep us locked up in here, maybe we could learn those things they are trying to teach us in this cell. Silent scream.

The next bell finally rings and on to the next cell I go. In this one they try to teach me how to keep a business running. I ask a question in there and they all jump on your back because you are already supposed to know the answer. I sit there and try to understand it all, but the words go on faster and faster. I just can't understand it all at once.

Soooo, I try to ask another question, but I just get jumped on again for not understanding. They did teach me one thing—never ask questions. The bell finally rings to go on to the next cell which is the feeding cell. They feed us garbage-like soup with mice parts in it and hamburgers made with oatmeal and desserts with bugs in it. Then they wonder why you don't eat the stuff they feed you. The bell rings and time to stagger to the next cell after throwing away the garbage from the garbage they served you.

In this cell, they try to teach you how to put your hands on little black keys and press them down and "bingo" you see words on a piece of paper. If you can't press down the keys fast enough, then you won't do very well because you are timed to see how fast you can go. Please ring, Mr. Bell. He finally does and onto the next cell.

If you were born in Mexico, this would be the perfect cell for you. They try to teach you how to speak another language. I can't even speak my own very well. I don't know how I am going to speak a different one except that I really would like to. Just as you start to get the hang

CHAPTER 8 ~ The Horrors of High School

of it, the bell rings and off you go to the next cell. This next cell is the big one.

This is the one where you get physically educated. That is the one good thing about this whole jailhouse. You get to goof around for a little while in the gym. This is one area I am good at because I am strong from the other jailhouse chores. The bell rings and it's off to the last cell.

I don't know what they are trying to teach here, really. It's very mixed up. I just do my homework and then, if it's wrong, well that is your own tough luck. The last bell rings and I escape to the outside to wait for my ride again. I am glad to see my ride because I can go home now for a while and do work around the house. I'm in jail in the day and in the night.

Tomorrow I have to wake up to another day and go through the same routine all over again. And people wonder why you hate jail. In case you haven't guessed by now, what I call jail by day is what most people call school. They should really consider issuing us black and white striped uniforms.

Trapped in JAIL

Long steel cylinders
Striped vision from behind
Distant freedom
Desires to be obtained
Part of the scenery
Never even noticed!

9

I Killed My Oma

Blessed are those who mourn, for they will be comforted.
Matthew 5:4

During my high school years, Mom developed lupus and couldn't walk, forcing her to be bedridden for months. At one point, a tumor burst inside of her and she was taken to the hospital, where she stayed for ninety days. There was hushed talk that she wouldn't make it home ever again. She was finally discharged, confined to a wheelchair.

Besides going to school and my regular chores, my father expected me to fulfill my mother's duties now, as well. I handled the cooking, cleaning, and laundry. But I couldn't handle being his wife.

My father saw this as an increased opportunity for sexual pleasures. He never did the bad things in front of my mom, but now it was open season on Alice. If I tried to refuse, he beat me and locked me in the ground cellar until I begged to come out, sorry and willing to do whatever he demanded. One time, I was in there all day and all night with the mice. Keenly aware of the secret room off the cellar, I stayed as close to the outer door as I could, talking gibberish to Jesus. Because of those days locked in dark dankness and hunched up small in a corner, I developed claustrophobia. I hate the dark. I can't sit in the middle of a row, only at the end, to escape quickly if panic sets in. No MRIs for me, either. Thinking about any closed spaces gives me the willies.

After my sentence had been served, my father was actually a welcome sight when he released me from the dark tomb of the locked cellar. I have to admit, it was probably the only time I was ever glad to see him. In fear of being locked down there again, I tried to be compliant to his deviant sexual demands knowing what the alternative would be.

CHAPTER 9 ~ I Killed My Oma

After a few weeks of trying to manage all the household duties during mom's hospital stay, I arrived home from school one day to find Oma Elise visiting. It was like Christmas! She was the best surprise ever and greeted me with a bear hug that felt safe and warm. I didn't want to let go. Oh, how I wished she could read my mind and somehow know what was going on in my home. I held tight to her and didn't want that hug to end. She always smelled nice. If love and goodness had a smell, it would be Oma Elise. She wore mom's apron and the house smelled like freshly baked bread. She smiled and told me she was going to stay a while and help with the cooking and cleaning. I was so relieved.

Father became William while Oma was in the house; except for the times she went to visit Mom in the hospital. Then, the Monster prowled around and tried to ensnare me in his sexual trap.

Oma remained with us only a few weeks before she got sick and could hardly walk down the hallway. Doctor Steffy came to the house and said Oma was severely dehydrated and should have lots of fluids. But Oma only seemed to weaken more and had to stay in bed. She couldn't climb the stairs, so that meant she slept in Mother and Father's room. Father was forced to sleep upstairs in the attic which was closer than ever to my bed. I slept with one eye open—if you get what I'm saying.

My expanded list of chores now included caring for Oma. She had to drink lots and lots of fluids, so I took her water and juices throughout the day because she was too weak to get out of bed. It was hard to get her to drink since she didn't feel well, but I insisted she try. I desperately wanted her to get better. Instead, she actually got worse, even though I kept taking her drinks, just like the doctor ordered.

One day while I was at school, the ambulance came and took Oma to the same hospital mom was in but admitted on a different floor. My mother, somewhat improved, kept asking about Oma. No one wanted her to worry, so they didn't tell her how sick she was. Everyone acted like everything was okay. But it wasn't. Things were never okay.

My father called his sister, Mollie, to come stay with us. She didn't like me because my father told her how bad I was. She called me Baby Alice since I peed the bed almost every night. When Aunt Mollie and the Monster went to the hospital in the evenings, I was relieved. I wanted to go, too, but if I stayed at the house alone, I

CHAPTER 9 ~ I Killed My Oma

could play with the cats outside and not worry where the Monster was hiding.

Oma's condition worsened to the point that the family decided to tell Mom. She visited her only if a nurse was kind enough to push her wheelchair to Oma's room, since my father refused to take her. After twelve and a half weeks, my Mom finally came home.

The very next day, my Oma died suddenly.

I was heartbroken that Oma Elise was gone. I loved her so much and she was the only adult whose hugs felt soft, warm, and friendly. When I heard that she died because she had a kidney problem and too much fluid in her lungs, I knew that somehow it was my fault. I was sure of it. If only I hadn't forced her to drink so much. *My Oma died because of me! I killed my Oma! How can I live knowing I killed Oma? Am I a monster now, too? Am I now like my father?*

To this day, I don't remember my Oma's funeral. I do remember when I saw Opa for the first time after she died. He was crying. I told him I was sorry, and that it was my fault.

"No, Alice, it was not your fault, and God will help us day by day." I wished I had been able to go to the hospital to visit my Oma. I never got to say goodbye. I wished a lot of things, and I especially wished that I hadn't killed her. *Does everything and everyone I love have to die?* I asked God that night not to let my mom die. If God wanted to take my mom too, then I asked that he take me first. I could not live alone with a monster on the loose.

The Secret Society of the Serpent
A Word to Clarify the Realities of Satanic Ritual Abuse

For our struggle is not against flesh and blood, but against the rulers, against the authorities, against the powers of this dark world and against the spiritual forces of evil in the heavenly realms.
Ephesians 6:12

Satanic ritualistic abuse is never easy to write about, talk about, or think about. Before sharing more details of my story, I want to take a moment to share a few backstory details about the secret world in which I was held captive for so many years.

It is difficult to comprehend that anyone, especially someone you know, could be a full-time employee of evil. In the underbelly of the devil's workshop here on earth, secret networks of drugs and deviant sexual behavior exist. These groups practice blood rituals with animals and the human sacrifice of innocent babies and children. The practitioners of such atrocities are loyal to Satan and his demonic minions. They are captive to a powerful binding force void of morality or reason. Sexual indulgence achieved through the infliction of pain upon their victims in service to their Master—their holy one—is their goal.

These precepts defined the group of hooded figures that met in the hidden basement chamber of the house I grew up in. They called themselves the Secret Society of the Serpent or the SSS. The Monster was their lead predator. I was their prey.

No consent was necessary on my part. The depraved degenerate I called the Monster always took without asking and demanded the blind faith of his so-called "followers." They took ownership of whomever they chose for their rituals without any personal regard. Vile brainwashing techniques stripped the mind as psychological

CHAPTER 10 ~ Secret Society of the Serpent

manipulation impaired, destroyed, and stole each victim's freedom of thought and reasoning abilities.

Some satanic ritualistic groups exist to promote wealth through the drug trade, pornography, or human sex trafficking. But in the case of the Monster and the SSS, they gathered to indulge in pure, unadulterated devil worship for deviant sex and power over others. In the dark, behind closed doors, they zealously embraced everything opposite of what we were taught in church on Sundays—the same church where, in daylight and in public, my "dear old dad" was a deacon.

Drugged before each terrifying session, I was forced against my will into the chamber rituals. I remember some specific details, but others, by the grace of God, are forgotten. The so-called "religious rite" was a parody of a Christian church service, mocking Jesus with an upside-down crucifix over the stone altar. There was nothing holy about this liturgy. It was a pure feast of violence and carnality.

The first time I was taken there, as an eight-year-old child, was an initiation rite. After that they expected—actually demanded—that I take an active part in all the rites, especially the sexual ones. Faceless men and older teenage boys DEPAR me on the stone altar too many times to count. Then, they forced me to ingest blood, feces, urine, and semen as a ritual meal. I spell DEPAR backwards. It was many years before I could say or write the word "rape."

Eventually, I learned that the gatherings were part of a pattern of eight Sabbaths and Festivals according to the lunar cycle: Candlemas in February, the Vernal Equinox and Beltane (also known as May Eve) in spring, the Summer Solstice and Lammas (Feast of the Sun God) in June and July, the Autumn Equinox and Halloween (the highest satanic holidays) in the fall, and the Winter Solstice in December. A follower's birthday provided another reason to gather—especially the high priest's birthday.

In addition to the ceremonies in the chamber, some were held in a clearing in the center of the wooded acreage behind our house. As a child, I never dared to go that far back into the woods. On ritual nights, I had no choice. My captors took me there where I saw an enormous stone rock with a flat, smooth top surface placed in the center of the clearing.

As an adult, with the terrors of my childhood left far behind, I never felt brave enough to venture back there to see if the giant rock truly existed. However, one day I used modern technology in the

CHAPTER 10 ~ Secret Society of the Serpent

form of my computer and Google Earth to take a look. I hoped to satisfy my curiosity about the hazy memories that haunted me. You can hide a lot of things, but you can't hide a ton of rock. And indeed, there it was. The satellite cameras from space found it. I gasped out loud and enlarged the picture on my screen just to be sure. Somewhere deep inside my brain, memories sharpened into clear focus. I shivered. Then smiled. Further proof that I was not crazy. Hateful and horrible things did happen to me there, and in the basement chamber.

Let me tell you the worst of it.

The Innocents

*Their feet rush into sin; they are swift to shed innocent blood.
They pursue evil schemes; acts of violence mark their ways.*
Isaiah 59:7

Nightmares don't always terrorize at night. Sometimes you live their horror by day.

By age thirteen, the Monster determined that I was ripe for impregnation during one of the fertility rites. The ritual required me to wear an oversized, flowing white, cotton gown with a braided gold belt. I stood by the altar holding a clear glass jar with a lit candle inside. I feared I would drop it due to the heat on my hands but was soon distracted by the sickening sweet smell of something burning on or near the altar.

The hooded figures stood within the circle lit by candle jars on the ground. The ringing of a bell signified the start of the ritual followed by droning voices that seemed to come from everywhere at once. The low hum grew louder and louder, sometimes sounding like words in a language I did not know.

Soon, the attention turned to me. They stripped off my gown and tied me down, naked on the altar, with leather straps. The cold, unforgiving stone pressed into my head, back, and legs, all buckled tight. Trapped.

I panicked! Bile rose up in my throat as I swung my head from side to side. One of the gowned figures stepped forward and held my head still. I squeezed my eyes closed and thought about the picture of Jesus with the children that hung in the Sunday school room at church. Reality faded in and out in my mind as the horrid ritual progressed.

Under each of those black hooded robes, my perpetrators were naked. Then, the robes came off, but the hoods stayed on their heads. I lay fully exposed on the stone, cold, naked, and afraid as my

CHAPTER 11 ~ The Innocents

own father DEPAR me first, followed by others whose voices I did not recognize.

After the Monster's defilement, something switched off in my mind. I don't know where I went; somewhere into a deep dark void where memories fracture, sealed away and locked up. I came to when I heard the clang of the bell. *Today's torture is ended!*

Frozen in place I felt someone untie me as one of the figures whispered in my ear with a hissing voice: "Tonight you were reborn into the Secret Society of the Serpent. You are lucky to be a part of this. After tonight, no one else will want a filthy ugly worm like you." They gave me a silver cup with the grape drink and ordered me to sip it down. That drink always came before and at the end of ritual time in the chamber. The next thing I knew it was morning.

The impregnation ceremony of that night succeeded in its depraved goal. Soon I learned I was pregnant. Although my mom wasn't present in the chamber to my knowledge, she looked for signs that I had become "with child."

Every morning at breakfast she asked me how I felt, "Do you feel sick?" The question seemed strange and quite different from her usual chore reminders. "Did you remember to give the chickens water? Did you turn the water off at the hose? Are you sure you gathered *all* the eggs?" I expected normal questions about the animals, not about my thoughts or feelings.

In addition to the baby I carried, I bore the truckload weight of shame, guilt, and confusion. I didn't go to the doctor once pregnancy was confirmed. Instead, every morning Mom dispensed a pill she claimed was a vitamin. I had no reason to doubt her.

The SSS child-bearing rituals were timed to coincide with the three-month summer school break. No one explained anything to me during those long months. I didn't know what to expect. At school, I carried my secret around plain as day, but no one suspected a thing since I overate and gained weight quickly. I counted that time as a good thing when I saw how the Monster left me alone and didn't visit in the night hours.

After five months, I sensed the baby move inside and felt very protective of it. *What a weird experience!* I knew monsters were responsible for its creation, but determined that I, Alice Fisher, would be the best mother to the innocent little life I carried in my body. I fantasized about the possible names I'd choose and the things I'd do as a good mother to my baby. *If you are a girl, you must be*

CHAPTER 11 ~ The Innocents

named Heidi. I'll dress you in a pink dress with matching polka dot ribbons like Hope, my bunny. Tea parties with real cookies will be served, of course. I'll improve my reading skills and tell you stories with happy endings at bedtime. I will protect you from the monster, you can count on Mama. If you are a boy, you will be named Tyler. I'll call you Ty-Ty for short. You will grow up big and strong; powerful enough to fight off any monster that gets in your way. Mama loves you already.

A calendar from a local feed and grain store hung on the wall next to my bed. I X-ed out each day as it passed with a red pen and waited for my dear baby to come.

At the beginning of the eighth month, Mom handed me medicine and said it was to help the baby. In fact, it induced labor. Although drugged, I still felt an alarming level of pain and thought I was dying. I heard strangers' voices and shuffling about the room in a frenzy of activity. My eyes refused to open. After the last painful push, I thought my insides had slid out. A gruff male voice proclaimed, "It's an 'effin girl."

Heidi entered the world!

For the next few weeks, I was excused from all my chores. But mother took charge of the infant and when I asked to see her, she replied, "No, it's better you don't get attached to her." *What did she mean?*

Her meaning became clear on the third night when I was carried to the ritual chamber of terror. I was forced to play a part in offering my precious innocent on the altar of the unholy that night. Big, rough hands wrapped around mine clutching a glinting sharp dagger in the air, then thrusting downward with a slice. *I h-h-helped m-m-murder my tiny beautiful little Heidi. Helpless as a lamb led to slaughter.*

I recall a lot of blood and a high-pitched scream. At some point I realized that I was the one crying out from deep within me, in reaction to the searing pain of a broken heart. Commanded to be silent, I sensed my inner being fracture and split into pieces.

I didn't know how mail was delivered in heaven, but if I were to write my Heidi a letter, I believed she would somehow know my love for her. There must be an eternal heart connection between a child and their mother.

> *Dear Heidi,*
> *I love your name, Heidi. I am not really sure why I like it so much, but I really love it. I didn't get to name you when you were born because I didn't have a chance before they took you from me. Before you were*

CHAPTER 11 ~ The Innocents

even born precious one, I knew if you were a girl that would be your name. You were here for such a short time. How I loved you and wanted to keep you. I have agonized over your tragic death for all these years. It has been heartbreaking for me to keep our secret of your brief existence and demise. Please know that I loved you and would have gladly cared for you had I been given a chance. I would have given my life for you as Jesus did for me on the cross. That's how much I loved you. I wish I could have gotten to know you, hold you, rock you and comfort you. You were a squealer when were born and a screamer when you died. How could you not be? The people that took your life were evil. They forced me to be a part of it and for that I ask your forgiveness. I am glad you did not live through the hell I have lived through. I wish with all my heart that you never had to be conceived or born so that you never had to experience any of what you did in your very short life. I vowed to protect you before you were born, and I could not. I am sorry I was not able to do so. I know you are in heaven now with Jesus and he is gently holding you and nurturing you with love every day. One day, we will be together again for all eternity. We will celebrate our reunion. Until then, I will never forget you and I will miss you, but I know I will see you again. I love you baby Heidi,

Your Mama, Alice

After that night, I stored up a mountain of unshed tears. My life was wretched; my insides blazed with hate and disgust. *How will I live with myself? I feel darkness creeping in around the edges of my soul.*

All the remains of the animals used in the ceremonies were burned in a fire pit out in the wooded clearing, near a man-made pond. The day after those rituals, it was my job to go back to the site and scoop up the ashes left in what I called the Hole of Death. I inherited that chore from Billy. The ashes were then carried to the pond and thrown in. I waited for a moment when the wind didn't blow. Otherwise, the ashes of death flew back into my face and hair.

The day after that horrible night, I was expected to do my job at the Hole of Death. The Monster stood at the edge of the woods. He watched and waited while I completed the gruesome task of shoveling what was left of Heidi into the ash bucket. My heart beat loud and fast. I knew HE could hear it where he stood. My insides squished like jelly. The pain of that moment paralyzed me deep inside my fractured heart and mind. Sweat broke out on my shivering body. I refused to vomit. I was determined to not allow my breakfast

CHAPTER 11 ~ The Innocents

to come up and desecrate her precious ashes. Squeezing my eyes shut, I prayed a quick, simple prayer, *Jesus, help!*

I shoveled up the ashes and carefully carried them to the pond where I knelt down on one knee. Time stood still. So, too, the wind. As I scattered the ashes, I repeated the words *"I'm sorry"* again and again in my mind. When I finally stood up and turned, the Monster had vanished.

The following year it was decreed that I would be the chosen one for the fertility rite, once again. The Monster told me I should be thankful for the honor. I became pregnant for the second time. This time I knew more of what to expect and dreaded the future of the helpless life growing inside me.

One morning, in my fourth month, I tripped and fell coming out of the hen house. Three dozen eggs cracked or spilled out like guts all over the ground. Father appeared out of nowhere, like some bad magic. He grabbed me roughly by the arms and jerked me up, then sucker punched my stomach spewing the words, "That ought to teach you!" *Teach me what?*

I lay on the ground stunned for a time; the wind knocked out of me. My shoulders ached where the monster had grabbed me. I gently touched my stomach, writhing in a knot of relentless pain. Humiliation and egg splatter covered me from head to toe. My throat ached and I hurt so badly, but somehow made it to the house.

I didn't go to school that day, and it was a Friday. The only day I looked forward to because of gym class.

I lay crumpled in my bed groaning in severe pain, reciting the ABC's in my head to help distract my mind. By nightfall I was bleeding from my girl parts and screamed for Mother. She knew what was happening, even if I didn't.

Mom led me into the bathroom and told me to sit on the enamel white chamber pot with red trim. I last saw this when Oma was bed-ridden at our house. She grabbed my hands and told me to push when the next pain came. I felt something let loose and slide out into the pot with a dull thud as it hit the bottom.

Mother insisted I stand even though I told her I couldn't. I leaned on her while she placed a folded, tattered white towel between my legs to soak up the blood. She guided me to bed, but not before I glanced into the pot. I saw a partially formed baby blob and lots of dark red fluid. I settled in under my bed covers and drank the grape juice Mom handed to me.

CHAPTER 11 ~ The Innocents

No one ever talked about that day, and I never saw that white and red chamber pot again. I lost another precious innocent. Secretly, I felt pleased and thankful. I didn't want to re-live the night Heidi's life was brutally snuffed out.

In my heart, I knew it had been a boy. I named him Tyler and called him Ty-Ty, just as planned. Another letter was delivered to heaven from my heart:

> *Dear Precious Ty-Ty,*
> *My dear sweet boy . . . this is your Mama writing you a love letter. Every time I go to write this, the tears start flowing as I remember the day you came into this world much too early. You were not allowed to grow into a big healthy boy that would cry when he was taken out of me. It is so hard to write this, but I am going to do it as I love you so much. I am sure if your birth were different you would want me to hold you. I know you would feel safe in my loving arms. And if you grew to be a toddler, you would hold up your arms for me to pick you up. Oh Ty-Ty, we should have had many special memories together. I am so sorry that your short life had to begin and end in such a cruel way. I know that you are now with the kind man named Jesus, up there in heaven. I know heaven is a place where there is no sadness, no pain, no tears, no suffering, and no monsters. You are in a better place and I know one day I will be with you again and we will celebrate on that day. You will get lots of hugs and kisses from your Mama. Until I am with you, I will always be sad. You probably already met your sister Heidi. I love you always and forever my innocent sweet Ty-Ty.*
>
> *Love, Your Mama*

12

Escape

*They will come to their senses and escape from the trap of the devil,
who has taken them captive to do his will.*
2 Timothy 2:26

I first met Miss Mary Miller at Hillside Church and Cemetery. She never married and had no children of her own. Some might call her a spinster, but that didn't affect my opinion of her. She demonstrated kindness to me every Sunday morning when I saw her at church. I often wished she was my mother. I even imagined she adopted me and took me home with her. There we'd live happily ever after in a house filled with cats and dogs destined to die of old age, instead of the unspeakable ways I had witnessed throughout my life.

I suspected she had a sitting room with shelves and shelves of books on every conceivable topic. On the center of her mahogany coffee table would be a worn Bible, lovingly placed and opened to read, just like at Oma's house. Every afternoon, tea would be served at four o'clock and all animals, the stuffed ones and the real furry ones, were welcome to come.

One Sunday during my middle school years, Miss Miller called me over to the side of the classroom. *Had I done something wrong?*

She whispered, "Alice, I know things are difficult for you at home and school. If you ever need someone to talk to, or help you in any way, please let me know." She paused, then continued, "Do you understand what I am saying?" I nodded my head.

Why did she think I needed help? What exactly did she know of my troubles? Did someone violate Rule #1: Don't tell? I certainly didn't.

After that strange encounter, whenever I saw Miss Miller, she always looked at me, gently nodded her head, and smiled.

Why was she being so nice to me? She could clearly see how fat, stupid, and worthless I was.

CHAPTER 12 ~ Escape

Who Can I Trust
Author unknown

I'm just a child
  Going this way and that
Running away,
  Like a mouse from a cat.
Which way do I turn?
  Which way do I go?
Who can I trust?
  How will I know?
A present in one hand,
  A blow in the other.
How can I trust...
  This one or some other.
I'm just a child,
  Which way do I go?
Who can I turn to
  How will I know?

The Sunday before my seventeenth birthday, Miss Miller stopped my father as we were leaving the church service. She explained to William that her Aunt Kathryn died just before Christmas and gave her some antique furniture and a serviceable car. "I have no need for a second vehicle," she said. "After careful and prayerful consideration, I have my heart set on gifting it to Alice. She will be graduating next year and undoubtedly will need transportation to a job."

My father's face flushed from pink to crimson in seconds. He swallowed and flatly decreed, "That's a very nice gesture Miss Mary, but one we will be obliged to decline."

Miss Mary carelessly waved her hand as if to sweep the power of father's words away and replied, "Well, it's already been decided, and I won't take no for an answer. I'll be in touch." She turned and hurried away.

That is how I came to own a 1963 Mercury Comet four door sedan in cobalt blue. My first bonafide miracle! Opa taught me how to drive. It helped him fill the lonely hours since Oma's departure. He secretly gave me gas money too. His driver education plan included a stop for ice cream at the end of each session. I tucked

CHAPTER 12 ~ Escape

these wonderful memories into the file cabinet of my mind under the label, *God Things*. I placed Oma, Opa, and Miss Mary's names behind the letter G.

Once I got my driver's license, father granted me permission to drive to school and church on my own. This little taste of freedom kept me lying awake at night plotting for more. An invisible chain had stretched from the Monster to me since I was a toddler. Even though I had a car, he still held my reins tight. Often, he conveyed his control over me with the stern reminder, "Don't think you're going anywhere."

By this time, I understood that the punishments the Monster subjected me to by day, and the torments and terrors of the night, were not normal. I didn't want any part of the candlelight ritualistic miseries that invaded and darkened my mind. Confusion was a constant companion as I often found myself in places around the property with no memory as to how I got there. I double checked my work because I couldn't recall if I did it or not. If it was done, I questioned whether I had actually done it. Nothing seemed certain. Day in and day out, life swirled around me in dull shades of grey.

One night, while fighting a cold, I couldn't stop sniffling. The Monster decided this was an intolerable offense. He grabbed a worn leather belt to teach me a painful lesson. It wasn't the worst thrashing received by his hand, but it put me over my limit. It was the proverbial straw that broke *my* back.

Without any clear plan, I packed up my grief, shame, brokenness, and meager possessions in the middle of the night and carried my heavy load to the car. Part of me was terrified that the Monster would discover me in my flight. Part of me didn't care—even if it meant getting caught and shot. I didn't think about my mother, Sandy, Billy, or the beloved animals I left behind. On a clear and quiet night, I sped away to my future with no backward glances and no regrets.

I lived in my car and ditched school, even though I was halfway through my senior year. In constant terror that the Monster, or one of his fiends, would find me and drag me back to Hell, I remained vigilant at every turn.

Then, in a moment of weakness, I broke one of my own rules to never ask for help and looked up Miss Miller's number in the phone book. Her gentle, but strong voice soothed me when she answered my call. In trembly, stuttering words, I told her that I left home, but

CHAPTER 12 ~ Escape

didn't say why or where I was for fear trouble might find her if I did. She invited me to stay with her temporarily, but I declined the offer, ashamed to face her and admit that the car she gave me was now my home. She suggested I look for a job at a daycare center in a nearby town. She prayed for me and asked God to give me courage and peace. My voice quaked when I thanked her. After I hung up, my heart beat fast with fear. But hope swelled there too.

Much to my surprise, the S&G Day Care and Learning Center hired me on the spot. I believe Miss Miller put in a good word on my behalf with the center director. My job became my comfort zone, my little place in the world. I loved everything about it. Soon, I moved from my car into a room at the YWCA and, when I saved enough money, I relocated to a studio apartment. After completing a course of study at evening classes, I received my General Education Diploma (GED). There would be no dates, no prom, and no graduation cap with a tassel for me.

No matter. I loved the children I cared for like I imagined Jesus loving the children gathered around Him in the picture at church that once captivated me. For the first time in my life, I thought about my future. I wanted to improve my reading skills so I could read aloud to my little charges with more confidence. One of the assistant teachers volunteered to tutor me. As I worked with her and grew in my abilities, a world of possibilities came to life for me through learning. I craved knowledge like an addict needs a fix. Nothing and no one would stop me.

Maybe I wasn't so stupid after all.

Whenever I traveled to and from my apartment, I had the creepy sense that I was being watched. One day, I spotted the Monster across the street in the shadowy store front of the Five and Dime. He knew exactly where I was and wanted to make sure I knew he lurked about.

I escaped my daytime abuse, but not the dread of the nighttime hours. There was no escaping that. I became aware, deep within, that more than one person lived inside of me. *Is that even possible?* Odd things piled up like evidence that something was terribly wrong. I couldn't solve the mystery regarding small gaps of unaccounted time or how I came to be in possession of certain things I didn't remember buying. *Could I have stolen them?*

I had escaped from one torment. But now, something indefinable had worked its way inside of me. *Would I ever escape that?*

Part 2

TOO MANY ME'S

*"She was making me sound like a freak.
How would you even get this way?"*

Knowledge Quest

*For wisdom will enter your heart,
and knowledge will be pleasant to your soul.*
Proverbs 2:10

Midway through the 1970's, I worked full time at the local Basinville University as a custodian–a fancy word for janitor. I knew how to clean and could do it well. This job paid better than the S&G Day Care.

Although I needed the extra money from the job, I despised it. The one bright spot was my cleaning assignment in the library. I had never seen such a magnificent structure and couldn't have imagined all the different categories of books sorted neatly on so many shelves. As a benefit of my job, I could check out books and take them home. What a delight to touch them, smell them, and hold them close to my heart like a discovered treasure. Thus began my one true love affair: reading.

Books transported me to any time in history where I let my imagination run wild, inserting myself as the main character into the adventures I devoured. Reading allowed the inner darkness and harsh realities of life to be held at bay for a little while.

My father continued to follow me. His spy game involved my brother Billy, too. One night, after my late shift, someone attacked me in the alley behind my apartment building. I gasped for breath after being shoved to the ground. As I struggled to sit up, I saw the attacker wore a black ceremonial hood before I passed out. If the goal was to keep me on the edge and unnerved, the dark side was winning. Brave Alice, who lived inside of me, wrote these words:

Secrets by Alice

*Words spoken softly, secrets they unveil
Can you even hear me? Promise you won't tell*

CHAPTER 13 ~ Knowledge Quest

Shout them from the mountain tops, so all the world will hear
EVERYONE will hear me, no more secrets to tell
Yes, I was bad, but you were too
It wasn't only me, as I believed.
You are just as guilty, if not more so
I was just a kid, you were all grown up. (I hate you!)

Silence is not golden, and memories can be an unrelenting enemy. I couldn't go to sleep without doing a monster check. I peeked under the bed, opened every closet door, and looked behind the shower curtain.

Then, I prayed. *Lord Jesus, I pray . . . well, I don't know what to say. All I desire is to be. The person You want me to be. All I see, all I feel, all I want is seeing the way you see. Change my life, change my heart. All I want is that you shine through me. Live in me. Be my life, be my way. Be the truth that guides my thinking. Make me less, You be more. I'm crying out, please come soon, but in the meantime, make your home right here in my heart. Amen.*

During my years as a campus custodian, I often visited the chapel and slipped into the last pew, sight unseen, for services, sure to make a swift escape before the student masses hit the door after the final "Amen." I found peace there and tried to pocket it so I could take it home with me. Miss Miller called me, on occasion, just to see how I was doing—always a bright spot to my day. With each conversation, she nudged me to apply for college and fulfill my dream to be a teacher even though I expressed fear to take that step. I missed the daycare children and their infectious smiles. With a teaching certificate, I could re-enter a classroom at a higher wage fulfilling my dream and my need.

Miss Miller's cousin worked in the admission department at Sweetwater Christian University near Chicago. She offered to enlist her help to get me into college. College! *Should I? Could I?* The negatives seemed to outweigh the positives: I had no money, no brains, and no end of doubts. However, I did have a strong desire to learn and resolved to let Miss Mary Miller help me take a giant leap from here to there. I hoped to land far enough away where monsters weren't allowed to cross the borders.

At the age of twenty-one, I entered college full-time, majoring in Elementary Education under a probationary status, but I was in! Sweetwater introduced me to a new world of wonder and an opportunity to start over. No one there knew me as a retard or slow-minded. I didn't fear getting beat or *DEPAR*. I viewed Sweetwater as the waiting room for Heaven.

College opened doors to a whole new world–so much to experience, to see, smell, and hear. I had lived so sheltered from the real world. Now, I saw endless opportunities for anyone willing to do the hard work. I was willing!

But my studies proved difficult and challenging when distracting thoughts invaded my concentration. Frustration welled up within me as long-past images of family relationships battled for my mental attention. Weary in the fight, I tried to eat the pain away, and packed on more pounds as a result. Awkward hugs set me off with manic scenarios swirling in my mind. A simple touch felt detestable to me.

Anytime I became overwhelmed, I thought about all my future students. It motivated me to keep pressing on and not give up—a constant temptation. *What will I do with all this knowledge? With my life? Will I be remembered? Will anyone ever learn anything from me?*

I dreamed of one day being a wonderful teacher. I fantasized about how I would be loved by my family and the Monster would leave me alone. I entertained the thought that I might open a school for children who had been abused. I could help them with their reading, writing, and arithmetic, but also teach them about how to manage their emotions. I'd teach them that it is okay to cry, to hate, to laugh, to love, and to be hugged. I dreamed on and dreamed BIG. And wrote my thoughts in a journal . . .

Reflections on College Life

Year after year, my dreams materialized into reality. I was free from my father in college. I've struggled—with feelings, beliefs, values and–with people in general. In the struggles, I have learned. I learned how to laugh again, to cry real tears again, to love, to feel. Too many people take feelings for granted along with the ability to express them. Feelings can be paralyzing, but you may have to invalidate your feelings in order to survive.

You experience hurt, deep bitterness, loneliness and sorrow, but if you allow it—happiness, excitement, and joy can leak in and surround the negative. I've learned that I am an imperfect human and Christ loves me as much as anyone else on this campus. I choose not to be an object to be used when desired and then thrown in a corner like trash. I've learned that Jesus isn't hung up on legalities, but He is more interested in us as His treasured ones. If I can only begin to view every

CHAPTER 13 ~ Knowledge Quest

person I meet through His eyes, then I will have learned the most important lesson I can learn here.

None of us is any better than another, different, yes, but better— no! I've grown, I've changed. In order to grow, you have to change; it is inevitable. Only dead people don't change. The changes in me are enormous. People here don't know my history; and, therefore, change is easier. I've broken off the 'stupid image' imposed on me—I'm making it! Or-am I fooling myself? Is this progress real or just a mirage?

Intellectually, I have achieved here. Emotionally, that's another story. I understand the value of a person in light of the Scriptures. I adopted that belief on an academic level. However, to internalize truth in regard to this person called me is extremely difficult.

Walls built by anger and hostility are all around me. Some anger is directed; some is not. It's always there to frustrate and hurt by its passive stubbornness, displaced aggression, and mixed feelings about other people. I have an interpersonal attitude of combined hostility, fear, and the overwhelming need to love and be loved. My need for love cannot easily return the love. Where do I go from here?

I must purpose to continue dreaming, learning, struggling, growing, changing. I have to move forward, to keep going, and striving. Hopefully, I will never give up and lose my desire to do these things. I want to see the world as Jesus does, not the white middle class world, but through the eyes of the One who walks beside me each day and accepts me as I am with His unconditional love. When I don't have the strength or the guts to keep going, then this Jesus is strong enough to carry me. I want to be like that Jesus for others. When Jesus is in me, my participation in the world around me is essential and it counts for something, right?

At the intersection of Future Road and Dream Corner, I desire to be teaching as my gift of participation. It doesn't begin or end there. SCU (Sweetwater Christian University) is part of the real world, it's where my involvement is and I don't take that lightly. There are many needs right here on campus that are overlooked. Hurts are hidden as the primary focus is preparation for the real world. Isn't SCU part of the real world?

I'm sure I'll never make the headlines and that is fine by me. I would rather have it that way. I prefer being behind the scenes in the shadows where the spotlight doesn't shine. I am determined to be like Mother Teresa. She didn't do anything extraordinary in one sense; she did what lay before her day after day, caring for the lowly and outcasts.

CHAPTER 13 ~ Knowledge Quest

She put into practice her values, beliefs, and Christ's principles. That is what I am striving for—to be a servant, but not an ignorant one. One that reaches deep down inside for what is truth. I don't want to become stagnant, but willing to explore. After all, what I believe today could change because of what I learn tomorrow. Well, this is me, a struggling wiggly worm, the lowest of creatures.

Behind the Books

And God is able to bless you abundantly, so that in all things at all times, having all that you need, you will abound in every good work.
2 Corinthians 9:8

Throughout my time at college, my parents never visited me. When other parents helped their children set up dorm rooms at the beginning of the semester or visited on Parent's Day, mine were nowhere to be found. This created a seesaw of conflicting emotions within me. I wanted to be like the students who hugged their parents goodbye while their mom wiped tears away on an embroidered cotton hanky. But on the other hand, college was my personal safe place. *Did I really want my father invading that space? Once you let a monster in, how will you get it out?*

My parents knew where I lived. I sent greeting cards home on family birthdays and expanded letters at Christmas. I wrote an over-the-top account of my busy college life, secretly hoping the infused positivity would anger my father.

Occasionally, a letter arrived from Mother. *What good news could she bring?* When I saw the return address, Hateful Alice hoped it would bring news of a certain monster's death. Instead, she wrote a mundane account of day-to-day events on the farm and glowing details that all was perfect in "Sandy-world." Billy, still home bound, worked like a pack mule under the command of Sergeant Know-It-All. *"Billy, why? Why do you stay?"*

Mother's world never varied. She laundered on Mondays, grocery shopped on Tuesdays, ironed on Wednesdays, sewed on Thursdays, cleaned on Fridays, baked on Saturdays, and reserved Sundays for church. Planting, weeding, gardening, canning, and a host of other chores filled the rest of her schedule. What she said in her letters didn't trouble me. What she *didn't* say in her letters gave me goosebumps.

CHAPTER 14 ~ Behind the Books

During freshman year, I stayed at the college in a dorm room with a noisy roommate named Lucy. I'm certain the name Lucy means parrot; she-talked, squawked, and talked some more. All. Day. Long. Silence had always been my faithful companion, so I had a difficult time adjusting to my roommate's constant clamor. To muffle the endless stream of words, I wrapped my pillow around my head. She asked questions I didn't want to answer like: *Where did you grow up? What is your family like?* Perhaps I should have told her. Then, she would have run away screaming, never to return so I could enjoy peace and quiet—just me, and me alone. When I didn't speak in response to her chatter, Lucy thought she'd angered me. Sometimes, she stomped out and slammed the door. Little did she know that I just wanted her to SHUTUP.

Keeping busy outside of my dorm room and away from my annoying roommate, I found solace in the library when not working in the cafeteria as a dishwasher or volunteering for campus security.

I constantly checked the job boards for opportunities to earn extra money in order to pay more on the negative balance between my grants and student loans. My parents didn't give me a penny toward my education, and if they had offered, I would have taken great pleasure in saying, "No, thanks!" I'd die first before taking money from the thief of my childhood.

When everyone left for summer break, I spent my time camped out in the near empty dorms. I scored a job with the International Student Program. Undergraduates from all around the world came to SCU for eight weeks of integrated study. I enjoyed interacting with these friendly students on their annual visit. I related to their feelings of stepping into unknown territory where they had to rely on others to help them navigate unfamiliar waters of a foreign country.

When I first came to SCU, I felt like Alice in Wonderland. I understood their concerns. I felt needed when I helped these students find their way—an enchanting but strange feeling for me. It helped me focus on the needs of others and not think about the horrible things that went on at Shivering Acres.

One semester, I befriended Nkechi from Swaziland, Africa, and Hannah from Alberta, Canada. They expected nothing of me, which was a relief. In my life, only Oma, Opa, and Miss Mary had shown me the love of Jesus, but Nkechi and Hannah were my first Jesus-loving friends who accepted me despite the physical weight and heavy burdens I carried. They didn't try to poke behind my façade

CHAPTER 14 ~ Behind the Books

too much and I appreciated that. I looked forward to seeing them every semester they visited. Hannah and Nkechi became lifelong pen pals.

In fact, I saved this treasured note from Hannah:

> *Alice,*
> *You may find this unnecessary; I don't know. You have been one of my closest friends during my time at SCU. I feel indebted to you for all you have given and done for me. I have felt loved by you; I honestly have. I want you to feel your own personal goodness. I sense this is difficult. So, I hope you understand my awkwardness and lack of sensitivity at times. I don't know where or how to begin. Just know that I love you. I thank God for the beauty I see in you. I know we will remain friends beyond the walls of SCU.*
>
> *Signed,*
> *Hannah*

Does God have a giant Wheel of Fortune in heaven to spin on our behalf? Some days it seems we're out of luck and other days we hit the jackpot. During my first eighteen years of life, the spinner must have been broken to always point to Out of Luck. But slowly, I began to suspect that God arranges things for good in due season; even directing when the spinner lands on a golden ticket.

The president of SCU and his family lived on the edge of campus in a stone villa, named Young Manor, after the first SCU president. The villa's attached efficiency apartment was annually awarded to a deserving low-income student. At the end of the summer after my freshman year, I won the jackpot prize—the golden ticket—the apartment at Young Manor. I had been noticed by college administration officials and applauded for excellence in my on-the-job responsibilities and commitment to the International Program. My probation status disappeared, replaced with three years of paid room and board. Miracle number two had arrived!

By senior year, four months prior to my cap and gown moment, I student-taught a wonderful class of second grade special education students, bringing me another step closer to my dream of teaching full time. In the spring of 1982, I graduated with a Bachelor of Arts degree in Elementary Education with minors in Social Science and English. I was even listed in *Who's Who in America—College and University Edition of 1982*. After graduation, I worked to secure a teaching position, built my bank account, and continued my

CHAPTER 14 ~ Behind the Books

knowledge quest in pursuit of a master's degree. I was a rising star, at last!

All these good story elements of my college experience may cause one to surmise that Miss Alice Fisher was finally on her way to something well deserved after growing up with the twins—Devastation and Despair. Hopeful Alice recounted those four years of college with cheerful celebration.

But Alice, Queen of Malice, tells the tale of those four years with less enthusiasm. Much less.

Read on.

Behind the Curtain

*Trust in the Lord with all your heart
and lean not on your own understanding.*
Proverbs 3:5

In the movie *The Wizard of Oz*, Dorothy and her companions make it to the Emerald City and shakily face the great and mighty Oz. Toto scampers off and pulls the green curtain aside, exposing the manipulation and trickery of an ordinary con artist from Nebraska. Turns out he was not so powerful, after all.

Throughout my time at Sweetwater Christian University, I felt like a con artist. Behind life's curtain, things happened I didn't want exposed. I struggled internally between the Alice I was and the Alice I wanted to be. These two went head to head many times, each wanting to go their own way. Hopeful Alice always had to be on her toes, trying to think straight every day. She managed work schedules, volunteer duties, wrote papers, studied, and interacted socially. Of course, *that* Alice was always on time and kept her goals in the forefront, thinking of those future little ones who needed a loving, caring teacher in their lives.

Malice Alice, with all her hatred, suicidal thoughts, and self-loathing, lived behind the curtain. I knew she dwelt there, but I didn't know how to tame that part of me. She scared me. *She wants to take over my life!*

I refused to allow the venom of her miserable existence to poison the good I had tried to achieve. It is said, "We are our own worst enemy." I knew that to be true. I fought Malice Alice, the ugly part of me. She lurked from deep within, circled around the episodes in my daily life, and surfaced at the most inconvenient times.

For instance, in my freshman Creative Writing class, we were instructed to write down anything we deemed important to our life and well-being. I purchased a journal with a cover that looked like a blue denim pocket which had a small red label attached that read: *My*

CHAPTER 15 ~ Behind the Curtain

Anything Book. Malice Alice decided this would be *her* private diary. Here's a peek behind the gloomy curtain to see what she thought while the other Alice went on with life as usual:

I'm so sick of this d*mn life! No one ever promised life would be easy, but no one told me it would be hell either. Why can't there just be a balance? I feel like I am losing touch with reality—and I like it! It is easier to cope that way. I just hope I don't go off the deep end.

*It's not easy being alone! But it's probably not easy **not** being alone either. People say they understand, but they don't really, how can they know, unless they're alone too? NOISE—I can't stand it! Every noise seems to be louder and louder. The clock ticks so loud and the chimes—oh, how they bother me. Take them away! PLEASE PLEASE PLEASE—before they attack me. TICK TOCK TICK TOCK—my head is ringing, bursting, please stop the noise before I explode. Can't you hear me. . . !??*

Blocked. No matter what I try to do. Walls built by anger and hostility are all around me. Some of my anger is directed, some is not, but yet, it is always there to frustrate and hurt. Is it passive stubbornness, displaced aggression, or mixed feelings that I have about ALL people, including myself? All of Alice needs love. Where do you go to find that to fill in the spaces around the hate and anger? I am broken. I am tangled. I am shattered. I feel scattered.

Please care!
Hate me if you want
Hate me if you have to
Beat me, even kill me
But, please know I exist!
I exist, don't you see?
Can you not see…
the different parts of me?

I am
Unnecessary
Unlovely and
Probably
Unlovable
Abnormal

CHAPTER 15 ~ Behind the Curtain

Weird
Fat
But
I am
Now what?

The dark shadows are moving closer and closer each night. What will I do when they overtake me? Don't tell daytime Alice, she has enough to worry about during the daylight hours.

Late at night when the entire world is sleeping, here I lay in darkness softly weeping. The moon hangs in the tree top and its light streams through the window down upon my face pressed tightly against my pillow. The tenseness of the moment is worn on the lines of my forehead and in the glazed blur of my eyes. My body, shaking uncontrollably, strains to keep the turmoil in. As I lie here, I feel so hurt I think my heart will break. It's just too hard to take. The moon still alight in the tree top draws me to the window. I gaze out into the stillness of the night and wonder how long I can keep hanging on.

My trembling hand, cold against the windowpane seems so different now than it's ever felt before. The physical wounds have formed their scars leaving reminders of past tortures. The personhood has not yet formed its defense against the enemy's continuous attacks. Slowly all hope is oozing out. No healing salve can seal the flow; only delay termination.

I turn back to bed and affix my eyes on the glimmering sharp blade that beckons me. Only minutes, maybe hours and pain would be no more. It would be so easy. "Oh my God, the moment could be no closer, please help me lay it down."

Daytime Alice lived in a state of euphoria and delusion. One year, she concluded we would go home on Christmas break. Home. It should conjure up pleasant memories of family gathered around the table eating a plump, juicy, turkey dinner with all the trimmings. The scene would include brightly wrapped gifts sitting under a freshly cut Christmas tree, filling the room with a pleasant outdoorsy scent. When the gifts were distributed, we would create memories of laughter and maybe Kodak pictures to place in a scrapbook for a lasting treasure. Mother humming, father smiling, brother whistling

CHAPTER 15 ~ Behind the Curtain

and sister clapping her hands with delight—these are the elements I dreamed of living out on a trip home for Christmas—like a scene in a children's picture book.

But such dreams could never come true in a house with the name of Fisher on the mailbox. *What kind of Christmas miracle did Hopeful Alice, the grand believer in a holy God, expect?*

She falsely believed that the protection and shelter she felt in her new college life made her invincible. *Hopeful Alice, what were you thinking?*

Emotions are like a storm. They darken and swirl around you. Sometimes, a loud thunder crash jolts you with a warning of worse to come. The lightning may strike you unaware. Storms are unpredictable. There can be calm in the middle of one, but then, the rain pelts you into a puddle of despair.

> *Beware of the storm, Alice. I tried to warn her, Hopeful Alice. I tried to warn her.*
>
> *Help me if you can*
> *I'm feeling down*
> *I'm homeward bound*

The Decision

*My soul is weary with sorrow;
strengthen me according to your word.*
Psalms 119:28

Journal Entry:

    I never forgave my father for killing me, especially at such a youthful age and in such a horrible way as EPAR while I was just beginning to grow up. I've hated his name and hated his authority and cannot let him be close to me ever again. Though the memories are stored in the deepest cabinet, I can hear him faintly knocking.

    I foolishly let him in with the hope of change from revenge and hatred to compassion and love. Oh, so disappointed! I'm continuously disappointed because he always rips me into shreds without a single word and leaves me lying there for dead. In my twenty-fourth year, I can still feel that tormenting pain.

Yes, Alice, Queen of Malice warned me.
Yes, I thought I could somehow handle it.
My Christmas break that year destroyed any preconceived notions or fantasies of how I thought people might change. My time spent at home was a game of cat and mouse—with me as the defenseless mouse. Again. Caught in a trap the third day home without anywhere to run or hide.

EPAR

*Death, repeated…death
sore, ripped, opened, bloody
limp body
repeated thrusting
agonizing torture
wet, hot smelly*

CHAPTER 16 ~ The Decision

clothes tearing
nakedness
madness
pregnant

This was the gift my father gave to me that Christmas. Our Heavenly Father gave us the Christ Child, and my earthly father gave me a child conceived in sin and hate.

I don't remember how I wound up back at school. I must have driven because my car was clearly there. The gift I opened on Christmas day with the tag "To: Alice—From: Mom and Dad" was lying on my bed when I arrived home from work one day. The jeans. They were completely cut to shreds. *How did this happen?* If it was me, I don't remember. I couldn't imagine my roommate Lucy doing such a thing. *Should I ask her? I'm afraid.*

I picked up all the ripped fabric pieces. *Who will pick up the pieces of my life?* But, shredded blue jeans were easy to toss away and the mess cleared. I had a bigger problem. My other gift was growing inside of me.

Journal Entry:
How can I write about an unwanted child? How can this be happening? The Monster has planted his seed? Ugh! Revolting! What to do? What to do?

Mother is daughter
Father is grandfather
Child is conceived
Hatred dominates
A decision is needed

The struggle had begun. A decision had to be made. My gut churned. I was a mother once and the child was ripped from me, taken before I could claim her love for my own. The child, innocence given over to darkness. A life snuffed out. *Guilt, guilt, guilt.* I was forced to participate in such an unholy act. *Guilt, guilt, guilt.*

"Lord, can you hear me? I have strayed from you again. Will I ever feel worthy of your love? I dream of a time when you will accept me with open arms? Will you forgive me for all I have done wrong—or is that impossible? Why did I go back to the hell house? Couldn't you have

CHAPTER 16 ~ The Decision

stopped me? Maybe you tried and I couldn't hear your voice among all the other voices vying for attention. I'm sorry I keep screwing up! What do I do? To get rid of this child, like garbage—isn't that murder, Lord? Then, it would be by my own hand, how do I live with that? I am barely holding on here. To allow this cursed seed to grow in me, day by day—I cannot comprehend a way to love a child like this, spawned in hate. It would be a daily reminder of the Monster's power. I can't! I can't! I don't want to! You said you are powerful and mighty—so show me the way! Maybe the answer is closer than I think–I could shrivel up and die. You won't allow that–or will you?"

I had to call the doctor the next day. A decision had been made. *What will he say? What will he do? "Lord, no! no! Please, I beg you; take me to where You are. Just let me die—let me get out of here. Don't You see, I'm not worth the bother. I'm beyond help! I don't want to be this way—I'm afraid. Terror."*

I breathed deeply and picked up the phone.

A child's voice whispered in the dark as I wrote.

> *I am*
> *Unwanted*
> *Unlovely and*
>   *Probably*
> *Unlovable*
> *Bred in darkness*
> *Abnormal*
>   *But*
> *I am*

D*mn indecision! The doctor called back, "Alice, you are with child, full to the brim, what is your decision?"

I thought on these things . . .

> *You tied me down*
> *I couldn't move*
> *You laughed*
> *And I cried*
> *You forced yourself*
> *Upon me*
> *Your final bow*
> *Was urination*
> *All over me*

CHAPTER 16 ~ The Decision

You covered me up
Like a corpse
Left me for dead
Laughed again
Walked away
Morning stirs
You came
Loosened the ropes
To set me free
But a prisoner
I'll always be
Go, please go
Leave me alone
To shower
And try to live again
Now, I carry a child
Conceived of hate
"What do I do?"
And God is love?
Yes, he'll care for me
He'll love you too
Tell me how
Where is love
When torture strikes
Show me love
Then, I'll believe
I'm tired, so tired
Of empty words
What now?

We've decided!

The voices decided. Voices in my mind. There was so much conflict in my head, so many thoughts, swirling, whirling. I stumbled, attempting to regain my balance in my dizziness and disorientation. My mind battled in a tug-of-war, back and forth, until the rope frayed from the center into two ends with only one small strand of fiber to hold us together. Take-Charge Alice was a definite "no" vote. Malice Alice voted "yes." In a burst of fury, she yanked the rope to its breaking point. The choice was made. We scheduled a date.

CHAPTER 16 ~ The Decision

On appointment day, I scribbled a journal entry in childlike handwriting, back slanted, small with wavy letters; different from all my other writing:

> *How do you expect me to write about abortion when that is a decision that has already been made? What's the point? Abortion can be a release. You can continue what you were doing before. It's less expensive. You don't have to face the hatred. There's finality. Words like murder, cruel, irresponsible, fear, garbage, and guilt come to mind. How will I cope? What chance do you have, child, in this big cruel world? It wasn't your fault and it wasn't mine either. I wish you could talk to me and tell me what you want, but now—it's been decided. The deed is done!*

In deep despair, I wrote this:

> *I'm alive, the baby is no more*
> *I'm rocking, screaming silently*
> *"What have I done?"*
> *More secrets.*

Shattered

If we confess our sins, he is faithful and just and will forgive us our sins and purify us from all unrighteousness.
1 John 1:9

Once the child was detached, I wailed and moaned, I wanted to cry, but no tears came. Empty, I felt so empty inside as I wrote:

> *Wind whispers through the trees*
> *Trying desperately to do its job*
> *In a quiet kind of way*
> *Hanging on fiercely*
> *Leaves are shouting for the wind to stop*
> *Yet, the wind keeps blowing*
> *Never taking a rest*
> *Still suspended, watching,*
> *Another empty limb*
> *From where their partner fell*
> *Observing, as he is carried away*
> *To shrivel and die*
> *Somehow Lord, the last leaf*
> *Holding on*
> *By one tiny hand*
> *Is me*

Wrapped up in an excruciating realm of pain, it didn't matter how many times I showered. I couldn't scrub away the guilt. My sorrow overflowed and washed down the drain, never-ending. My life was one gaping wound, oozing out poison without a bandage big enough for the mess of me. *Who can heal me? Where do all the healers go when there is no emergency? Help! Help! Is anyone listening? Lord, are you home today?*

CHAPTER 17 ~ Shattered

I was afraid to make decisions. I questioned the difficult one I had just made. My heart battled on the frontlines of an interior war. I grew weary in the fight. Malice Alice and her darkness perpetually invaded me—body and soul. She thrived there, trying to take the lead in my life. Hope had always been my strongest weapon when I battled darkness—a beacon to guide me. But now, that light seemed diminished to a sputtering flame. Hope eluded me. *How do I keep Hope alive?* I was determined not to follow Malice Alice in the death march.

Though I silently screamed for help, I rejected it when rescue arrived. *How do I accept help from others? I'm tired of being isolated, all alone, afraid to touch and be touched. Please, someone, anyone, come and hold me. I might try to push you away, but just tell me I'll be okay. That I'll make it. Lie to me, if you must.*

When someone did come alongside of me to help, I felt no different after their promises. *Are the people all around me blind? Can't they see me beyond the fat, the half-smile, the silence, the pain of me? Oh, they say they'll pray, but will they? Or do they just go their way, feeling all self-righteous?*

Like a wild animal pacing in a cage, I needed to be tamed. I made my cage of steel barriers that grew stronger and taller with each passing day. *Who will tame me? Am I able to be a friend to those around me? Someone take the time! I promise to be patient, to learn, to listen. If I can't change, if I can't be tamed, I must be caged. I am afraid of humans. They are not all monsters, but how do you know who to trust?*

Like glass fallen and shattered into a variety of sharp, jagged pieces—too many to piece together—I lay littered on the ground. I looked up in prayer, the place where elusive Hope resides:

> *Lord, I will lay these pieces on Your altar. Is it too late? You can do the impossible. Is this possible? If anyone can help me, it's you. You are the only one who knows I exist. I feel my inward parts ripping, rending and fraying. I am split apart. Please, I beg You to forgive me and put me back together, before the enemy wins this death battle.*

18

Living the Dream

Be strong and courageous. Do not be afraid or terrified because of them, for the Lord your God goes with you; he will never leave you or forsake you.
Deuteronomy 31:6

Days passed in a blur. Strong Alice reorganized our interior world attempting to refocus our life to move singularly forward.

Six weeks before graduation day, my sister Sandy sent me a help-wanted ad from Orchard Grove Christian Academy in my home state. They needed a teacher for grades seven and eight. The school was only an hour and a half north of where I grew up, but too close to the root of all evil. Sandy, in her excitement, insisted I apply. Her college friend, Debby, was already teaching fourth grade there.

So, what?

Sandy announced her engagement the year before and planned a fall wedding. She prattled on about me being closer to the action and how she needed my help with wedding details. I didn't know anything about wedding logistics, but I needed a job. My number one goal was the dream career of teaching. I prayed and reluctantly applied for the position, reasoning that if God didn't want me there, the answer would be a big fat "No!"

An immediate response and job offer arrived two weeks before graduation. I believed this proved the hand of God rested upon me. With a degree in hand, I packed up my dreams and wishful thinking and headed back to Pennsylvania. I found an affordable efficiency apartment a short three blocks from the school.

My anxiety and internal struggles moved in right along with my meager possessions. I discerned a time-bomb residing within me. *I am a bomb!* I heard it . . . *tick tick tick*. I felt it vibrating deep inside-- its fuse growing shorter and shorter with each passing day. Each facet of Alice sensed it, too. *When the timer runs out, it will destroy everything. Nothing will be salvageable. Nothing will ever be the same. It's only*

CHAPTER 18 ~ Living the Dream

a matter of time. Please Lord, make me deaf to the ticking so I can get on with my new life as a teacher here. These kids need me, and I need them!

Teacher Alice organized my books and binders, and I began what was to be a seven-year relationship with the school. Life settled into a busy routine. At first, I struggled to make ends meet and took a part-time job to fill my evening hours at Walmart.

My students became my world. My surrogate children.

Teaching rejuvenated me. Watching a sense of wonder light my young charges as they tackled challenges and projects filled me with great satisfaction. It was something I had missed in my childhood. Thoughts expressed. Ideas shared. Questions asked. Answers discovered. Intangibles grabbed and formed into creative, tangible evidence of learning was an exciting process to behold. The open honesty and simplicity of trust my students communicated about the people and the world around them refreshed me. The beauty of an untainted childhood inspired me. Their humor, boundless energy, and spirit captivated me and made me smile. Hope heightened knowing these young hearts would be leaders one day, and I, Alice, had played a part in their success. I was blessed to be a teacher.

Teaching responsibilities filled my life with lessons to plan and papers to grade. This eased my panic in the night hours when the minions of darkness teased, attacked, and attempted to overrun my life. A battle constantly raged inside me, but Strong Alice was vigilant to push back the dark so it would not steal my light. Still, the bomb ticked on, unrelenting.

If I listened carefully, I heard it . . . *tick tick tick*.

Teacher Alice perfected her teaching skills and looked forward to each day knowing twenty faces counted on her to fill their minds with knowledge about life and the world around them. She tacked inspirational reminders and some of my favorite quotes throughout the classroom:

- *God loves you just the way you are, but too much to leave you that way.*
- *God has no grandchildren.*
- *Christians have more fun, especially later.*
- *I've read the last chapter!*
- *What you are is God's gift to you; what you make of yourself is your gift to God.*

That last quote captured my heart's desire. I wanted to be *that* child of God, to make something of myself as a gift to God. I didn't

CHAPTER 18 ~ Living the Dream

want to remain captive to the life of pain and abuse I'd lived for so many years. *Oh God, I don't know how to be a gift worthy for You to receive, but I can certainly encourage my students in that direction!*

In the fall, I traveled home for my sister's wedding. She asked me to participate as a bridesmaid. Brave Alice agreed. Hesitant Alice did not. No way did she want to stand up in front of an audience, fat as a house and be seen! I would have been more comfortable sitting in the farthest corner seat of the last row watching the whole thing unfold from there.

But love for my sister won the wedding battle and there I was, big as you please, in her wedding photos. Wedding days are meant to be treasured and remembered. That day blurred by, and I longed to be done with it and safe at home. I wanted to be joyful for Sandy and her new husband, Michael, but part of me was jealous, too! Their love for one another appeared genuine. *Would I ever experience that kind of love?*

Throughout the wedding weekend, I was constantly aware of the movements of my father; like reverse stalking. I wanted to be far away from wherever he stood or sat. I set myself on High Alert Status at the wedding and at the house the day before. I would not allow myself to be alone with Father for one single, solitary moment. On her last night in Hell House, Sandy and I slept in the same room. I knew the Monster would not dare creep out of his den.

As I lay in bed, I realized another monster lurked nearby. He went by the name of Sneaky Thief. He stole my childhood and now he wanted to steal my sanity. Sleep evaded me as he roamed about the dark room where I tossed and turned on the night before my sister's wedding. I was exhausted. *Tick Tick Tick*

I noticed how Sneaky Thief also stole time. I discovered event programs and ticket stubs wondering where they had come from. *Did I sit in Row C, Seat 4?* Groceries appeared that I had no memory of buying. *Where did they come from?* I was puzzled and alarmed. *Tick Tick Tick*.

Organized Alice needed to stay on top of all the strange events as they unfolded. I kept a record to see if a pattern developed. The Monday after the wedding weekend, I called out sick from school. I wasn't physically ill, but seeing the Monster stirred up the quicksand around me. That entire day, I tried to erase the image of his face imprinted on my mind, tormenting me.

CHAPTER 18 ~ Living the Dream

It didn't work. *Jesus, I'm sinking! Lift me up out of the pit. Help! Throw me a lifeline!*

I'm sure Principal Kevin Stryker suspected some sort of unspoken issue going on in my life. I thought I hid it well, but he and his wife Carlene regularly inquired, "How are you doing, Alice?"

"I'm OK, why do you ask?"

"Well, we care about you and just want to be sure you're okay." Kevin and Carlene had three children; five-year-old identical twin girls, Amy and Beth, and a two-year-old toddler boy named Brian.

One day, after church, they approached me about the possibility of babysitting so they could have a date night. Though baffled by their personal request, I felt honored and accepted that they thought me worthy to look after their children. This launched a peaceful interlude of happy times spent with their family at dinners, picnics, fireworks, birthday celebrations, and game nights. One year, they even included me on their long weekend summer trip to Bushkill Falls. *Why would they bother with the likes of me.*

It didn't take long until I thought of them as my adopted brother and sister and their kids as my Godchildren. Between my times spent with the Stryker family, church, my part-time job, and teaching in the classroom, I pretended that everything was normal.

The last item on my nightly checklist included turning the light on. I'd push fear into the hall closet and shut the door tight. The bomb still ticked. Always threatening. For three years, my life had been void of any interaction with my parents. Everything in the *outside* world was calm.

Then, Brave Alice decided to go home for Easter.

Tick! Tick! Tick! BOOM!

Undone

Even though I walk through the darkest valley, I will fear no evil for you are with me; your rod and your staff, they comfort me.
Psalm 23:4

Easter Day Journal Entry:

> Jesus, you are alive!
> Faith-filled Alice celebrates you!
> I'm excited about possibilities
> Something good will surely happen
>
> I am tense with anticipation
> Hoping . . . a miracle awaits, around the corner
> You were in the tomb for three days,
> You were dead, now alive, out of the tomb
>
> The house feels the tension today
> Even the dog's eyes grow wide
> Smelling the aroma of the ham
> My anticipation grows stronger
>
> The table is set with Oma's china
> Cotton napkins carefully folded
> The dinner bells rings
> Announcing all is ready
>
> We gather for the feast
> William offers thanks

CHAPTER 19 ~ Undone

I wasn't listening
Loaded shotgun in the corner calls my name

I look away, I see Billy
Sandy and Michael,
The two-eyed Monster, mother
Then there is me, me, and another me

My head spins
As we silently fill our stomachs
My anticipation shrinks
Dishes done, I have to run

I drive away
I glance in the rear-view mirror
Catch a glimpse of a hooded figure
In the doorway of the barn

Keep driving Alice
Don't look back
There is no miracle here
You have been left in the tomb, all alone

Easter break meant no school for a week. After a disturbing Easter visit to my parent's house, I drove home to my safe place on autopilot. I would never escape the Monster's grasp! Like a magnet, I had been pulled back into a lie by an unrelenting force. Foolish Faith-Filled Alice trusted where she should never have trusted.

Numb and paralyzed inside my home and myself, my apartment became a tomb that week. Like an oversized rat racing through a maze with no possible exit, I was trapped. Shadowy figures in the back of my mind worked their torments overtime at night. Now they dared to show up in the daytime hours. My jumbled, disordered mind stirred my anxiety. Take-Charge Alice was nowhere to be found to put things in order. *Who would take charge of my life, now? Surely*

CHAPTER 19 ~ Undone

Teacher Alice would return in time to go to school on Monday. I tried to hope but didn't count on it.

My life was like an unsharpened pencil with no point, no point, no point! I couldn't see straight, blinded by pain and shame. Like a broken record, my thoughts mocked me. *Shame! Shame is your name! You are an enormous fat burden to everyone. Dirty! Dirty! Not quite thirty!*

My memory was my enemy. I didn't want to think, feel, or do. Anything. I was uncertain if I even wanted to BE. *Who cares? Will anyone miss me?* I whispered, "9-1-1, 9-1-1, 9-1-1!" *Is anyone listening? Live or die? Die or live? Is there really a choice?* Darkness–everywhere darkness.

A vision of that loaded shotgun swirled into view. Yes, so easy, one quick pull of the trigger. Too bad that I didn't own a gun. But I did have a knife. A sharp, pointy steak knife. *Do I dare? God, where are You? I call out Your Name. If You are speaking, I can't hear You. I call on You again. Fresh out of the tomb, did You forget about me? Here I am. You said the eyes of the Lord are everywhere, watching evil and good. Well, can You see? Are Your eyes closed? Do You see the shadows lurking, surrounding me? They have a strangle-hold on me. Loosen their grip, Jesus.*

NO, don't! I want to die!

Is there a safety catch on self-destruction? Perhaps a password would stop the madness. Again, I muttered, "9-1-1, 9-1-1, 9-1-1."

I was alive. I was breathing. But I was dead on the inside. A stab to the heart would make it official. I would become just another suicide statistic. Just another someone who didn't make it.

My tomb has no bottom—a pit of dark torment. Shine your flashlight, Lord. Extend Your hand! My head hurts from the tick—tick—ticking. It's so loud, loud, loud. Stop the noise. I'm trapped! I need a miracle! Resurrect my soul. Bring me out of the tomb before the bomb goes off. Dark—so dark.

My turbulent week of Easter vacation finally ended. Teacher Alice showed up Monday morning at 6:00 a.m. She seemed to have everything in control, so I allowed her to think that. *Where had she been while the threads of my life frayed and the tick tick tick grew louder in my head? Did she even care that I had lived a whole week of agonizing days and nights?*

I hoped Teacher Alice wouldn't notice the bandages across our chest where the knife left jagged lines as a reminder of how we survived the week. *I can't stop hurting myself! I'm out of control and can't stop myself.*

CHAPTER 19 ~ Undone

"Somebody, please take over," I cried aloud. Teacher Alice stepped forward. Maybe Faith-Filled Alice was right. Jesus answered the 9-1-1 call. He rolled the stone away from the tomb just enough for a little light to shine through. That sliver of light kept us alive. For the moment.

Teacher Alice arrived at school wearing an outfit I didn't recognize as one I owned. *I'll worry about that later.* The inside of my chest rumbled, like aftershocks in the wake of an earthquake. I was so tight, my entire body, wound-up in a rubber band about to snap with parts of me springing out in all directions, littering the ground. I murmured to myself throughout the day. Every noise agitated my threadbare nerves.

Miss Alice Fisher tried really, really hard that day. Just before the dismissal bell, Peter, the most challenging eighth grader in my class, broke his pencil in two. When I heard the snap, something deep within me snapped, too. Like that rubber band I'd had a vision of earlier.

"Are you stupid?" I uncharacteristically yelled at Peter. "Were you born in a barn? Are you the son of a donkey? Do you expect to amount to anything?"

The tension in the room was palpable. The class gasped as I reduced a smart aleck teen to tears. Fortunately, the dismissal bell sounded, and the students scurried out of the room like frightened mice. The school day was ended.

An hour later, Principal Stryker wandered into my classroom to see why the lights were still on. He saw me huddled in the corner on the floor, arms hugging my legs pulled tight to my body, rocking, trembling, teary-eyed, muttering incoherently, "Pencils, tombs, shadows, tick tick ticking . . . where did Alice go?"

Baby Alice peed herself.

Mr. Stryker called his wife and then 9-1-1.

Broken

*The Lord is close to the brokenhearted
and saves those who are crushed in spirit.*
Psalm 34:18

Journal Entry about the Shameful Incident:

> *Sirens screaming,*
> *Rescue squad arrives*
> *Picks up the pieces of me*
> *Loads them on a stretcher*
>
> *Why did you let this happen*
> *Who's to blame for this*
> *Once cracked*
> *You're never the same*

Transported to the Emergency Room at Mercy General Hospital, doctors admitted me to the psychiatric unit where I remained for 40 days, 960 hours, 57,600 minutes, and 3,456,000 seconds.

After evaluation, I was placed on suicide watch. *Suicide Watch! Did they really want to watch me take my life?* It wasn't enough that I had gone to hell and survived the ordeal of living at Shivering Acres. Now, a multitude of professional caregivers wanted me to talk openly about everything I'd lived through. I was sorry I didn't just do the deed and have it over with. Trapped. Again.

I tried to escape. I set off alarms. I was introduced to my new uniform, the straight jacket, after the inner wildness in me gave way and exploded. I resisted, kicked, twisted—all to no avail. Placed in isolation, I had to earn my way back to a regular room through the practice of controlled behavior. People entered and exited my cell

CHAPTER 20 ~ Broken

on a continuous basis: psychiatrists, psychologists, therapists, assistants of this and that, counselors, nurses, aides, social workers, and chaplains paraded in and out. They brought their clipboards with questions, their needles, and cocktails of pills morning, noon, and night.

I heard phrases like "repressed trauma," "PTSD," "paranoia," "cognitive therapy," "hallucinations," and "crisis resolution." The list stretched as long as each day. I was numb, but scared. When asked, "How do you feel?" how should I respond?

"Do you feel sad?" *Yes!*

"Depressed?" *Yes!*

"Do you want to die?" *Yes!*

I also didn't want to talk to anyone. I didn't want to eat. *I want to die. It would be so much simpler. I'm tired of trying and not getting anywhere. Leave me alone to die in loneliness. The way I lived!*

Hatred gripped my bones. I was pregnant with hate! My tears backed up, refusing to flow but for one drop that eked out and dripped down my face. *Is that all I have to show for the turmoil inside of me? So much hurt. So much hatred. If only I could put them to sleep. Why do things haunt me? I am never good enough. I never will be. Never, ever! I am so bad, bad, BAD! I need to get out of here, but where do I go to escape this insanity called life?*

I wrote a prayer in my journal:

> *Father in Heaven, maybe sometime if You are not too busy, You can help me understand how to leave the past behind and press on and live. Show me how to live. I will admit to You, as I know You keep secrets, part of me wants to live. You say Your yoke is easy and Your burden light. Sorry Lord, but it isn't easy right now. I know, You probably want us to grow through hard times. Well, I'm sick of growing. I hope You understand that. Hurt surrounds me and tries to sweep me off my feet. Why do you allow it God? Is it a result of sin? In my case, maybe it's true. But in the case of those little babies, my little babies, I hardly think so. I don't understand. I keep seeing the endless hours of torment—years of agonizing torment. Show me the way Jesus, which way is out from this death march? Give me a break before I break. I cry out to You with all that I have left within me.*

I eventually settled into a routine of individual counseling everyday along with group sessions. I spent time in the gym to expend the pent-up energy that filled me like a balloon ready to

CHAPTER 20 ~ Broken

burst. Every day. The physical release felt good and my weight miraculously reduced as well. I looked forward to music and art therapies when they were assigned. No one visited me, but I was fine with that. I didn't want to face anyone, especially Principal Kevin and his wife Carlene. The hospital chaplain prayed with me each week. He seemed genuine and caring. He suggested I write a letter to God, so I did:

Oh, Dear God,
  It's me again. Alice.
  Which one? Take your pick, we're all a mess. My heart is breaking! I am so sad. I long for friendship, but don't know how to accept that which is in front of me. My heart longs for a special person. It hurts me to see so many people happy and relating to one another. Is it proper to consider God a friend? If so, OK then, maybe I do have at least one friend. I know I'm feeling sorry for myself, but what is it about me that backs away from people, from the possibility of friendship?
  My future seems so uncertain right now. I just don't know what to do. Of course, it would help if I consulted You and get to know You on a daily basis. I have been so bad in regard to my relationship with You. How do You put up with wretched me? Oh God, help me to thirst after you. Please God, I need You so much! My heart is breaking even more right now. It seems like I'm not even in the picture so many times. I have faded out. The staff and the people in here seem to care, I have to accept that. I don't feel worthy of the bother. I am a botheration!
  I have now failed at being a teacher. You saw what happened. All this chaos abounds because I didn't trust in You and Your love. I felt so mean; I don't want to be like that! I don't ever want any monster DNA. Help me to rely on You and You alone. Be my comfort so I can think clearly, give the answers to help get me out of here. I have begun to cry real tears now. They come flooding out when I least expect it. Your peace and Your love are what I need to survive this. Not just this hospital, but this life! I don't want to be separated from You any longer; I am miserable, so unhappy. The games are getting old. Sometimes I even feel jealous of those around me; they seem to have it together, why can't I? Please God, come to me in a special way, I am broken, and I surrender!

Your friend,
Alice Iris Fisher

Who Am I?

Then you will know the truth, and the truth will set you free.
John 8:32

Halfway through my psych ward stay, the head psychiatrist's office summoned me to see Doctor Val Spitzer. She diagnosed me with Multiple Personality Disorder, now called (as of 1994) Dissociative Identity Disorder (DID), a severe condition where a person's primary identity splinters or fragments into two or more distinct personality states.

The primary identity of a person suffering from DID is passive, dependent, guilty, and depressed. It includes periods of time loss and memory gaps regarding personal history, people, places, and events, too extensive to be explained by ordinary forgetfulness. A disrupted identity manifests as a change in a sense of self, plus changes in behavior, consciousness, memory, perception, conditioning, and motor function. These symptoms cause significant distress or impairment in social, occupational, and other important areas of functioning.

In essence, I understood Dr. Val's words to mean that another personality, or Alternate (Alter), had taken over my life. This personality had its own distinct history, self-image, and identity. I was already scared just being in a hospital psych ward under a suicide watch. Dr. Val's diagnosis caused me more anxiety. *I don't buy this! She makes me sound like a freak! How does a person get this way?*

She further explained that DID is a direct result of severe physical and sexual abuse, particularly during childhood. The disorder can surface at any age. Post-Traumatic Stress symptoms such as nightmares, flashbacks, and startle responses may also be present.

CHAPTER 21 ~ Who Am I?

Something clicked in my understanding. *That part makes sense to me.* "So, supposing this is true. How do I recover from this . . . this disease?" I asked. "What is the cure?"

"Well, Alice," she said, "please understand, this is not a disease. It's a disorder. The primary treatment for it is long-term psychotherapy with the goal of deconstructing the different personalities and uniting them into one. There are no specific medications that treat this disorder, but continuance of antidepressant and anti-anxiety drugs will help control the symptoms. With proper treatment, I believe you will be able to improve and have the ability to function in your teaching occupation and other aspects of your personal life. More than seventy percent of DID patients have suicidal tendencies and self-injurious behaviors such as you have presented. Treatment is crucial."

Her words were hopeful.

She continued, "Alice, quite often patients describe a sense of being observers of their own speech and actions. They may hear voices, like that of a child, or have multiple streams of thought that they have no control over. You might experience strong impulses or emotions that you don't feel ownership over, too. People have reported that their bodies suddenly feel different; like a small child. They may experience a shift in attitudes or personal preferences before shifting back again." She passed me some papers. "Here's a pamphlet further describing what I have spoken about. Read it through, think honestly about this diagnosis, and we will meet again tomorrow to discuss it further."

A fellow patient gave me the following verses. I copied it into my journal because it described exactly how I felt:

I'm So Many People
Author Unknown

I'm so many people,
At least, that's how I feel.

Sometimes I can't make up my mind.
Which one of us is real?

One wants to go one way,
Another disagrees.
It really is confusing,

CHAPTER 21 ~ Who Am I?

To be so many me's!

One would like to hurry,
And be grown up today.

One likes being small,
And have lots of time to play.

One wants to find adventure,
And travel everywhere.

One just wants to stay at home,
One would like to share.

My deepest inside feelings,
With someone else, but one.

Would never, ever talk about,
Those things to anyone.

One really likes MYSELF a lot,
One thinks I'm not so good.

How can there be so many me's?
I wish I understood.

How can I keep from being pulled apart?
Can they all agree?

Or if they can't, how can I tell,
Which one is really me?

I had a lot of information to process. *Does Dr. Val think I'm possessed? Like some kind of a character in a cheap horror film? Is that what she meant? I have heard it said that God doesn't make junk. Would he make a cracked version of me?*

Somehow, I knew enough to answer my own question. *God doesn't make mistakes. If I am split apart, then I know it's the Monster's doing!*

I admitted to Dr. Val about the unholy trinity of abuses—physical, verbal, and sexual—but I didn't have the courage to talk about the dark secret stuff. I remembered how Father warned, over and over again, "They are everywhere. Watching."

CHAPTER 21 ~ Who Am I?

Could they possibly be here, in this place? I resolved to remain mute and not reveal anything about the appalling acts of darkness.

I lay in silence that night and prayed as best I could:

God, You created me. Your Word says that You have a plan and a purpose for us. It includes hope and a future. I can't imagine a future beyond this place. My hope seems to have leaked out. Is it too late? Is what Dr. Val said true? Is there more than one of me? How can that even be? You can do anything, so show me a sign that I shouldn't give up no matter what I have to face. Help me not to give up and give in. I don't want the enemy and his gang to win. I belong to You, so help me out here.

Amen

No sooner than I had said a silent *Amen*, I shifted around my pillow and heard what sounded like wrinkled paper. To my surprise, I discovered a folded note under the pillow written on lined notebook paper. *Should I open it? Could this be from God? Ridiculous thought!* The moon shone bright through the upper window, spilling onto the paper as I carefully unfolded it and read:

Alice,

You have one of the prettiest faces. Your features and mannerisms are very attractive, especially when you talk. But I am not so sure you know this. You have six friends in this room. Each of us waits for a chance to reach out to you for your benefit; not to use you in any way. You are very good at blocking us out. (Me, Patricia, Cindy, Pam, Susan and Judy) I have a feeling that all the people in this room—you included—are not going to give up. The enemies we all have to face will not win!

You are smarter than a whip. You tell it like it is. That is courage! You are clever and to the point. Sometimes the truth hurts you and others, but you are willing to take the chance to get it out in the open. It may seem like it is rebuffed, but sometimes what you say is so powerful, it takes people awhile to think it over in their own minds. They want to come to grips with it before they can respond. You are a pleasure to listen to. Your perception is really clear. You are capable of putting yourself in anyone's shoes. This is a rare talent. You are a true survivor and a personal inspiration.

People are waiting, longing to get to know you because of who you are. You don't have to wonder about being accepted, you already were a long time ago. Your understanding is deep and needed in this world.

CHAPTER 21 ~ Who Am I?

You are needed! Your abuse was not all for naught; neither was mine. Maybe we learned so much more than others who never knew pain. Maybe they never found it necessary to get in touch with who they really are at the deepest level. You have truly learned about people somewhere along the line. Keep going, don't give up!

Love you,
Carol (bed 1, by the other window)
Smile

I read this treasure of a note three times. *Incredible! I just prayed and the answer was there the whole time, right under my pillow. God, You do work in mysterious ways.*

I still felt like a fraud. What would these roommates who declared themselves as friends really say if they knew the whole terrible truth? I viewed this as a paper olive branch, extended in open honesty and love. I would honor that and vowed to be friendlier.

Sleep evaded me as I mulled over the events of the day including the delivery of my official diagnosis. I wasn't crazy—as in insane, but I had an inkling of truth as I pondered the question, *Who Am I?*

My name was Alice Iris Fisher, but there were many facets to Alice Iris. There was definitely Malice Alice, Organized Alice, Teacher Alice, Faith-Filled Alice, Hesitant Alice, Brave Alice, and Baby Alice. My mind raced to other names—Hurtful Alice, Forgetful Alice, Hateful Alice, and Alice who cuts her skin until she bleeds. *Could there be more?* I considered the lapses of unaccounted time, items I couldn't remember purchasing, and people who acted like they knew me, but I couldn't remember meeting. The facts spoke for themselves. The truth weighed heavy upon me. I allowed it to slowly seep in and believe that Dr. Val was right, after all.

22

I Am Me

You have searched me, Lord, and you know me.
Psalm 139:1

Journaled from a group session hand-out:

I Am Me
Author Unknown

In the entire world, there is no one else exactly like me.
There are persons who have some Parts like me,
But no one adds up exactly like me.
Therefore, everything that comes out of me is authentically mine because I alone chose it.
I own everything about me,
My body, including everything it does.
My mind, including all its thoughts and ideas;
My eyes, including the images of all they behold.
My feelings, whatever they may be—anger, joy, frustration, love, disappointment, excitement.
My mouth and all the words that come out of it; polite, sweet or rough, correct or incorrect;
My voice, loud or soft;
All my actions, whether they be to others or to myself.
I own my fantasies, my dreams, my hopes, my fears.
I own all my triumphs and successes, all my failures and mistakes.
Because I own all of me, I can become intimately acquainted with me.
By so doing I can love me and be friendly with all my Parts.
I can then make it possible for all of me to work in my best interests.
I know there are aspects about myself that puzzle me, and other aspects that I do not know.
But, as long as I am friendly and loving to myself,
I can courageously and hopefully look for the solutions to the puzzles,

CHAPTER 22 ~ I Am Me

and for ways to find out more about me.
However I look and sound, whatever I say and do,
  and whatever I think and feel at a given moment in time is me.
This is authentic and represents where I am at that moment in time.
When I review later how I looked and sounded,
What I said and did and how I thought and felt,
Some Parts may turn out to be unfitting.
I can discard that which is unfitting and keep that which proved
  fitting and invent something new for that which I discarded.
I can see, hear, feel, think, say, and do.
I have the tools to survive, to be close to others, to be productive and to
  make sense and order out of the world of people and things outside
  of me.
I own me, and therefore I can engineer me.
I am me.
And I am Okay.

I left the hospital even though I couldn't fully embrace or understand my new diagnosis. I decided to work on setting limits in my life, my self-esteem, my compulsive need for friendship, my fears, my guilt, and my self-injury tendencies. Follow-up therapy was scheduled. *Do I really have time to attend these sessions? How can I manage my teaching job, church, and now therapy, too?*

Discharged on a Friday, I returned to the classroom and my students the following Monday with no questions asked. A miracle! I had missed the smiling faces, the laughter of my students, and the safety of my classroom. That was the best medicine; better than the numerous prescription medicines piled up on the counter at home.

I faced Principal Stryker first thing. He extended forgiveness and grace in a natural, generous way, just how I imagined Jesus would. My students welcomed me back with caring gifts of flowers and treasured hand-written cards that touched my heart. The month of June brought the finale of the school year and graduation for eleven eighth graders. What a joy to witness the accomplishments of each individual. I looked back upon the school year and pretended the horrible day when everything fell apart didn't exist.

While life seemed to be flowing along during school hours, it was rather bumpy when I returned to my home after working hours. I lived two separate lives divided by the sun and moon. Nights were hard. I cut myself to ease the never-ending pain. Pills helped, but the pain was stronger than pharmaceuticals could handle.

CHAPTER 22 ~ I Am Me

Reflection written by an unnamed Part of Alice:

Walking slowly down the street
You see a brightly colored poster
Pasted on a tall pole
The wind grabs at a corner of it
Carries it reeling across the street
Like some grotesque monstrosity
Slams it into a brick wall
It lays there in a pile
Writhing in the wind
Like a broken body
Trying to get up
And then it starts to rain
Now a disintegrating mess in a dirty puddle!

I discovered numerous writings on bits of paper all over the apartment. There were some notes in handwriting I recognized and others that appeared to be written by strangers. Some were penned by a left-handed person in a back-slash sort of way. Others, in block letters, and fancy cursive with squiggles and flair endings.

The messages written backward, which I deciphered by holding them up to a mirror, puzzled me the most. One time, I found a note on my dresser and dared to hold it up to reflect and read the strange writing: *I hate myself. I can't put the knife down. My name is Kris. Kris?*

It took me only forty days to muck things up again. The day after eighth grade graduation, I reluctantly showed up for my appointment with Dr. Irene Barrett, the therapist who had been assigned to my case. Someone, I won't say who, lifted up her shirt during the session and exposed the carved word *HELP* scratched on her abdomen by the sharp end of a knife. The next thing we knew, Dr. Barrett admitted us to the psych unit, once again.

The routine continued as before: a parade of specialists, therapy sessions, and the attempt to surrender a multitude of irrational ideas that existed deep within me as part of my daily mind-set:

- The idea that it is a necessity to be loved by everyone.
- The idea that you should be thoroughly competent and adequate to consider yourself worthwhile.
- The idea that certain people are wicked and should be severely punished for their evil deeds.

CHAPTER 22 ~ I Am Me

- The idea that it is awful and catastrophic when things are not the way you would like them to be.
- The idea that our unhappiness is solely externally caused and that we have little or no ability to control our sorrows and disturbances.
- The idea that if something may be dangerous or fearsome, you should be terribly concerned and dwell on the possibility of its occurrence.
- The idea that it is easier to avoid than to face certain life difficulties and self-responsibilities.
- The idea that you should be dependent on others and that you need someone stronger than yourself on whom to rely.
- The idea that your past history is an all-important determiner of your present behavior.
- The idea that something which once strongly affected your life should indefinitely affect your life.
- The idea that you should be upset over other people's problems and disturbances.
- The idea that there is invariably a right, precise, and perfect solution to your problems and it is catastrophic if this perfect solution is not found.

For the next forty days of my confinement, I had a lot to work through, hour by hour, minute by minute. In forty days. Out forty days. In forty days, more. From the Bible, I remembered the story of the Israelites wandering around the desert for forty years. I knew Jesus' temptation by Satan when He was in the desert lasted for forty days. I related to these Bible stories and felt like a nomad in the desert being tested.

> *Lord, if this is a test what is the name of it? How to Be Whole Again? How to Stop Cutting in Three Easy Lessons? How to Take the Too-Many-Alices and make them One? How to Survive the Attack of the Monster? How to Make and Keep Friends? How to Keep a Job While Going Crazy? Tips on Pretending Everything is Just Fine? Okay, Lord, whatever this test is, help me stop roaming alone in this desert. Help me to pass the test. Is there an oasis called Hope, just ahead?*

Therapy

*Surely you desire truth in the inner parts;
you teach me wisdom in the inmost place.*
Psalm 51:6

After my hospital discharge, I decided to embrace therapy and discover who I, Alice, truly was—including all my Parts or Alters. I attended church faithfully and sought answers directly from God. I hoped He would love me enough to help me.

I grew comfortable with my new therapist, Dr. Lillian Chambers. I committed to seeing her twice a week and began to open up to the reality of my DID diagnosis. At first therapy was difficult. I trusted no one. I heard myself talking, but "Others" did the speaking.

I cracked open the door of my mind just enough for Dr. Chambers to get a foothold. She asked about previous events. She told me that one of her main goals was to gather a history of each Alter. She needed to know who they were, when they came about, and why they appeared. She also wanted to determine where they fit into the personality system and the function in my life that they served. After many therapy sessions, she concluded that I had child personalities, protector personalities, and persecutor personalities with names.

These therapies were overwhelming and exhausting. After each session, I just wanted to escape, which manifested in a tendency to overeat or self-injure. I barely coped at home. One of the Alters, named Iris, took over my day hours. Kris was the one with extreme self-loathing. She scratched our chest with straight pins and carved words into our abdomen. I wouldn't have known her name except for the fact that she had signed the note I found which led to our latest hospital stay and therapy sessions.

CHAPTER 23 ~ Therapy

I grew moody and emotional, particularly after sunset. Any little thing triggered anger and disgust. Waves of fear crashed over me, the weight of which tried to pull me under into a darker world. Memories were my enemy. The daily fight left me exhausted. Nights were challenging and unbearable. Greater periods of unaccounted time surfaced. I was afraid to bathe not knowing what new patches of raw flesh I would discover, or new words etched into my skin. When I got up in the morning, there were often dried rusty colored spots on my nightgown where I had bled from self-imposed artwork.

Daytime Alice/Iris held it together somehow and performed well at her teaching job. She conducted my teaching job with integrity. She was organized, efficient and appeared calm and in control on the outside. But if those around her ever glimpsed what was going on inside, they would run away shrieking!

In the new school year, I was assigned to the 4th and 5th grade classroom. Many of the children in my new class came from difficult backgrounds. Iris convinced herself she was making a difference to help her focus during the day. She genuinely loved her little charges and found her identity in teaching with joy as she watched over them.

As the school year drew to a close, it was difficult to keep up the illusion that everything was okay. Feeling like a "botheration" to the people around me put me in a stranglehold. Dr. Chambers constantly reminded me that I was not a burden, but rather, I had a burden to carry. It seemed too heavy even for Iris to carry, or all of us combined. My hope diminished.

Faith-filled Alice, or Allison, as I came to know her in therapy, saw to it that I fulfilled my commitment to attend church each Sunday. We walked to a lovely little chapel not far from our apartment every Sunday morning for a 10:00 a.m. service.

Pastor Terry Snapp, a seasoned pastor in his late seventies, possessed an ever-present smile on his wrinkled face. I could look directly into his compassionate eyes without fear. It is said that the eyes are the window to your soul and Pastor Terry's eyes revealed a soul of kindness, forgiveness, and warmth. He reminded me of Jesus, but without the beard. I trusted that He preached the truth. I just couldn't believe it was for me. For us.

His wife, Millie, was a powerful prayer warrior intercessor. She frequently asked if she could pray for me. I allowed her to do so and was comforted in her presence. She prayed with confidence, like she could see straight into my heart. She saw my pain and hurt but never

CHAPTER 23 ~ Therapy

asked me directly about it. I knew that she knew, and she knew that I knew that she knew.

Millie spoke a lot about forgiveness. She shared how Jesus died on the cross taking on all our sins. She firmly stated that if I was the only person alive, Jesus would have died for me. I heard the Easter story every year but was convinced that Jesus loved everyone else more than me. *Why would Jesus die for someone like me?*

AND . . . forgiveness?

How could Jesus, if He loved me, forgive the Monster? Jesus wouldn't forgive monsters, would He? Aren't some things so very, very bad that they are unforgivable?

I didn't want the Monster to be forgiven. But, beyond that, how could I ever forgive myself for the decision I made in college to end my baby's life through abortion? Jesus surely wouldn't forgive that. He was a life *giver*, not a life taker.

No! Forgiveness is not attainable for me and certainly not for monsters!

Attending church should make you feel better, but it only emphasized the weight of all my burdens instead of easing them. Each challenge was like a stone piled on my back, getting heavier to carry each day.

I'm just a fraud going to church!

I tried to leave Dirt, Filth, and Stench outside the doors of the church each week. But, like faithful companions, they were always there waiting to cling to me again once I walked out the doors. I wanted Hope to be my friend. But Hope appeared to be turning its back on me.

Without Hope, what was left?

24

The Storm Inside

But when you ask, you must believe and not doubt, because the one who doubts is like a wave of the sea, blown and tossed by the wind.
James 1:6

Meditating on James 1:6, the verse for the day in my devotional reading, I marveled at how perfectly it described me—a wave on the sea tossed by the wind.

The turbulence of uncertainty left me feeling like the ebb and flow of restless waves. One moment I would stand steady, only to be grabbed violently by a wave of doubt—like a fierce undertow pulling me under to the deep unknown.

The verse reminded me of an article I once read in Campus Magazine during college entitled, *The Storm Inside*. I identified with each word and ripped it out to file it away and keep for reference. I hurried to my office and pulled it out of its file to read again. It confirmed how my churning and shifting emotions were a life-threatening storm swirling around me. I saw myself helpless, adrift, bobbing up and down on deep waters, struggling to keep my head above water. *I need a life preserver. Who will throw me one?*

My devotional reading continued in Mark 4:35 where Jesus miraculously calmed a raging storm. I closed my eyes, clutched my legs close to my chest, and rocked back and forth mumbling a prayer:

> *Jesus, I wonder, are You asleep? Can't You see I'm drowning? The storm raged all around when Your best friends were in the boat and yet, You slept. The waves rose higher and the boat began to take on water. They were afraid of sinking. So am I! Waves of fear and doubt slosh about inside me. I feel seasick, like I might have to vomit. The darkness within fills to capacity. I'm afraid it will overtake and drown me. Then what? My spirit is sinking. I can't stay afloat. Please take over! Please lift Your hand over me and command these emotional waves to settle down. Calm the maelstrom within me! You asked the*

CHAPTER 24 ~ The Storm Inside

disciples in the boat that day if they had any faith. I ask that of myself now. Help! Help! I'm drowning! Do You have a life preserver? Are You the life preserver? Maybe I'm just not worth saving.

Courage

*Have I not commanded you? Be strong and courageous.
Do not be afraid; do not be discouraged, for the Lord your God
will be with you wherever you go.*
Joshua 1:9

I likened myself to a master juggler who broke the world's record for keeping countless balls in the air for a sustained period of time. Eventually there is one ball too many to keep aloft, and the master juggler tires in the frenzy. My internal frenzy exhausted me.

As the school year ended, I decided against my counselor's advice. A change needed to happen. If I packed up my possessions, along with my troubles, I could load them in my car, drive away, and start over. *No one would know me. Good idea, right?* If I decided to end my existence, I'd be further away from people I knew and wouldn't be a botheration to them. *No one will actually miss me if I leave this world.*

Even Faith-Filled Allison and Brave Iris, the strong ones within, struggled with anxiety in their daytime roles. The situation and circumstances weighed heavy on all of us.

The idea of running away to . . . somewhere else . . . appealed to me more and more. I could no longer move forward staying where I was—not even in baby steps. The voices in my head grew louder. Even the meds didn't silence them.

Dr. C. gave me a list of things to work on:

- My speech—sometimes I stuttered or broke out in baby talk
- My inability to make decisions
- My weight and eating habits
- My constant thinking that I was a botheration to people
- My ability to relate to people as an adult
- My consistency with Bible reading and journaling

CHAPTER 25 ~ Courage

What an overwhelming to-do list to navigate amid the swirling storm within me: *The list requires me to work on my inability to make decisions. But every time I make a decision and tell my counselor, she says it's unwise. And after seven years of teaching in a career that I love, what if the others inside me jeopardize and ruin who I work so hard to be in the daylight hours. What if hate-filled Kris cuts me on my face at night? It will be seen in the day. I'm on the edge of a panic attack just thinking about that! Everything seems about to unravel! The Alters are restless! So many voices chattering in my head. I can't tune in to what they're saying! What am I to do? I'm drowning in indecision.*

Even so, I did decide to make a change of pace and scenery in the hopes of calming everyone down. I applied for jobs out of the area and, to my surprise, was hired by a multi-marketing company near Philadelphia. Tearfully, I gave my notice to Principal Stryker at the school that summer. I told everyone I was leaving to earn more money and save for my master's degree in social work at the University of Michigan. Technically, I didn't lie as Iris did dream of gaining a higher education towards the opening of an orphanage someday.

But there was more to it than the increased salary. A new job would come with mental health benefits that I needed to continue therapy. Some of us inside wanted that, while others feared it. With Dr. Chambers' list of recommended therapists in hand, I promised her I would make therapy a priority. During our last session, I was astonished that Dr. C looked sad to see me go and asked permission to hug me. I reluctantly allowed her to do so. Some of us would miss her and others, opposed to counseling, would think, *Good riddance! We don't need her to pry into our lives!*

Dr. Chambers gifted me with a framed watercolor lettered in calligraphy that said: "I have the courage to keep going." With tears in my eyes, I thanked her. I would hang it in a special space in my new home where I could view it daily. We all needed the reminder to be courageous and keep going—and she knew it.

Since this was about starting over, I sold or gave away all the furniture that I'd purchased from thrift stores. With only meager possessions in my car, it seemed crowded with more than just my stuff. I identified different Parts of myself and counted at least six Others taking up the same space in the car. *Could I trust this crowd? Hmmm.* Uncertainty shoved into the front seat. Fear and Panic hitched a ride in the back seat. I shouted aloud to them, "Get out of

CHAPTER 25 ~ Courage

my car! You are not coming with me this time!" There seemed to be more room momentarily, but if they did get out, they cleverly snuck back in before I pulled out to start the journey. Although invisible, they were still there, lurking in the background.

I set my GPS for the YWCA in Philadelphia, which became my home until I found an available place near my new job. The drive was supposed to take around four hours and forty minutes without stopping. We were on our way at 11:00 a.m.

My car pulled into the parking lot of the YMCA by late afternoon. I glanced at the time, astounded. *Is my watch broken?* I shook it. *It can't be 4:00 p.m. already!* Paralyzed, I sat hunched over the steering wheel. *What happened? How did I get here?* The last thing I recalled was pulling out of the parking lot, ready to hit the open road. I remembered blowing the horn a few times in farewell and whispering, "Goodbye old life, hello new!"

Unless I entered the twilight zone, transported through a wrinkle in space and time, I couldn't, just couldn't be here already. I looked over to the passenger's seat and spied a gas receipt and a crumpled bag with golden arches. A drink cup with a straw sticking out of the lid was in the holder. *Where did that come from?* I took a sip. But it wasn't root beer, my favorite. *Yech, who ordered this?*

For a full hour I sat in a stupor trying to puzzle together how I arrived and why I couldn't recollect a single detail of the trip from there to here. I pounded on the steering wheel in anger and frustration shouting, "Why? Why? Why?"

Finally, it dawned on me that one of us was a better driver than me. I took a deep breath and resolved to follow the advice of my counselor, repeating my new refrain—*I have the courage to keep going.*

Beginning Again

*See, I am doing a new thing! Now it springs up; do you not perceive it?
I am making a way in the wilderness and streams in the wasteland.*
Isaiah 43:19

I found a small efficiency apartment within the first month of my arrival in Philadelphia. It consisted of two large rooms and a closet-sized bathroom. Living in Philly opened me to a new world of sights, sounds, and culture. Though warned about pickpockets, vagrants, and beggars, I wasn't afraid. They were threats I could see. The threatening things I couldn't see were the ones that frightened me. In fact, I felt quite at ease around the homeless individuals I saw on park benches or begging on the street corners. If I had loose change or small bills, I smiled and gave them away willingly. *That person could be me someday!* After all, I was one step away from sanity and the ability to care for myself, too.

I wandered the city in the evenings and night hours like a nomad, often traveling miles in every direction. *Maybe I can walk off this restlessness. Will I ever have a normal home and a life surrounded by people who love me?*

Along with the historical sights, I discovered the delicious foods famed in Philadelphia which fed into my comfort eating. Cheesesteaks, hoagies, soft pretzels, pork roll, tomato pie, peanut chews, and the best of all—Tastykakes! The only Philly food that didn't sound appealing was scrapple. Anything with the word scrap in its name was not worth it. Bring on more varieties of Tastykakes! But my taste-bud delight turned to horror when I stepped on the bathroom scale. I'd inched up two sizes since relocating!

One day, while mindlessly driving around the city, I spied a beautiful antique walnut bureau tossed to the curb and partially hidden by other unwanted junk. An ornately carved wooden framed mirror sat next to it waiting to be attached. *So what if it has a crack*

CHAPTER 26 ~ Beginning Again

down the center of the mirror and the leg is a little broken on the dresser? I'll adopt these sturdy furnishings and give them some well-deserved TLC! My good intention turned to frustration as I learned how uncooperative furniture can be when attempting to load the heavy bureau into the trunk of my car and the mirror onto the back seat. *Perhaps I should buy a truck?*

After setting up my reclaimed find at home, I glanced into the mirror and startled myself. I stopped. I focused. The jagged crack in the mirror fractured my face and skewed it to look split in two. I didn't recognize the face looking back at me. *Who is that?* I stared and stared, afraid to look away. When I finally pried my eyes from the mirror and the face staring back at me, I ran for a spare sheet and covered it. *Who is that stranger in the mirror? I don't want to know.*

Holidays never failed to be difficult. As December 25th approached, I found myself work-free for Christmas week. I considered going to church, something I hadn't done since I came to town. Thoughts of Miss Miller and her green felt board with her Bible figures revolved through my mind. *What a failure I am if can't at least go to church on Christmas Eve! Even heathens know if you call yourself a Christian, you should attempt to go on Christmas and Easter, at the very least.* I reminisced about the carols I enjoyed singing, the smell of pine, and the brightly lit candles. Embracing the joy of the season was tempting. Even so, I sighed. *I. Can. Not. Do. It! Look! The snow! Too much snow! I'm locked down like Ft. Knox. Just can't go to church. No way. No how.* Epic fail!

Home alone that Christmas, I meditated on the Christ Child, so innocent—a gift to the world. Baby Alice came to mind, so innocent—a gift to no one. Random thoughts floated through my mind as I pondered the horrible things that happened to Baby Alice and Little Alice. Then some of the Big Alices became enraged. I wrote in my journal all the things that angered me regarding Little Alice or Alli as I came to know her:

- *Wetting myself and getting peed on*
- *Not taking care of my sister good enough and then having to spend time in the metal garbage can with the lid on it*
- *Being afraid and not being able to talk about my fears*
- *Being sad, but not allowed to cry without getting something to really cry about*
- *Being smelly and getting made fun of*

CHAPTER 26 ~ Beginning Again

- *Getting bullied and beat up at school and on the bus*
- *Having to lick up the floors, even dirty ones*
- *Making mistakes—not holding my pencil right, my chores not completed good enough or fast enough, accidentally spilling my milk*
- *Getting hurt repeatedly causing bleeding, but not able to get help; left to suffer*
- *Having my pets killed*
- *Getting DEPAR by lots of monsters in the secret place*
- *Getting tortured (many types of this, but I have locked the details in a file drawer of my mind.)*
- *The pond and all that happened there—ashes, ashes, and more ashes*

We made it through the Christmas season without dialing 9-1-1, but it was a close call. The pills were in my hand, ready to be swallowed. What stopped me? The framed words gifted me by Dr. C: "I have the courage to keep going."

Is it true? Do I have the courage to go on?

I fell asleep on the floor. When I woke up all the pills were back in the bottle. I'm not sure who put the lid on, and I didn't know whether to be happy or sad about that fact.

The one gift I gave myself Christmas Day was the word J-E-S-U-S carved on my upper thigh. I desperately desired Jesus to be a part of my life. If I branded Him there, He would always be with me. Blood rose to the surface of the cuts and dripped down my leg. *It's just like Your blood dripping down the cross! For me, Jesus? For me?*

Happy Birthday Jesus!

The Power of Three

*And now these three remain: faith, hope and love.
But the greatest of these is love.*
1 Corinthians 13:13

As the page turned for the New Year, three wonderful things happened that were cause for celebration. My sister Sandy had a baby boy on January 1st. Their increase to a family of three made me jubilant, not jealous, as I thought I might be. I now possessed a new name to add to the list of others: Aunt Alice.

I loved this precious new baby, sight unseen. They named him Samuel, a strong Bible name meaning "name of God" or "God has heard." Still holding the birth announcement in my fingers, I dropped to my knees and asked God to protect him from the strong arm of the Monster and his cohorts. The peace of God surrounded me. He heard my prayer. *Thank you, God, that Sandy and Michael live many miles away from where we grew up.*

Though I hadn't communicated with family in a long time, I sent out a Christmas update letter to a chosen few, my mother included. But with the arrival of Samuel, a congratulations by phone was in order. Sandy assured me the birth was uneventful and motherhood agreed with her. It sounded like an answer to prayer when she shared that her husband, Michael, was fiercely protective. I couldn't wait to meet, hold, and rock my new nephew, hoping the deep ache in my soul from my own unspeakable losses might be eased.

A new baby in my family was the first good thing to kick off my new year.

The second blessing came after receiving permission from my landlord to adopt a pet. I went to the local shelter and picked out a soft, grey tabby kitten. I stood at the metal enclosure gazing at a six-week-old litter of five fluff bundles wondering how I could choose

CHAPTER 23 ~ The Power of Three

from among them. Then, one little fur baby wobbled up to the gate and mewed loudly as if to petition, "Don't leave me behind!"

I named my new kitty Comet, a nod to his fleet feet scurrying about the house and a clever homage to Miss Mary Miller who gave me my first car, a Comet. Having a pet to love and care for gave me a reason to go home at night. This small critter to love, and who loved me back, made me smile.

The third thing on my joy list was a letter that came in the mail from Dr. Chambers. *Wow! After all these months Dr. C. didn't forget about me!* I eagerly read:

Dear Alice & et al,

I was delighted to receive your Liberty Bell postcard. Because of maternity leave, my response has been delayed. Sorry for the time lapse. Yes, I had a baby in November, a precious little girl, I named Lauren.

I appreciate your honesty in telling me that you have not begun further therapy. I know how painful it can be and what courage you need to keep going at times. Remember, you have that courage! I am pleased you are enjoying city life. I know the teacher in you is appreciating all the historical sites Philadelphia has to offer.

I hope you are continuing to embrace your new career. You have always been a hard worker, and I'm sure you are appreciated. It's wonderful you get to travel a bit around the surrounding states as part of your responsibilities. I trust you are also finding respite in your new home. PLEASE consider therapy and write me an update when you can. Address it to the Department of Psychiatry at the hospital.

Take care.
With sincerest regards,
Dr. Lillian Chambers

After reading the letter several times, I felt a mix of happiness and sadness. I was happy Dr. C. took the time to write to me. *She must be so busy caring for an infant. And she still thinks to write to me? She really cares about me, right?* Sad, too, because her words pierced my heart. I promised that I would continue therapy when I got settled in Philadelphia, but months passed. I hadn't followed up with a call to a new therapist. I vowed on Monday I would pick up the phone and honor my promise to Dr. Chambers.

I took a deep breath, watching Comet skid across the floor and land by my leg, reminding me of my three incredible blessings. Mom

CHAPTER 23 ~ The Power of Three

always said that things come in threes. I relished this flood of terrifically tremendous treasures that had come my way.

But . . . *what if there are three BAD things lined up for me, to follow these three GOOD things?*

I exhaled a long, anxious sigh. *I won't hold my breath!*

To Go or Not to Go

Do not be anxious about anything, but in every situation, by prayer and petition, with thanksgiving, present your requests to God.
Philippians 4:6

Days passed. I made inquiries at a local counseling center about getting back to therapy and begin attending group sessions for abuse victims. My third meeting resulted in a particularly debilitating day. I never knew what I should or should not say, always anxious I would blurt out something wrong or inappropriate. After the last session, I wrote these thoughts in my journal:

> *The questions asked are challenging to answer—like the one tonight: "Was I ever pregnant?" I became distressed to admit I was once, well actually more than once. How do I explain what happened to the babies? The fact they were fathered by monsters is more than I can bear. I could not, would not talk about that! Anytime I hear the word abortion it sends me to a desolate place. Once I get there, I am weighed down, making escape impossible.*
>
> *I have given a lot of thought to pregnancy and wondered if I could even get pregnant again. Perhaps that would be my ultimate punishment. Who knows? Physically and emotionally I don't allow anyone to get close to me. Being intimate in that way makes my skin crawl. In marriage, sexual intimacy is supposed to be something beautiful and special, not a lesson in pain and torture. Maybe one day. Some days I hate being a woman having been cheated of so much. I presume that's why I don't bother with make-up, wear unisex clothing, and sport a short blunt haircut. I even plan my next vehicle will be a truck—useful, although a bit manly.*
>
> *Another question I was asked tonight: "Why am I so nervous?" I don't know the answer. I'm nervous around most people. I don't know how to relate to them. I can handle being around children and animals more so than adults, male or female. I have so much to learn*

CHAPTER 28 ~ To Go or Not to Go

and work on to become a whole person again. Lord, I want to be whole! Help!

My inner identity struggles worsened. *If I just check out of this world, I could solve all my problems. I'd be out of everyone's way—no more botheration.* It became harder and harder to stop myself from cutting or taking a handful of pills that called to me.

Then, my mother called. She asked me to come home and drive her to visit a distant cousin who was not well. *A six-hundred-mile drive from her house? Twelve hours in the car? What would we talk about?* And the clincher? She requested I stay a few days at Shivering Acres. "I just don't understand why you don't visit anymore," she said. *Is she freakin' kidding me? How can I survive even one night in that house?*

I despised my life. I told her I would think about it since I'd have to take time off from work. I promised to give her an answer in a week. I wished I could hate the bad and embrace the good, but it was getting harder to find the good in anything anymore. Even reading the Bible seemed dull without clear personal application.

Should I actually take this trip? The list of "cons" far outweighed the "pros." There were only two reasons to go: I loved my mother, and while I was in the general area, I could visit my sister and spend time with Sammy, my little nephew. *But too many things could go wrong. I wish I had a trusted friend to take with me as a buffer against the pervasive darkness at Shivering Acres.* I couldn't take Comet. Though he would have been a comfort to me, he wouldn't be safe from my monster of a father.

I daydreamed and wrote in my journal about the qualities a perfect dad should have. My heavenly Father was a perfect example with all the qualifications. *Lord, could you please give a few of these to my father? Maybe then, I could call him Dad.*

I dusted off my Bible like a long-lost treasure and held it close to my heart. *God, please help me see what a perfect Dad would look like if I could order one directly from you.* I imagined him to be engaging and fun, someone who wanted to spend time with me. He would be nurturing and give me hugs, my defender by day and a comforter by night. He'd always be available to me and I would be the apple of his eye. His love would be unconditional, no matter what I had done. He would be patient with me when I did something wrong and when he did something wrong, he would say he was sorry. He would be someone I could count on, not a man of secrets, but of truth. He would seek to understand who I was and help me fulfill the dreams

CHAPTER 28 ~ To Go or Not to Go

in my heart. If I did need to be disciplined, he would do so in love. But none of these fanciful thoughts came close to describing William or the Monster. *Lord, I guess the year I was born, no father models like that were available for me.*

But my Heavenly Father loved me, even though I didn't regard myself as loveable. A song I learned many years ago in Miss Mary's class often played in my mind:

> *Jesus loves me, this I know,*
> *For the Bible tells me so.*
> *Little ones to Him belong.*
> *They are weak, but He is strong.*
> *Yes, Jesus loves me.*

I sang *Jesus Loves Me* to myself over and over again, especially when in despair. It calmed me. I tried to accept the truth of the words. I think of Jesus as my Dad, but still long to have a good earthly father and belong to a loving family. I prayed that my life would work out in that way. Somehow. Someday. I grieved for the loss of it in my life, and all the losses created by being a part of the Fisher family.

I watched the news one night about the war in Kuwait. As I listened, I wrote down some thoughts as they occurred to me:

> *I've been saying a lot lately that I'm tired of fighting—that there is no more fight left in me. I'm tired of the war, I am battle weary. I made an analogy as follows: Kuwait was invaded (DEPAR) by Iraq and the land and peoples' lives were destroyed. All kinds of dark atrocities were committed to the people. With the war now over, Kuwait will rebuild with little help from the Iraqi people. Similarly, my life was invaded, and I was DEPAR for many years by different unnamed people. The actual physical war is over, the enemy has departed. I, too, must rebuild my life without any help from my destroyers. The damage is extensive, but with help, I can be re-created. Letting go of all I had to defend myself from is not easy. It is hard to let go of things you've carried around for years. But, as painful as it is, the new should/ could be much better. I need to leave the old, crumbling shattered remains behind and rebuild something new. That is the goal of war-torn Kuwait and maybe I can set this as my personal goal. But first, do I take that trip home?*

Road Trip

*Do nothing out of selfish ambition or vain conceit.
Rather, in humility value others above yourselves.*
Philippians 2:3

I had absolutely no reason to feel guilty, but I did. *Why?*

Mom promised to visit Cousin Dianne without first confirming her travel arrangements. Having promised, she needed a pushover like me to transport her there. Father considered this trip a waste of time, and my sister wasn't a likely candidate to drive that distance with the baby. Mom used the ultimate guilt tactic when she phoned for my final answer: "I'm your mother. I gave you life. Is it too much to ask you to do this ONE thing for me?"

Seriously? Maybe you shouldn't have given me life and, yes, it was too much to ask.

Being a people pleaser, I said, "Yes, but I will not sleep at the house. I'll visit Sandy first, sleep there, and pick you up in the morning." Mom agreed. Even so, this whole business stirred up a nest of uneasiness within me.

At the last minute, I decided to take Comet with me for company on the long drive. I'd have to keep a close watch on him and keep him out of the Monster's reach. I wouldn't put it past the weasel to try to destroy another thing I loved and treasured. I vowed to be on the highest alert possible. I prayed and asked God to protect us while on Shivering Acres property which wouldn't be a second longer than necessary.

On the drive, I daydreamed about the possibility of moving again. My job's home office recently asked if I would consider a move to the Lancaster, Pennsylvania area to help unravel all the problems at the field office there. The head director was pleased with how I got the Philadelphia office in tip-top shape, while also

CHAPTER 29 ~ Road Trip

traveling to the surrounding states of New Jersey, Delaware, and Maryland.

The few times I visited the Lancaster area I visualized myself living there among the rolling hills. The simplicity of the Amish people appealed to me: traditional, simple, and faith based. They lived separate and apart from worldly influences. It sounded so peaceful—the complete opposite of my tangled and complicated life, even though I consistently worked on the faith part.

The country lifestyle would be a respite from the big city noise of Philadelphia. I was attracted to the slow-paced life of the Amish, evident by their horse and buggy mode of transportation and gardening skills. One lonely, gratifying memory from childhood involved digging in the dirt. I enjoyed it and loved the reward of harvesting a bounty of vegetables or flowers.

I also fell in love with the brightly colored patterns of hand sewn quilts displayed throughout the country shops. If I learned how to quilt, that might help me in the night-time hours. The Pennsylvania German heritage of the region reminded me of my Oma Herman. I missed her so much.

I'd recently started to read again, too, and singled out Beverly Lewis as a favorite author, specializing in Amish tales about the simple life. A life without complications. Could a move to the Lancaster area be the answer to a quieter life for me? Deep down, a part of me wanted to make a change.

Daydreaming made the drive go faster and, before I knew it, I was at Sandy's house. On the back seat two shopping bags overflowed with picture books and toys I imagined boys would enjoy, even though Sammy was too young for most of it. Little Allison helped me shop for gifts she knew would be appropriate.

Sandy seemed genuinely pleased to see me, as did Michael. I asked for permission to hold Sammy, elated to rock him to sleep. Thoughts of my own babies, Heidi and Tyler, flitted through my mind, and I ached for what I'd lost.

Sandy and I had an unspoken agreement that we wouldn't discuss anything concerning our father. Although we both grew up in the same household, she never revealed what she knew or saw. *Did father abuse his princess after the ugly sister left?* Her silence on the topic of our family suited me, and I was relieved to not get lectured about visiting Mom and Shivering Acres more often.

CHAPTER 29 ~ Road Trip

After dinner, Michael bathed Sammy while she shared disturbing news about our brother Billy. He'd been caught drinking and driving and received a hefty fine and DUI citation. Billy still lived at home, and I thought it odd Mom hadn't mentioned anything about it. But there was more. Billy had a serious drinking and drug problem. Police discovered pills in the car during the arrest. *Was he numbing his pain with drugs, just like me with food?* More than likely his immediate future included jail time. *Whoa! Now we have a jailbird AND a monster in our family, not to mention the tangled mess of me!*

When I left in the morning, I promised Sandy that my visits would be more frequent. I also invited her to visit me, too, and blurted out that I might have a new address soon. We awkwardly said goodbye. No hugs involved—those were still beyond my comfort level.

My next stop would be to pick up Mom, who was waiting and ready to roll when I arrived at Shivering Acres. There she sat on the rocking chair in the living room with her avocado green Samsonite overnight train case by her side. She looked old and frail. Living in that house, who wouldn't be? Bad Boy Billy helped at home after working full time hours. *Who would do the manual labor if Billy ended up in jail? Maybe Mom wants to escape, too.* My mission would be to bless her with three Monster-free days. *Does she feel any love for the man she married?*

I didn't ask about my father. He was nowhere to be seen, and I was okay with that. As we headed out the door, I shivered when I noticed the shotgun propped in the corner like a sentinel on duty. It still held a place of honor—always within easy reach. My breath quickened as I hurried Mom out the door.

I opened the car door for Mom and happened to glance up at the second story of the house. Oh—that mysterious window again! The one that I couldn't match to an actual room according to the layout of the house. On the return trip, I vowed to play Nancy Drew and solve the mystery of the unknown window.

30

The Closet

*There is nothing concealed that will not be disclosed,
or hidden that will not be made known.*
Luke 12:2

The road trip went better than anticipated. Mom and I chatted about Oma and Opa Herman, but not about our own lives. Mom reminisced about her own childhood, and for once in my life, she seemed real to me—not the wife of a monster. I remember the trip fondly, as a rare treasured time with Mom.

Upon arrival at Shivering Acres, Mom tried to convince me to stay for dinner and overnight. *What was she thinking!* No way in the land of Hades would I do that!

We opened the unlocked front door. A hastily scrawled note on the table read: "If you get home before I return, start dinner. I took a load of straw over to Flury's Feed & Grain." My prayers for protection from the monster were answered. Father's absence was a gift from above, but I had to escape before he returned. There was one thing I had to do with him gone. I told Mom I needed to use the bathroom upstairs while she unpacked and started dinner.

As I stepped gingerly up the creaky stairs, my stomach knotted. *Is this how an intruder feels?* Standing at the top of the landing, I squeezed my eyes closed. *Think, Alice, think!* I reviewed the layout of the house and pictured where I'd spied the mysterious small window from outside. It wasn't the bathroom, so I eliminated that. The bedroom where I had slept was at the back side of the house along with the storage room, so it couldn't be either of those. I looked in my sister's old room, now officially mother's sewing room. No, it wasn't in there. So, it must be Billy's room!

The door was ajar. Slowly pulling it open, I scanned the room, thankful for daylight. Walking to the middle of the room, I realized the window must be in the closet. There was no other place it could

CHAPTER 30 ~ The Closet

be. *Strange, why would a closet have a window?* My trembling fingers turned the knob and opened the creaky closet door. I heard myself breathing heavily and sensed an evil presence. *A stupid thought. It's a closet, just a closet!* Moving the hanging clothes to the side, I prayed I wouldn't see anything that would validate Billy as a criminal. He had "girlie" magazines in the barn loft I once discovered by accident. If that was his only problem, he wouldn't be facing jail time.

Peering up at the top shelf, I noticed a square cut in the ceiling with hinges on the right side. Closer inspection revealed a thin rope wrapped around a hook. The glare from the light fixture made this difficult to spot. *What can I stand on to reach that rope?* I hurried to Mom's sewing room and grabbed the chair by her sewing machine that I'd seen earlier.

I balanced myself carefully with shaky footing and stood on the chair to inspect the door and string. It was a hatch with a pull-down ladder. Once the rope was unwound, I tugged on the cord and a squeaky staircase descended within a foot off the floor as I moved the chair aside. Part of me knew I shouldn't go further, yet part of me pulled forward. A magnetic force of curiosity dared me to take the first step. *Should I or shouldn't I?*

The window puzzle begged to be solved and I was on the threshold of discovery. I counted to five, took a deep breath, and ascended step-by-step. My head rose over the edge of what appeared to be a secret room, and I saw the mystery window. *So, I'm not crazy after all.* Sunlight flickered through the grimy glass panes adding an air of mystery. I reached the step, almost at the top and saw THEM!

The men of the SSS—The Secret Society of the Serpent stood there! At first glance it looked like them. In a hidden room of hidden secrets, dark ceremonial robes hung in line like soldiers suspended on a wire. I gasped for air and started to hyperventilate. In a hasty retreat, I held tight to the ladder sides, bypassed all the steps, and slid down in a heap.

My stomach clenched. *No! No! No! Don't vomit!* I hurriedly retracted the ladder and rewound the rope. I'm not sure if I returned the chair in my escape, but I bolted to the bathroom and hurled. My ears pulsated with my rapid heartbeat as I heard Mom calling me in the distance. "Coming!" I choked out in response. Once in the kitchen, she must have seen how disturbed I looked. I had no problem convincing her I didn't feel well and couldn't stay for dinner.

CHAPTER 30 ~ The Closet

When I woke up the next day, I tried to remember how I got home. The last thing I recalled was dropping Mom off after our road trip. As I clasped my hands in prayer, I noticed something alarming about them. The palms of my hands were filled with numerous tiny splinters. *Where had they come from?*

The Straw

He has delivered us from such a deadly peril, and he will deliver us again.
On him we have set our hope that he will continue to deliver us.
2 Corinthians 1:10

During the daylight hours of my nine-to-five job, my Alter parts co-operated with each other to manage a successful career. I felt fulfilled in my work. Proof positive that I was not as stupid as my Father had led me to believe.

No matter how much my mother might beg me, I vowed not to go home anytime soon. Maybe not ever. Especially after my most recent encounter at Shivering Acres. The discovery of the secret SSS closet stirred-up nighttime Alice. When the sun lowered at the end of the day, a dark dread crept over me. Each morning, I climbed my way back to the sanity of a new day. *Kris* left *Iris* a note one morning that could only be read by holding it up to a mirror.

> *Iris, Didja really think that cross necklace you wear everyday would protect you from evil? Howja like those straight pins Monique and I stuck in your boobs last night? That oughta teach you! Get your effin act together, why don't ya? We're dying in here! Kris*

We? Oh, she was a clever. This is how I discovered *Kris* had a nighttime helper. *Monique? Where did SHE come from? How many are there?* My body continued to be a canvas where they etched their outrage. My coping mechanisms were shaky at best and I allowed *Iris* to take over as it appeared that she was the one who managed daily operations. Therapy taught me how to let go and fade out. *How is it possible for the same person to oversee daytime events and experience stability, but come undone at night?* I cried out to God for answers. My finger

CHAPTER 31 ~ The Straw

clasped the cross necklace around my neck which normally gave me solace. But sometimes, it felt more like a millstone.

The only solution that came to mind to mend my messy life was to MOVE! Move forward, move to Lancaster or . . . take the pills and be done with it. I longed for a quieter life, a life where the background chatter would be muted. Therapy? I didn't want to face it and the daily struggle it required. I had little inner strength left to hold me together.

Iris finalized the decision to relocate. Details lined up in an incredible way. Maybe God was at work after all. Just outside of the charming town of Lititz, Pennsylvania, I found and purchased a small two-bedroom cottage. This proved to be another personal step in canceling out my father's words, "You are never going to amount to much."

My mother's sewing skills had rubbed off on me. I stitched every curtain throughout my new home. When spring arrived, I purchased a lawn mower to cut my sizeable lawn and enjoyed it so much that I mowed several of my neighbor's yards, too. Focusing on hard, physical work proved to be a blessing and made me happy inside.

The time seemed right for Comet to have a sister. I adopted a black cat with white feet and named her Frosty. The two pets immediately bonded and were a cherished delight. I reveled in watching them scamper about the house, batting a catnip mouse back and forth.

The local Victory Community Church advertised its services in our *Penny Saver Magazine.* They had several adult Bible classes and the option to attend either a Saturday night worship service or an early or late service on Sunday morning. They even had a weight loss class, which I could make use of. Since the church was bigger than any I had ever attended, I thought it might be easier to fit in and come and go without being questioned on every detail of my life.

I hadn't found a new therapist, yet. It was #2 on my "to-do" list right under finding a church. *Maybe I should move mental health to the top of the list as my meds were running low. Are pills even a necessity at this point?* I hoped the idyllic feeling I enjoyed after settling into the move would last a long time. But the proverbial "other shoe" always seemed to drop when I least expected it.

One day, not only did the shoe drop, but it kicked me to the curb. An eerie feeling came over me that day. I couldn't shake the sense that someone or some *thing* was watching me. Every time I had the

CHAPTER 31 ~ The Straw

nerve to turn around and check, nothing was there. The strange notion followed me as I walked through the weekly farmer's market picking out fresh produce. Even though it was a warm day, I felt a chill outside under the sun. I told myself that it was only my imagination. I knew my imagination well and it was capable of running to pitch-black places.

However, I knew that I knew that I knew as soon as I walked in the front door someone had been in my home. Nothing seemed out of place, but the presence of evil hung in the air. I dropped my overflowing market basket and tried to move, but my feet seemed stuck, as though encased in cement. Fear gripped my heart. Possible reasons for this strange sensation swirled through my mind, but the most overwhelming thought was—*they found me!*

The Brotherhood of the SSS had a long arm, able to reach out to remind you that you cannot escape and had better keep your mouth shut. I had done the second part well.

In a stupor, I slowly moved around the house calling Comet and Frisky. They hadn't given me their usual greeting when I walked in the door. They didn't answer and I teetered on the edge of a panic attack. *What if they've been catnapped—or worse! No! No! No! Not my precious kitties!*

My heart hammered through my chest as I checked each room. I tiptoed into my bedroom and spotted visible evidence left by the intruder. Written on the cracked mirror in red crayon were the words:

WE KNOW WHERE YOU ARE

Alarm bells rang, like clanging bells, in my head. I broke out into a cold sweat. My heart pounded. Pee trickled down my leg. I felt DEPAR, violated. *How dare they!?*

I stumbled to the bathroom and grabbed all my prescription meds. *One bottle isn't enough! Maybe if I combine all the pills, it will be a lights out cocktail. I will never be able to escape! This ends now! Fear won! They won!* Rational thought bolted from my mind as hope slipped away.

I flopped down on the bed, not caring about my wet pants. Comet and Frosty raced out from underneath the bed frame where they had been hiding. Relief washed over me at the sight of them. I sobbed for joy that they were alive. I sobbed harder knowing the time had come to say goodbye.

CHAPTER 31 ~ The Straw

"I love you my furry babies. Please forgive me. I am no longer a fit Momma. You deserve better. Take care of each other." *Courage, where are you now?*

I swallowed the handful of pills and rubbed Comet and Frisky's ears as I closed my eyes and leaned back on the pillows. *There is no way out of this madness. I am unraveled. This invasion has penetrated my soul. It is truly the last straw.*

Hope

"For I know the plans I have for you," declares the Lord, "plans to prosper you and not to harm you, plans to give you hope and a future."
Jeremiah 29:11

Thank God for my recently widowed next-door neighbor, Mr. Harvey Mason. He was quite lonely as he loved to jibber-jabber about the weather or the latest news headlines whenever I encountered him. Because I was single, he appointed himself as my personal overseer, but not in a creepy kind of way. Normally, this would make me uncomfortable. But instead, he reminded me of my Opa.

As I lay drifting away on my bed, Mr. M. got his mail in for the day. He noticed my Chevy Silverado in the driveway. He knew I had gone to the Farmer's Market because he asked me to purchase a honeydew for him. It's a good thing he did. Knowing I was now home, he thought he would save me the trouble of delivery and pick up the melon he'd ordered.

He thought it odd when I didn't answer the door after he knocked several times. He turned the knob and found it unlocked. As he entered, two distressed cats greeted him with loud meows and growly sounds. They scampered toward the bedroom and he followed, discovering me in a semi-conscious state, unable to speak. The evidence of the empty pill bottles told him everything he needed to know. He phoned the rescue squad and bagged the scattered medicines. His quick action saved me from slipping away into the blackness of death.

The details of my time in the emergency room remain sketchy. I remember the pain and discomfort of getting my stomach pumped and the unrelenting throb of my throat aching for days afterward. This was a gift from the hand of the Lord that kept me from further suicidal attempts. *I don't want to go through that again!*

CHAPTER 32 ~ Hope

While the staff evaluated what to do with me, a deep sense of loss, abandonment, and emptiness swept over me. I'd never felt so alone as I did in that hospital room. I wept uncontrollably for hours, unable to decide if I was happy to be alive or disappointed that I would have to face another day.

Eventually, the doctors transferred me to a well-known psychiatric hospital in the area. *Ah! The psych ward. I know what to expect here!*

Yet, when I became fully aware of my surroundings, I heard moans, screams, and gibberish coming out of a variety of rooms unlike my last experience in a psych ward. Looking around the common room, I winced at the sight of several patients drooling. One even had a large bib tied around their neck. *What am I doing in this place? Am I the only sane one in here?*

The unit was locked down. Claustrophobia gripped me from the inside out. *Why would someone as sane as me be placed with these psychotic freaks?* My surroundings petrified me, and I wondered if my life would end in a place that professed to save you.

At the time, I didn't realize the complexity of my true condition. My life had been an illusion. The Alters attempted to keep up with daily life, though sometimes one didn't know what the other was doing.

During my five-week stay in the psych ward, I struggled to handle the confusion and was grateful when one of the Alters took the lead. My sanity hung on by a thread. *There are too many me's! How can all these parts of me be brought into unity? Into wholeness?*

The therapist explained the situation, "There will be hard work ahead but, if you fully embrace my diagnosis and treatment plan, you can live a fully integrated life."

Oh, goody. That may be your goal. I need to decide if it's my goal. It seemed unreachable.

Some Parts of me weren't happy or helpful, but antagonistic. I'd arrived at a fork in the road and had to choose. *Do I want to get better or am I going to be content with my life the way it is?*

I was NOT content or at ease with my life in general. In fact, I hated most aspects of my life. I functioned only because the other Parts of me helped in their own unique ways. *How long before my brain explodes? It's getting very crowded in here!*

After one of the group sessions, a patient named Cathy asked to speak to me. I secretly admired her in the group as she appeared

CHAPTER 32 ~ Hope

positive and determined to make it this time around. She had struggled for a long time. I needed a dose of her positivity.

"Alice," she spoke confidentially, as though entrusting me with a great secret, "I heard you state your faith has been an anchor at times. I, too, made a personal declaration that I would anchor myself to Jesus and cling to Him as never before. I vowed to include Him into every facet of my recovery." She paused, then went on. "Listen to this verse from Philippians 1:6: *'Being confident of this, that He who began a good work in you will carry it on to completion until the day of Christ Jesus.'* I know He has begun a good work in both of us and will help us. Alice, just ask Him."

Her words replayed again and again in my mind as I sat alone in my room. *Lord, I am guilty of calling for Your help when it's convenient. I understand that I need to be intentional about my faith. I want to practice what I've learned.*

In a flash of Holy Spirit insight, I recalled a verse I'd hidden in my heart years ago when I memorized it in Miss Mary's class: *"Rejoice always; pray continually, give thanks in all circumstances; for this is God's will for you in Christ Jesus."* 1 Thessalonians 5:16-18

Can I rejoice or give thanks in these current circumstances? Pray? Yes! I can pray continually—a good place to start a more faith-filled life.

During one of my prayer times, I felt the whisper of the Lord gently telling me my life was not my own to take. I would have to wait for Him to determine my time—whenever that would be.

I set myself to dig in and dig deep to figure out how to overcome my fears, anxiety, and self-loathing, as well as my hatred for those who had committed such dark deeds against me. Forgiveness was key, but it might be a long time before I could hand that key over to Christ and trust Him to unlock all the hidden places of my heart so I could be healed.

One morning I was scheduled for Expressive Art Therapy, taught by Susan. This class birthed something beautiful in me through the gift of hands-on creativity. It proved to be a way for me to find my voice when I couldn't speak directly about my trauma. Susan was a compassionate, animated individual who exuded an artsy energy that transcended the doom and gloom bubble that surrounded me. A kaleidoscope of colors and patterns seemed to swirl around her. I admired her funky earrings, and her brightly colored clothes made a stylish statement. She was passionate to share

CHAPTER 32 ~ Hope

her love of art and see it transfer to each patient as a creative means toward healing.

Art therapy added a bright spot to my psychiatric stay. When it was suggested that I continue art therapy after discharge, I was more than willing to continue. I loved it! In locating a new psychotherapist for outpatient care, Susan suggested a colleague who had experience with Dissociative Disorders, Dr. G. Wallace. Even though he was a man, if Susan thought so highly of him, I would make an appointment for outpatient follow-up.

I felt like God had cracked open a door for me. Hope shined through. This was a door I didn't want to see close.

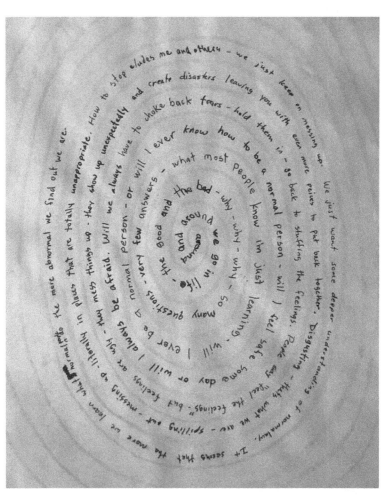

Around and Around I Go

Dearest Baby,

An overwhelming sadness
   wells up within me
   almost choking me
   with its intensity,
when I think how inhumanly
you were taken from me.

The tears furrow down my face
   forming a glistening pool
   which through misty eyes
   a reflection of anguish
   stares back.

I love you precious little one(s)
   so innocent and beautiful
and I'll cherish the moment
when one day I can hold
you in my arms and look
in your sweet eyes and smile
and face to face say I love you.

               Mommy

Dearest Baby

Disappearing Alice

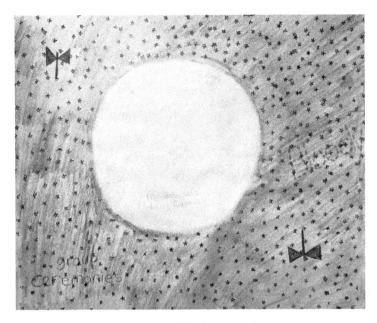

Full Moon

In the Woods

Kaleidoscope of My Soul

My Life in Pieces

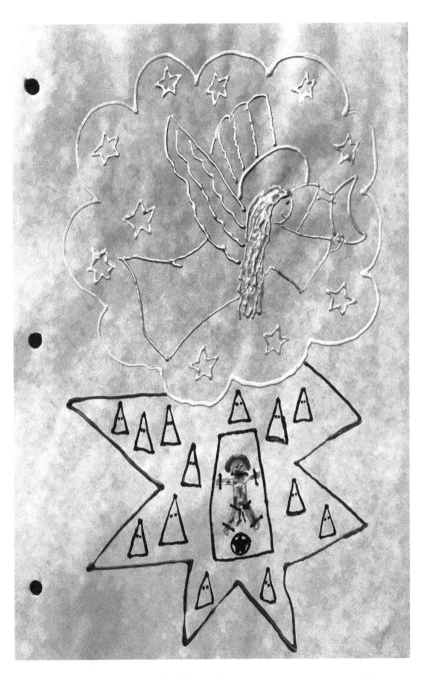

Life Over Death

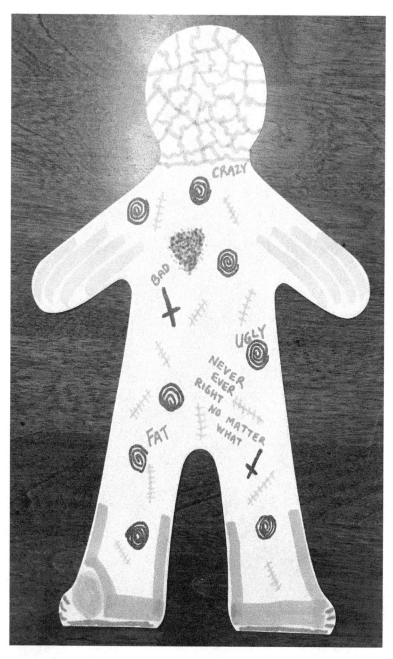

My X-ray Results

Not Welcome

Places in My House

Powerless

Searching for Alice

The Many Faces of Little Alice

Trapped

Too Many Alices

Persevere

Blessed is the one who perseveres under trial because, having stood the test, that person will receive the crown of life that the Lord has promised to those who love him.
James 1:12

As an outpatient, my art therapy balanced my traditional psychotherapy with Dr. Wallace. All the inner child Parts of Alice were discovered in my therapy sessions: *Baby Katherine, Alli, Tiny,* and *others.* They each had an opportunity to express their love of primary colors and the hidden emotions of a stolen childhood.

Susan guided me carefully and gained insight and understanding into the thoughts and emotions of the Alters, many of whom were often suppressed. I sometimes created brightly colored, zany artwork that spoke of how an Alter hoped their life might be. Then there were angry, explosive, dark works which sent shivers down the viewer's spine. Artistic representations of interactions with my family and my perpetrators surfaced revealing clear patterns. These works prompted a narrative for a deeper discussion toward healing.

What couldn't be spoken out loud could be demonstrated in different forms of art. Frequently, I created a collage with torn scraps of paper from magazines, books, or journals. Nothing was off limits in terms of objects used to form a footprint of my personal journey to hell and back. My art toolbox included string, yarn, buttons, gemstones, foil, fabric scraps, straws, paint, construction or tissue paper, ribbon, wiggly eyes, and feathers.

Mixing colors, shapes, and textures calmed my agitated soul. Other times a simple sketch with colored pencils proved to be a soothing exercise. Susan's expert suggestions pointed me toward the art form most useful to draw out the emotions I experienced. I employed this artistic approach at home when my emotions tangled up and needed an outward expression. I soon built a collection of

CHAPTER 33 ~ Persevere

art books recording the events of my life in loud, living color on each page.

Susan worked hand in hand with Dr. Wallace. It provided a secure feeling for me that not just one, but two people were teamed together with the goal of helping me heal to wholeness. I gave them permission to freely discuss what happened in each session as I understood it would benefit the ultimate outcome.

Little by little, I became more aware of the different Parts of me. Not all of them were on board with therapy. I didn't know why. Maybe they feared that being exposed, or exposing the horrid secrets hidden in my life, might result in punishment. Those Parts of me didn't participate in therapy. They weren't talking, in obedience to Father's rules which were not easily forgotten. They'd been hard wired into my brain.

I trusted both of my therapists explicitly and knew each possessed a great deal of wisdom. They certainly needed it for the likes of me.

I am not easily impressed by most professionals in the mental health field, but Dr. Wallace had a genuineness about him from day one. I believe God intervened and arranged an introduction to him. Though not religious, he had a gentle, kind soul. He wasn't quick to judge and accepted—even liked—the many Parts of me. I was truly comfortable with him. He took time to listen—not just to hear what I said, but to understand. He never seemed in a hurry but had all the time in the world just for me. I was misunderstood by most people, but not him. Some therapists I'd had in the past didn't believe me and thought I conjured up the horrors that followed me. *Who would make up such terrifying tales?* The positive effects of his help were significant from the beginning of therapy.

An entry from my journal:

What can I do to help myself when I am not in therapy? Here is a reminder list from Dr. Wallace of what I can do day by day.

- *Realize when you are demanding. Think about the words 'should' and 'must.'*
- *Start saying NO more often.*
- *Don't allow others to waste your time.*
- *Stop blaming your stress on outside influences.*
- *Put your energy into areas that you can control.*

CHAPTER 33 ~ Persevere

- *Realize there is a choice in every situation.*
- *Talk more; don't hold feelings in.*
- *Schedule a time of relaxation or exercise.*
- *Do your best but allow mistakes when they occur.*
- *Don't be a people pleaser.*
- *Allow time to play.*
- *Keep in mind what awful really is.*
- *Live in the present, not in the past or future.*
- *Be kind to others.*
- *Success comes from hard work and dedication.*
- *Count your blessings.*
- *Pray.*
- *PERSEVERE.*

34

Faith

*Now faith is confidence in what we hope for
and assurance about what we do not see.*
Hebrews 11:1

Seeing Dr. Wallace twice a week and Susan every other week along with a full-time job helped me stay focused. Nights were difficult as sleep often evaded me. Kris and Monique continued to be up to their self-injury tricks from time to time, etching into my skin unwanted and painful designs evident in the morning light. There were ongoing gaps of time I couldn't account for. *Iris* held down the fort for all of us and did a decent job of it.

Just as the Israelites of the Bible needed to gather manna day by day to sustain them, God bestowed a daily portion of grace to sustain me. Regular church attendance was important for spiritual strength critical to my recovery. The time had come for me to honor God by going into His house again, even though it would be difficult to meet people.

I'd seen a second advertisement for Victory Community Church and took it as a sign to go there. Stepping out in faith, I sat in the last pew on that first Sunday. In the subsequent weeks, I inched my way forward, pew by pew, until I settled myself each week in the middle of the sanctuary.

Since my childhood days at Hillford Church and Cemetery, I'd always been soothed and comforted by music. I took pleasure in the contemporary style of praise and worship music at my new church. Closing my eyes, I allowed the chords and melodies to sweep me away to a place of serenity. I felt united in spirit with the people around me as we sang, stirring happy emotions. There were songs about God, but I cherished the ones sung directly to God. I couldn't get enough of the music and powerful lyrics. For my own private

CHAPTER 34 ~ Faith

worship sessions, at home and in the car, I tuned into K-Love, a Christian radio station.

After six weeks of faithful church attendance, I signed up for the weight loss group that met on Monday nights with the goal of accountability as I sought control over my weight. This is where I first encountered Grace Shepherd, the leader of the fellowship group, called *God's Weigh*.

When I stepped on the scale, I closed my eyes as Grace wrote the total on my chart. I blinked in shock when I saw the result was as close as you could get to the three-hundred-pound mark: 299.9 pounds. This was the most I'd ever weighed. *How could I have gained one hundred pounds since my college years?* I blushed a bright shade of red, embarrassed, and took the paperwork from Grace. My weight was an outward indication of all that was going on inside.

Despite the weigh-in results, the eating plan appeared to be reasonable. *I can do this! I must do this!* The bonus of a faith tie-in with Scripture reading would be an additional benefit as I reached for my goal.

The meeting went well until the end. Grace asked us to get into a circle and join hands for prayer. *Circle? Oh no!* My heart raced. My gut ached as if an elephant had chosen that moment to sit on my chest. A full-blown panic attack rose to the surface and unleashed. I bolted out of the room.

I dashed to my truck and climbed inside, gasping for air. Leaving the meeting in such dramatic fashion without an explanation wasn't a good first impression. *What would everyone think? Can't I get even one thing right?*

I whispered a prayer, "God, please calm me. I need your help to go back and explain." *Explain!? How could I explain?* "Lord, I need courage, help me to be brave." *OK self, if Grace is still there when I go in, that is a sign to speak up and give her a reason for my escape.*

I timidly walked back into the meeting room and saw Grace hauling the heavy stand-up scale to the closet. The last of the other participants headed out the door. I took a deep breath and blurted out my apology. "Grace, I'm s-s-sorry I left. Be-c-c-cause of some things in my childhood, I can't get into a circle. It is a r-r-r-r-reminder of a very dark time in my l-l-l-life."

Grace stopped what she was doing and looked right at me. "Oh Alice, say no more, I am sorry to hear that." Her understanding words put me at ease. "Starting next week, we will arrange the chairs

CHAPTER 34 ~ Faith

in rows instead of a circle and do prayer a different way. Please don't be embarrassed by this. I had a difficult childhood, too. If you ever want to share further about it or have me pray for you, I'd be happy to do so. We are in this together."

Over the next months, I lost weight each week in small increments, and gained knowledge about nutrition, eating triggers, and specific Scripture to help in the battle of the bulge. My favorite Scripture verse was 1 Corinthians 10:13: *"No temptation has overtaken you except what is common to mankind. And God is faithful; he will not let you be tempted beyond what you can bear. But when you are tempted, he will also provide a way out so that you can endure it."*

Prayer helped me keep the Lord a partner in my weight loss adventure.

> *Father, I am a comfort eater. I eat my feelings, and there are so many different feelings to be considered. I find wrappers of food in the trash that I don't remember buying. This is a complicated process. Maybe one of us doesn't want to lose weight. If we become attractive to the outside world, it might mean attention and we don't want that, do we? Father, give me the faith of a mustard seed, the kind that can move mountains. Mountains of fat and mountains of unwanted feelings. Increase my faith in Jesus' Name.*

Friendship

*Therefore encourage one another and build each other up,
just as in fact you are doing.*
1Thessalonians 5:11

My new friend Grace was persistent in getting to know me. This usually irritated me. I wanted to be left alone, but I also whined about not having any friends. The Alters could always be counted on to confuse me with a seesaw of emotions. I learned to recognize the positive and negative influences of the different Parts of me. For instance, Iris usually made the final decisions, not weak and insecure Alice.

Grace invited me to dinner at her home after church one Sunday. When I arrived, I noticed the American, Marine, and Christian flags waving proudly from a decorative basket on a rustic bicycle in the front flower garden. Her husband Teddy, although quiet, kindly welcomed me into their home and gave me a tour while Grace readied the meal in the kitchen. Clad in a military tee shirt denoting his veteran status, he spoke about his service in Vietnam as a Marine Corps draftee. His bold patriotism won me over and raised my awareness of how blessed we are to be Americans. *What would it be like to be married to a man of integrity and courage like Teddy? Maybe someday I'll find out.*

Prior to my visit, Grace had asked me what my favorite dinner was, and I shyly told her my choices: pot roast, mashed potatoes, gravy, carrots, and peas. When I walked into the house it smelled like my mom's house on Sundays. Surprisingly, the aroma didn't trigger any craziness within me. *Why would someone go to all this trouble for me? It wasn't my birthday!* Homemade bread and applesauce rounded out the menu. *This is comforting. I hope you are all listening, especially you Kris and Monique!*

CHAPTER 35 ~ Friendship

When fudge brownies were served for dessert, I felt relaxed and secure enough to share a little about my story. In the past, after unmasking details of my life to others, I always felt regret. But not this time. Grace and Teddy had an air of trust about them. Their daughter, Penny, was currently on the mission field somewhere in Africa. *Impressive! I can't imagine having a child across the globe somewhere, not knowing if she was safe. I might learn a lot about life from Grace. But first, I need to focus and trust God to heal my fractured life.*

Grace and I continued to grow in our friendship and discovered mutual joy in many of the same interests. We had a shared love of country stores and loved to window shop or add rustic, retro, or reclaimed décor touches to our homes. Grace had a passion for reading, too. We shared and discussed books in a little book club for two. She introduced me to Karen Kingsbury, an author who writes life-changing Christian fiction. Her books showed me God is real and personal even through life's disappointments and tragedies. Grace and I had the pleasure of meeting Karen when she spoke at a conference in our area. We acted like stage-struck kids getting autographs and pictures with her.

Grace didn't have a green thumb like me, so I helped with her flower gardens. What a pleasure it was to share my fondness of gardening with another person.

I invited Grace and Teddy to my house one Sunday after church. It was the first official invitation to my home and personal space that I'd allowed, other than Mr. Mason. I didn't count him. He came by to pick up groceries he'd ordered or drop off mail he'd picked out of the box for me. Although I offered him leftovers, he never stayed for dinner. I needed more time to be comfortable with him as a dining partner.

But I wanted to return Grace's invitation to her house and serve my specialty crockpot pineapple pork, a favorite recipe from my Oma. Though nervous about hosting guests for dinner, I felt comfortable welcoming Grace and Teddy into my world. Grace was not a cat lover due to her allergies, but Comet and Frosty warmed up to her right away. To my relief, despite her sniffles, Grace enjoyed interacting with them. It provided entertainment to our day after much praise for my meal. My heart was full with the joy of sharing true friendship.

In time, we grew to share more about our mutual childhood abuse experiences. Grace confessed that her abuse went beyond

CHAPTER 35 ~ Friendship

physical and verbal to the sexual realm. *She trusts me!* I shared a bit of my story. But each time the subject of childhood issues came up, I never hinted or mentioned the dark stuff of the Secret Society. I thought it best to keep that buried and locked down.

One time after talking about my love of teaching and how I missed it, Grace asked if I ever considered volunteering in the Children's Ministry at church. I hadn't given it any thought, but the possibility stirred my heart and mind with excitement.

If the church knew about my psychiatric stay, I figured I would be ruled out. The application asked the question: "Have you ever served time in jail?" *They aren't talking about my high school years, so maybe I have a chance after all!*

I received my official volunteer badge after I met with Connie Robinson, the Director of Spiritual Education. She assigned me to His Kids, the 3rd and 4th grade classroom, once a month. *Perfect! I can't wait to get started.*

Over time, the kids taught me a lot. It felt more like I was the student, not the teacher. Being in the classroom again reminded me that I hadn't made any real effort to get my master's degree as I had originally intended. *I hope this doesn't become another one of my life regrets.*

Grace proved to be an extraordinary personal cheerleader. She continually encouraged me, whether the issue was physical, emotional, or spiritual. *Would she still want to be my friend if she knew there were a group of us. How do you confide a secret like that? Could our friendship handle the full exposure of my multiple me's and remain intact?* I needed to discuss this issue with Dr. Wallace. I believed all the Alters liked Grace. We didn't want to risk losing her as a friend.

In Honor of Grace

I will always remember you my friend for giving of yourself
Especially at such a crucial time
And in such a beautiful way as loving me
When I was just experimenting with trust.
I watched you from afar for the longest time
Without you ever knowing.
Your gentle ways and caring smile
Your home cooked meals and compassionate prayer
Cultivated my curiosity.
Your strong embrace, comforting me on a lovely afternoon.

CHAPTER 35 ~ Friendship

Who you are and what you mean to me are expressions of what life means to me. I am grateful that God allowed our paths to cross, to merge. Only the future knows how long we will travel the same road united by our common experiences. Let us enjoy the walk together and celebrate one another and the friendship that we now share.

Revelation

*Above all, love each other deeply,
because love covers over a multitude of sins.*
1 Peter 4:8

I struggled daily with my job and complained about it all the time, especially to Grace. I had this job for nine long years, and the travel from state to state grew old. The responsibilities increased while the pay didn't. Medical benefits were on the top of the list of reasons why I hung on. Even though therapy was a top priority, I had to cancel many sessions due to my ever-changing work schedule—so frustrating!

Grace worked as an executive administrative assistant at a nearby manufacturing company for industrial equipment. She frequently boasted how inspiring it was to work there. The owners were Christians who ran the company based on faith principles. A five-minute devotional time kick-started each workday. Chapel services, while optional, took place each Friday.

One day she told me about a job opening in the Product Development Department as an administrative assistant to the Vice-President. Her enthusiasm as she spoke bordered on bossiness, but I knew she had my best interests at heart. She offered to help me update my resume, and I agreed to the kind offer. With my application completed and submitted, I figured if it was meant to be, the job would be mine.

Within a few days, my face-to-face interview was scheduled and much to my surprise, they hired me on the spot. Wow! It was a lateral move in terms of salary, but the outstanding benefit package included 401k retirement and profit-sharing plans. What a jackpot! With over 1,500 other employees, HR assured me there would be plenty of opportunities to move up the ladder.

CHAPTER 36 ~ Revelation

Grace and I celebrated this good news at Mr. Softee with large twist cones. That's what two friends do whose lives are centered around food. "See, Alice," Grace said, "God knew just what you needed. He cares about you and all the details of your life."

Maybe, He does, Grace, but you still don't know all the details.

I loved going to church. It provided additional time for me to spend time with Grace and Teddy. I tended to avoid phone conversations, so Grace and I usually chatted on the go. Now that we worked at the same place, we shared rides to work allowing additional talk time. No subject was off limits and occasionally, Grace bravely asked questions about my family. Just to satisfy her, I gave her little bits and pieces, and could tell that she discerned there was more. *Will I ever have the courage to tell her the whole truth?* Parts of me were afraid and reminded me of the rules. Fear always held me back. And if fear had a name, it was Kris!

With my birthday right around the corner, Grace suggested we schedule a girl's only weekend. She purchased tickets to see the latest biblical stage production of *Ruth* at Sight and Sound theatre near Lancaster. In addition, she made reservations at our favorite bed and breakfast, Rose Cottage, run by Marian and Calvin Degler.

I gave Grace the head's up that I wanted to share something very important with her while we were away. After she begged for the tiniest hint, I revealed that I'd allow her to peek at my art books. Now that I let the proverbial cat out of the bag, I knew I had to go through with it or she wouldn't stop bugging me about it. *Could I do it?* The day had arrived!

Two art books that contained my darker drawings were selected. My plan was to give direct hints to Grace about the darker side of my life and allow the artwork to do the talking.

One of my favorite spots on the grounds was the beautiful, fragrant rose garden behind the B&B, hence the name Rose Cottage. A unique cobblestone path led to a gazebo at the center of the garden. Peace was planted there. I had the sense of being hidden from the world and all its turmoil. The perfumed air from the roses was heavenly. Occasionally butterflies winged their way past us, expressing their freedom of movement while showing off their colors—a serene environment in which to share secrets.

Grace and I strolled into the garden, taking time to smell the roses. My heart pounded and felt as heavy as the two selected art books I clutched tightly to my chest. The books were filled to

CHAPTER 36 ~ Revelation

overflowing with interpretations of my life story. *Lord, help! I am risking a friendship here!*

Grace could see I was uber nervous and tried to comfort me. "Alice, we are friends for life. There is nothing you can tell me that will make me love you or value you any less. But, if this isn't the right time, it is fine, I'm not going anywhere."

"I want to tell you. It's just d-d-d-difficult. Hard to s-s-s-speak it out loud. Saying it out loud makes it factual. I never know who is listening."

"Alice, may I pray for you?" she said. "I know God is listening, and so will I."

I nodded my affirmative answer since I couldn't speak.

"Gracious Father, we come to Your throne of grace. We are thankful You are a God of mercy and compassion. I pray You will help Alice share a secret that has kept her from experiencing true freedom. You see and hear all things, so You know exactly how to help her speak this truth. I am thankful for the trust she has in You and in me. Help me to always honor that trust so I can help her carry this burden. In Jesus' Name. Amen."

I handed Grace the first book with tears in my eyes. Tears for what she would see, but also tears in knowing that she wanted to share my burden. She was about to open Pandora's Box and I prayed that what spilled out would not affect her in a negative way. I cared about her too much.

Just as she was about to open the book, an Alter tried to get my attention to stop the madness of revealing to another living soul the Depravity of Humanity, namely, my father!

I pushed aside the fear. The Alters sat very still. We observed Grace as she viewed page after page. When she caught sight of the colored drawing of the Secret Society of the Serpent ritual taking place, she gasped. She gasped again at the cutaway view of my house, complete with the secrets of the basement. The hooded figures, the candles, the knife, and the altar with me on it, were all depicted there.

"Dear Jesus, surely not! How can this be?" Grace whispered with tears running down her face. "Oh, my dear friend! What have you endured? Who are these evil men?"

For the next three hours, I spewed out the truth about the Monster. I admitted to Grace how I coped with life. That there were many Parts of me who helped me keep sane and live my life.

CHAPTER 36 ~ Revelation

There was another picture at the back of the book I wanted her to see—a pencil drawing of my crowded mind. There were seventeen separate Parts of me drawn in the picture. They were the ones I knew about. Perhaps there were others yet to be discovered. Each Part or Alter held memories and feelings of their own, all serving a specific purpose.

"Grace, I have one more thing I hesitate to tell you, and this may be the most unhinged darkest truth of all," I said. Grace nodded her head, and I continued. "During one of my therapy sessions with Susan dealing with the Monster and his ritualistic deeds, the air inside her office grew oppressive and heavy. I found it difficult to breathe and the hair stood up on the back of my neck. I was terrified and knew there was an unholy presence in the room. My lips began to move in prayer. I sat frozen in my chair with my eyes closed willing this evil to vanish."

"Although I looked quiet on the outside, Alters inside me began to chatter. Some screamed, some cringed and tried to shrink and take cover for what might come. As quickly as this evil force crept in the room, it left.

"Susan seemed unfazed by it, and I wondered if she had put on a brave front for me. She noticed my frightened expression and told me to breathe deep, and count to ten.

"I fought for control while she reached for my artbook and began to sketch with a royal blue marker. I couldn't imagine what she was thinking. Minutes later, she showed me the drawing and told me that the satanic blood rituals I was forced to participate in involved a blood oath—like a marriage of my soul to the highest evil power, Satan. She told me that the malevolent presence that had just invaded our space was a straightforward reminder that I'm still tethered to this darkness, and I must break that bond!"

I looked into Grace's face to determine what she might be thinking and gave her a minute to process what I'd revealed. She reached over to me with her hand and gently touched my arm in assurance.

I continued, "Grace, the picture she sketched was something that looked like an old scroll—like what government declarations might be written on. It was huge—on 11 X 14-inch paper. In bold letters at the top she wrote: *'Divorce Decree. I proclaim from this day forward, that I, Alice (et al), is officially divorced from Satan. That marriage is now null and void.'* There were two signature lines on the bottom. One

CHAPTER 36 ~ Revelation

for me and one for Susan, as the witness. She also drew an official seal in yellow with a line to write in the date. I signed it immediately and hoped it would stop the demonic forces from appearing again. Married! To Satan? Grace, this is my great shame. I couldn't imagine sharing this with anyone before."

I saw by the look on her face, she was stunned and overwhelmed. This was not a run of the mill confession, but a lot to take in and process. Neither of us said anything for quite a while. Grace reached out and hugged me. We clung to each other and sobbed. She cried for little Alice. I cried for my innocent babies. She whispered, "The past is behind you, and I will always be your friend."

I was thankful to have Grace Shepherd as a trusted confidant. She was the first non-therapist person to whom I had revealed the entire appalling truth. Sharing my dark secrets released me of shame, guilt, and humiliation. Skeletons in the closet are a weighty baggage to carry by yourself and now I didn't have to. I felt lighter as we walked silently back to the room.

37

Highs and Lows

*Consider it pure joy, my brothers and sisters,
whenever you face trials of many kinds,
because you know that the testing of your faith produces perseverance.
Let perseverance finish its work so that you may be mature
and complete, not lacking anything.*
James 1:2-4

After the big revelation, Grace didn't treat me differently. What a relief! I noticed sorrow in her eyes. Often, tears welled up in them when we were together. It comforted me knowing Grace held a biblical counselor certification. In case her empathy was too overwhelming, she could lean into her training, partnered with her faith, to carry the burden. What Grace had seen between the pages of my artbook would have an emotional effect upon her.

Anger from one or more Alters surfaced, concerned that the truth escaped, spoken out loud. Monique left a note and asked if I'd thought that Grace might be in danger if some of the Alters found out. *No! I hadn't thought of that at all. What a big dummy I am!*

Grace casually informed me one day that she'd begun research about Dissociative Identity Disorder (DID) as a means to understand what I was going through. *God, she is such a blessing. I'm thankful she never sees me as a freak in a sideshow. What did I do to deserve a friend like her?*

Around that time, I divided my life into high points and low points and recorded them in my journal. In the high column, God took first place. Grace, Teddy, and Penny were listed next. Also making the list were my sister Sandy, her husband, Michael, and their kids, Samuel and Rebecca. Rebecca was definitely a highlight. She came into the picture three years after Sammy made his debut. I loved them both so much and spoiled them whenever I could. I needed to visit them more often.

CHAPTER 37 ~ Highs and Lows

Mr. Mason, my neighbor, also made the high list. I didn't see him often since he'd started dating again but was happy for him moving forward with his life. I knew how much he missed his wife, Reba, of forty- five years. My job ranked up there in the high column, as well. I enjoyed what I did. My leader, Errol, told me how much he appreciated my work ethic, and my paycheck reflected it. I could pay all my bills and had cash left over for my blessing account to shop for the perfect birthday and holiday gifts for friends, family, and co-workers.

While I appreciated my crowded high column, the lows of my life column only had two major things written in it that were painful and threatened to derail me.

The first low I recorded was my decision to tell my story to one of the pastors. *I can do this! I told the ugly truth to Grace. I should tell my spiritual authority.*

Grace encouraged the meeting, confident that it wouldn't be an issue at all. I scheduled an appointment with the assistant pastor who handled most of the counseling situations even though this wasn't what I considered counseling. I had my therapy for that. It was more of a personal confession session in what I deemed a safe space.

I overviewed my life journey to Pastor X, who, out of respect shall remain nameless. Nervously, I bared my story, often stuttering and shaking. At one point, I thought I might wet myself. Thank God I was spared that embarrassment. I presumed the Lord directed pastors to know what was sacred and under the atoning blood of our Savior. I believed Jesus Christ was the Savior of the world and forgiver of all deeds, even those we were forced to do in the name of the unholy.

After sharing, I sensed Pastor X might have thought my story was a figment of an overactive imagination—though he didn't say anything out loud. It was just an innate feeling in my gut to that effect. "I'm so sorry for what happened to you, Alice," he said. "Let me pray for you." Though I don't remember a word of it, I felt confident his words were sincere.

The backlash of that meeting came a few days later when Connie, the Director of Spiritual Education called to tell me that leadership had made a determination about me. "I'm sorry," she said, "but Pastor X feels that you can no longer teach the children or serve in the Children's Ministry." The force of her words triggered a stabbing pain deep inside my heart. A sense of betrayal left me helpless and

CHAPTER 37 ~ Highs and Lows

suddenly empty. She may have spoken further comments, but I stopped listening after the words "*could no longer teach.*"

I breathed. Then a surge of anger bubbled up only to recede in waves of overwhelming sorrow. *Who did he think he was? How could he have come to such a determination?* I phoned to confront him for an explanation, refusing even the thought of another face-to-face sit down.

"Alice," he said, "I'm sorry, but I am obligated morally to pull you from ministry by the nature of your confession. You recounted how you participated in a ritual where the life of your own child was taken. You can no longer hold a teaching position. I hope you understand. This is a decision that I didn't make lightly. Beyond your confession, it's about your own liability and protection, as well."

Stunned, I hung up and slid to the floor. My world crashed in around me. *He doesn't believe me. He's labeled me a murderer. Doesn't he understand I had no choice? How is it that my therapist believes me, but not my pastor? God, is this my punishment? Separation from children whom I adore?*

I felt stripped naked, judged, and convicted of murder in a court of public opinion. *Guilty! Guilty! Guilty!* The light inside me dimmed. I believed confession was the right thing to do. *How could I have been so wrong?* I was being exed out of church life as an undesirable, an outcast who couldn't be trusted around children.

"God you know I would never harm a living creature and definitely not one of your precious little ones."

God whispered a response, "I know my child. I know."

This incident ranks very high on the list as one of the most painful things that I ever faced.

Shortly afterward, another low point came into play. Comet's health rapidly declined, and the little guy was in constant pain. I made the excruciating decision to allow him to cross the Rainbow Bridge. My furry family member had been a joy and comfort to all the Alters, and Frosty, too. Deep grief settled over me like a heavy blanket weighing me down, my legs crumpling beneath me in weakness.

Although we experienced some highs along the way, the lows were truly low. It was hard to move through the Valley of Despair day to day while the Alters warred restlessly through the nighttime hours.

Feeling like a wiggly worm again.

Lost and Found

*But you are a chosen people, a royal priesthood, a holy nation,
God's special possession, that you may declare the praises of him
who called you out of darkness into his wonderful light.*
1 Peter 2:9

After the confession session at church, I no longer deemed myself worthy of going to weekly services. I felt defeated. How ironic that the church was called Victory Community Church. Every Sunday morning at 10:00 a.m. when service started, I sat home curled up and alone, either crying or picking at my skin with a safety pin. Self-injury didn't normally happen during the day, but this hurt went deep. *I am like Alice in Wonderland sliding down the rabbit hole. Who will save me?*

Adding to my distress, an odd emotion infiltrated my sleep with recurring dreams where I was literally lost. I decided to write the vivid details in my journal in an effort to make sense of it:

> *I am lost! It is dark, but I notice a tall beautifully designed building that I yearn to reach. I keep taking wrong turns. Am I in a maze? Left-right-left, no! I'm frightened! Night-time has arrived and I see the structure is now well lit and just steps ahead—finally! Everyone around me is certain of the path, but not me. Fear torments me with confusion. So many streets to investigate and I'm getting nowhere. I cut through alleys and climb fences. I run as if my life depended on it until I drop from exhaustion. I follow others thinking they might know the way, only to become lost again. The building is always in sight, but I can't find my way to it. Is this how a blind person feels?*
>
> *Giving myself permission to speak, I bravely walk up to the first person that is passing by. "Hey, stranger, I'm bewildered and going round in circles to get to that stately building just ahead, can you help me?"*
>
> *"Of course, you're almost there," the friendly stranger replied, "Follow me!" I was stunned. He took me straight away to that which*

was just out of reach. He delivered me to the massive jeweled front gate and bowed in retreat. What a dazzling sight! I knew instinctively that this was a safe haven. Before I stepped under the arch with the Welcome sign, I promised I would always remember how disheartening and lonely it felt not to be able to find your way.

What is the message? Hmmm . . . God speak to me. Are others besides me lost, wandering around aimlessly looking for safety? Am I courageous enough to look for them and lead them to their destination?

Recently, I heard a sermon on television about how Jesus left the ninety-nine sheep to find the lost one. That's how much He loves the one. *I'm a lost sheep, Jesus! I'm roaming around waiting for rescue. Looking to be found. To feel safe. Baaaa! In my heart I know you love me, Jesus. Help me to believe it. I want to rest in the loving arms of the Shepherd.*

Lord Jesus, You Are so Beautiful

*When I finally realized
I couldn't do it on my own
You looked down at me and said
"Alice, I love you!"*

*You didn't say I will love you if.
If you stay out of trouble
If you go out and change the world
You just simply said I love you.*

*Lord Jesus, I just want to praise you
Praise you because you love me
Praise you because you are my friend
And praise you for your beautiful creation.*

*Lord Jesus, I just want to love you
Not just love if you heal my family
Not just love if you help me when I need it
I just want to simply love you.*

*Lord Jesus, you are so beautiful
Because you just simply said, "Alice, I love you!"
And now I want to tell you
"I love you! Simply because you are you."*

CHAPTER 38 ~ Lost and Found

Notes from My Journal

Jesus, it's me, you know, the one who looks into the mirror these days and sees an ugly face that doesn't smile much anymore staring back. There is so much going on behind those troubled eyes staring back at me in the mirror. I get so impatient because I don't understand it. I'm bewildered and I'm frightened.

This world is such a cold place and I'm so preoccupied with troubles I don't fully understand. I don't know what to do and feel so afraid to ask for help. Guide me Lord Jesus. Remind me daily that I'm infinitely precious in your sight. Help me to believe that I matter to you even though I'm fat, ugly, and bad. I feel lost. No one can find all the parts of me except you. Alice and et al.

Oh Jesus, how it hurts to be me. I'm standing forlorn and alone because in the opinion of all the other ducklings, I'm not quite right. Oh Jesus, do outcasts have to exist? It's hard to suffer the pangs of loneliness that come with being a weirdo. I want to be an acceptable duckling. Is that too much to ask? I hear a firm rebuke from you. You don't want acceptable ducklings—you create glorious swans. Your ways are not my ways. You see the value of the weak and the funny looking. Maybe it is a preparation for something greater. I'm grateful there is no one more loving than you, no one more sensitive to the abandoned than you. You fling wide your arms of love and gather in the outcasts, misfits, abused, broken, scarred, and shattered ones. Oh, Jesus, can you open your arms a little wider and gather in this ugly duckling until I become a swan? Alice and et al.

One more thing Jesus—do we really have to love ourselves before we can love others?

Grace bugged me about missing church. She didn't understand how deep the Pastor X wound cut. How could she, she wasn't me. She spoke all the time about the importance of forgiveness. She said that to forgive the hurtful actions of others didn't mean approval of what they did. Even if the perpetrators weren't sorry, forgiveness would be released, and I would be free.

But I wasn't ready and told her so. "Eventually I'll go back, just not yet. I need a break. Not from God, but from God's people."

Everywhere I turned, confusion reigned, and direction wasn't clear. Like in the dream. In therapy, my progress slowed. Brain fog hindered my responses. *How can I find my way to being a swan? There are*

CHAPTER 38 ~ Lost and Found

many of us clamoring about inside, wanting attention. Lots of lost ugly ducklings each trying to find their way.

A year after the confession event at church, Grace's daughter, Penny, was home from the mission field for a brief furlough. She invited me to one of the local churches where she was speaking about her adventures and raising financial support. As she testified how she and her teams shared the Gospel message through song, drama, puppets, and Scripture, excitement stirred within me.

Is that You, God, stirring an idea within me?

Kids were impacted around South Africa as missionary teams visited school classrooms with the Gospel message. *Amazing!* As I listened to her, I added "mission trip" to my bucket list.

To close out Penny's remarks, Pastor Graham extended a powerful challenge to examine our hearts and pray about being part of a mission trip. "Repent," he said, "and confess anything that is holding you back from being everything God designed you to be. When your heart is cleared of lingering debris, invite Jesus to be the leader of your life and direct your feet."

> *Lord, it's me again. I'm asking on behalf of all the Alices who are tuned in. I release all the pain, bitterness, and unforgiveness to You. I invite You into all the locked places in my heart. I can't believe I just asked this! I dedicate my life to Your plans and purposes.*

Waves of warmth welled up from my heart and reached my cheeks. They turned red. *God, I thought You had forgotten me. I sense Your presence all around me. Is this how an ugly duckling feels after being transformed into a swan?*

I had arrived at church that day feeling lost. I left knowing I had found renewed hope. Like the song, *Amazing Grace*, "I once was lost, but now I'm found." Again!

39

All of Me

He has made everything beautiful in its time.
Ecclesiastes 3:11

Year after year, my therapies continued with both Dr. Wallace and Susan. We delved into other issues besides my childhood or dissociative disorders. Sometimes we dealt with frustration, overweight issues, challenges in the workplace, or the discovery of ovarian tumors and subsequent surgery.

Between art therapy, journaling, notes from Alters for Alice to find, and my regular therapy, twenty-one different Alters were identified. I listed them along with their primary roles:

1. Alice—21 parts; making up authentic me
2. Abby—Witness to death of pets, protector of animals
3. Alli—Little girl; loves to play games, collects stuffed animals
4. Allison—Co-manager; faith and hope are her strengths, comforter
5. Hope—Stuffed bunny, if she came to life she would save Alice and destroy the wrongdoers
6. Caroline—Imaginary friend; shifts to her during sexual aggression
7. David—Fun-loving, male protector, the personality she would like her father to be
8. Heather—Hand holder through trauma, optimistic
9. Iris—Co-manager of career and organizer of details, helper
10. Jackie (JJ)—Mirror image of Alice, but edgy
11. Jesse—Sassy teen; talks back to other Alters, knows everything
12. Joey—Male protector; feels safe when in danger, causes to dress male at times
13. Katherine—The perfect little girl; craves parental love

14. Kris—Aggressive, self-injures, would like to be in control
15. Lynda—Denies any abuse ever happened
16. Monique—Aggressive, self-injures, does what Kris tells her to do
17. Rose—Endures all, but numb; feels non-existent
18. Sally—Carries grief for all the children, frequently cries
19. Tiny—Infant; wishes she had never been born
20. Tracy—Unhappy toddler; demanding
21. Vicki—Sexual; believes she must have brought this on herself

At first, I was terrified to think there were so many Parts of me. *What if they peek out or shift at an inappropriate time and embarrass me? I won't even remember any of it!*

As I persevered in therapy, greater understanding and more control of the Alters fell into place.

Many times, during my ongoing therapy, different Alters wrote letters and spoke on my behalf. If afraid to communicate certain information or specifics I couldn't remember, one or more of the Alters did. Notes and letters written at different times during my extensive treatment reveal a more detailed view into the world of Dissociative Identity Disorder, otherwise known as My World.

Dear Susan & Dr. Wallace,
I'm going to write and fill you in on a few details on the trip "back home" this past weekend. It's easier than speaking it out loud. I am very disappointed in myself for not handling the situation better. I feel like I let Alice and the rest of the crew down especially since I call myself a helper. I believe I have let you down, too. I am sorry to everyone involved. Today is one of those days that I feel like giving up, just like Alice. I have a lot of learning to do like everybody else inside, and right now, I have failed in my role at helping. I am discouraged. The idea of talking and writing to people outside of Alice is a new experience and generally, it seems like a positive one, but not now. I am getting sidetracked.

When we were all at Shivering Acres, some of us got hurt. I know Alice isn't totally aware of what happened and in fact doesn't recall much of the trip at all. It is just as well for now, but she needs to face these issues at some point. Alice often has evidence of the physical and/or sexual hurts, but because she and other Parts often do things that are self-destructive, she doesn't realize that some of the hurts are from others

CHAPTER 39 ~ All of Me

outside of us. She figures that she hurt herself again but doesn't remember how or when. She is questioning her sanity and although she wants to believe you when you tell her she isn't crazy, she is not totally convinced.

On this particular trip, Alice did not get beat up very much, but EPAR did occur again. Just writing this brings tears to my eyes. I want to tell you more, but I can't seem to get it out right now, so I will change the subject.

Alice did go see the internist this week and did really great considering her fear of people. Today she sees the eye doctor and then is scheduled for a CT of her head. I have a feeling she may not show up for that appointment. Well, Alice needs to get to work and this has to get in the mail before she sees it.

Signed-Iris, who tried to help and failed

Dear Susan,

I am very sorry that I (or another Part) left you that message whenever that was. I don't like doing things that I don't remember doing. I missed seeing you when you were away. I hope your Mom is doing better now. I am sorry that she is very sick; I remember what that was like with my Mom.

Sometimes, there are so many things I want to talk about, but then when I come to see you, I can never remember. Why does that always happen? Most of the time, I can't even remember what we talked about anyway. Do you think other Parts of me remember? I don't want anyone else seeing what I am writing, except you and Dr. Wallace. That's all I can write for now.

From Alice or Parts unknown

Hi Susan,

It's me again! I have not been feeling well this week—I was hardly able to come to work. I did, but it is a struggle. It seems like, more and more, I just want to be dead—everything seems scary and I miss my kitty cat Comet so much. She was one of the few bright spots in my life. Why is life such a struggle?

Signed-Guess Who

Dear Susan & Dr. Wallace,

This is Iris writing to you. Alice wanted me to ask you some questions, but she never seems to get the courage to actually do the

CHAPTER 39 ~ All of Me

asking. I feel a bit awkward mentioning these things to you; however, my awkwardness is going to have to take a back seat for now and let my concern take over.

I think Alice is very sick, both physically and mentally. Several times recently Alice has vomited with no apparent warning. It has happened while driving, at work, and at home. It is usually accompanied by severe headaches and dizziness. I am no medical expert, but I think she needs to get this checked out. Alice has wanted to ask you if all of this is normal. She also has severe back pain and I believe that is a result of what happened on that recent trip back home. I want to tell you more about that, but I am hesitant to because if Alice reads this letter, I don't think she could handle it. A dilemma to solve.

Different subject—recently I thought that some of the little ones would like to read the book you lent Alice. You know, the one about the girl who went through the woods and got into the boat at the pond and went to a safe place? I thought it would give the little ones some hope. Just a thought.

Last, but not least. Alice is struggling financially. Between therapy, medication, and seeing Dr. Graves, the primary care doctor, she is spending over half of her take home pay. Some of the Others have spent Alice's money on non-essentials or given it away. I would like to continue with therapy, so I hope Alice can work these things out. I must rush this to mail, Alice is coming.

Signed, Iris

The notes and letters became key clues to the truth of a life hidden deep within my mind. During therapy sessions, memories came back, sometimes in a flood of swirling emotions that quickened my breathing. Therapy helped process whether childhood events were factual or a product of a twisted dream. *This was no dream!*

The anxiety produced by these events necessitated a twice daily cocktail of prescription meds. Vivid pictures of people and events materialized at various times during treatment like a movie on a big screen. Outside of therapy, I could be triggered while going about my daily business when wisps of memories floated in. A song at church, an object like a silver chalice, or a musty smell could lead to an episode of confusion, accelerated pulse, or a full-blown panic attack. These unpredictable moments swept me back into the twisted unholy world I couldn't otherwise have conceived of in my wildest dreams.

CHAPTER 39 ~ All of Me

The ultimate healing goal was to integrate all the Alter parts into one. I endured the daunting process of exposed details, each demanded to be apprehended, analyzed, and put to rest. *When, oh, when will this therapy game ever end?*

After seven and a half years of dedicated therapy and relentless, exhausting application of the process, the long-awaited day arrived.

Dr. Wallace looked up from his notes and smiled. "Alice, in my professional opinion I believe we have succeeded in uniting all the Alices into one!"

It seemed surreal. I sat stunned for several minutes and couldn't speak. An express train of questions coupled with resolve barreled through my mind. *Are the sessions really over, then? Can I make it without consistent therapy? How will I fill the time void? What if there's an Alter lurking in the background waiting to be discovered? I'm going to do this! My faith will sustain me and not fail me. It's time for the rubber to meet the road. It's time to embrace the future and put the past behind. Way behind.*

I left the office without making another appointment. *Today is graduation day! This is equal to the master's degree I always wanted to pursue. This master's degree is in Overcoming the Effects of Childhood Abuse. Lord, I am now all ONE. Back to Your original design! I can't wait to share this good news with Grace. She'll be so happy and proud I persevered in therapy all these years.*

A light-hearted smile formed on my lips as I walked to the car. *I am now fully, completely, born anew and overflowing with the knowledge that God is not finished with me yet. In this moment I sense Your love and presence with me. And, do you know what, Lord? I love me too. All of me!*

Susan agreed with Dr. Wallace's opinion to end psychotherapy but encouraged me to continue art therapy to express my sense of achievement. I readily agreed and looked forward to my creative sessions with her. They were worth every penny.

In honor of all the Alices, I wove together twenty-one colorful strands of yarn into one beautiful, solitary braid. At the end of each string, I attached the name of every known Alter part of me. We were one Alice! A strand of gold woven in the center, represented the One who created and protected me by allowing me to fragment into Parts as a child when my mind couldn't handle the trauma. *Why, this was a gift from my Heavenly Father! Thank you, Lord, that You didn't leave me in pieces, but lovingly restored me. How do you celebrate a miracle like this?*

Interlude

But now the Lord my God has given me rest on every side, and there is no adversary or disaster.
1 Kings 5:4

Starting my new lease on life simply as Alice intimidated me. I was grateful for the Alters, especially Iris and Allison, and all their help through hundreds of intense therapy sessions. Integration was a gradual process, but now I couldn't count on anyone but me and God—quite an adjustment!

I enjoyed a wonderful, peaceful three-and-a-half-year interlude from turmoil. Grace, my forever friend, invited me to participate in almost everything she did including spending holidays with her family. She didn't immediately succeed at getting me back to church, but she did triumph fashioning a more updated makeover to go along with my new outlook on life.

Joey, one of my Alters, had me sporting a blunt, masculine hair style and clothed me in unisex fashions. Grace unknowingly changed all of that when she gifted me dangly birthstone diamond earrings for Christmas. For years they were hidden in the back of my underwear drawer since they were so not me. But the time had come to unearth them. I was a different kind of me now and selected a new hairstyle featured in *People* magazine. Grace gave me a thumbs up when I showed her and proclaimed me to be "chic and lovely." I smiled, brimming with joy—my heart full. No such words had ever been spoken about me.

We shopped at Dress Barn and purchased coordinating pants outfits and even dresses. There were zero dresses in my closet at home, so that was a big moment. A salesclerk named Patty helped me select colorful earrings for each outfit, and I indulged myself with a silver heart pendant. Although costly, a new me deserved some fashionable attire. My book group friend, Gerri, held a Mary Kay

CHAPTER 40 ~ Interlude

make-over demonstration one evening which interested me very much. *Maybe I could be a swan, after all.*

I visited my sister Sandy and her family once or twice a year. I loved my niece and nephew and enjoyed watching them grow through their various states of development. I savored spoiling them with an abundance of kid loot and sometimes pretended they were my children in an effort to ease the pain of my own losses. After our visits, I drove away with a sense of grief and depression. Any environment with children reminded me of the three that lived forever in my heart.

My brother Billy had been released from jail, but no one knew his whereabouts. Mom wrote to me telling me of the rumor around town that he was shacked up with an older woman and her two kids. It had been years since I'd heard from him.

Without fail, every time I phoned Mom, she begged me to visit. My standard excuse not to visit was that my job kept me busy with overtime. *Will I ever have the courage to tell her the truth about why I don't want to visit? How can I honor my mother from a distance? Does trying to live my best life before a Holy God count?*

Grace and Teddy planned to go on a mission trip to Poland with Victory Community Church and asked me to pray about going, too. The team would be led by her daughter Penny and another missionary friend, Anna. Since serving in missions was on my bucket list, I put aside any and all irrational concerns. *What if I'm not spiritual enough? What if I freaked out and came undone? What if? What if?* Then, I applied for a passport.

This adventure stirred mixed emotions within me. As required, I prepped spiritually with the team, practiced the dramas, learned the songs, and even enjoyed the puppetry training. Penny and Anna made it easy for me with their love and acceptance. Grace teased me that she had gotten me back to church after all. The groundwork for the mission trip happened at church, so technically, yes—she had gotten me back to church. I promised her I'd think about regularly attending after our trip.

It invigorated me to be part of a team and minister God's love along with the Gospel to the Poles in their formal church setting. They were kind-hearted and quickly warmed up to us. As a result, many souls were brought to a personal faith in Christ due to our efforts at the church services, kid crusades, and sports camps for youth.

CHAPTER 40 ~ Interlude

We also experienced a life-changing visit to the Majdanek Concentration Camp near Lublin which gave us a glimpse into the Holocaust. During the German occupation of the Second World War, the site was used to exterminate people on an industrial scale. An eerie quiet enveloped the sacred ground as we viewed the crematorium and memorial filled with the ashes of thousands of victims—souls lost in the horrific and chilling devastation. We were stunned to see the piles of luggage, rooms filled with human hair, and floor to ceiling wire cages packed with shoes. Knowing each pair of shoes represented the life of a fellow human being, a deep sorrow rose up within me. I was especially affected as I stared at a lone red shoe which stood out in contrast, shoved in the middle of the wire cage. *We have a common bond. Evil was unleashed here, and you witnessed it, just like me!* I shivered as tears welled up in kinship.

The curator explained how the poor souls slept side by side, as close as humanly possible. Then, on the count of three, they'd all roll over in sync. This systematic method provided needed warmth along with the comfort of human touch—something mankind needs at the very deepest level. *I know I do.*

Being so personally acquainted with Evil, I sensed it standing in the gas chamber, walking in the dormitories, and lurking in the medical experimentation room. God reminded me of an important fact as I viewed photographs of the victims: *Others have been ravaged by demonic forces of hell, too. I was not alone.* This truth penetrated my heart. *God, You spared my life, why didn't You spare these lives?* I knew with God's help, my purpose as a survivor was to share my story and help other victims whose lives have been touched by ungodly actions. I journeyed to Poland to minister God's love and found that His love ministered to me through the whispers of silence at the concentration camp.

Throughout the mission trip, God opened my eyes to the benefits of a grateful heart. Once home, I began to actively attend Victory Community Church. Pastor X had taken a teaching post elsewhere, so the decision to return was made a little easier. As I matured in Christ, in my heart, I came to understand that Pastor X had made the best decision on behalf of the children. Even so, accepting this didn't lessen my pain. I had not quite arrived in the forgiveness department. Still, God graciously continued to work on me.

CHAPTER 40 ~ Interlude

The mission trip bug grabbed me again, and I committed to the team heading to South Africa. Grace, Teddy, and twelve others were scheduled to go, too. Our mission was to assist Penny and Anna distribute a storybook version of the Gospel in the local schools. They were open to religious instruction as long as it taught much needed AIDS education along with it. The team presented the story of Jesus' life, death, and resurrection through drama, music, and puppets. We invited the children, their families, and neighbors to return in the evening for church services and free Bibles in their native language. Each school proudly greeted us with the angelic voices of the school children singing a welcome song. The beautiful patterns and bright colors of the school uniforms mirrored the spectrum of the rainbow. When I think of Africa, it is this beautiful portrait of sight and sound that pops into my mind.

Out of all the amazing things we experienced, there were several standouts I treasure from the trip. We toured a nature reserve which included a safari drive and observed Africa's big five: the lion, rhino, leopard, elephant, and Cape buffalo, in their natural habitat. We were invited into the animal nursery where we held and cuddled a baby lion. A wild, once in a lifetime encounter.

The team accepted an invitation to an orphanage established by a missionary ministry. Most of the children housed there were abandoned due to the AIDS pandemic. They asked our team for volunteers to spend the afternoon. They needed extra hands to care for the little ones in the nursery. My hand shot up. I couldn't say "Yes" fast enough. The four team members who stayed were tasked to simply love, snuggle, and rock the babies for several hours. I pretended these were my children with their sweet innocent brown faces. I sang and prayed over them while I held the precious little ones close. I whispered, "God loves you and has a beautiful plan for your life."

It was joy! It was heaven! It was an honor! It was contentment! I could have stayed forever. I wished I could adopt them all and daydreamed the entire time wondering what it would be like to run an orphanage.

God had another highlight and breakthrough event for me on that trip. We scheduled a stop at a women's prison. Anna asked me if I would consider sharing my testimony or a personal story. She told me that many of the inmates had been abused, both physically and sexually. *Oh God, You are a tricky One. You brought me thousands of*

CHAPTER 40 ~ Interlude

miles from home to share my story for the first time. I told Anna I was a willing, but reluctant volunteer. She suggested I write down my thoughts. I asked her to look over the three pages of notes I prepared and see if it was appropriate to share. As she read, her face displayed shock, even as she attempted to hide it well. She had tears in her eyes and she nodded her head in an affirmative way. What I wrote was satisfactory.

The appointed time came. I took a deep breath and openly shared details of the horrors from my childhood abuse and how God was my ever-present help in time of need. Although my knees knocked nervously, I felt liberated telling my story accompanied by a translator who echoed my words into the Swahili language for a ragtag group of women. At the end of my personal testimony, several fellow sufferers came to know the saving love of Jesus. They embraced hope. I was astonished that God used me in such a powerful way by opening my life story to them. I knew what it felt like to be a prisoner, even though the iron bars I hid behind were self-constructed and invisible to others.

Grace and I participated in other adventures during those interlude years. We travelled together to the Western Caribbean and celebrated a big birthday of mine on my first cruise. She collected birthday cards from everyone she could find. Every morning when I came out of the shower there would be a fresh pile of encouraging words and love on my pillow. *Is this what it's like to be a member of the royal family?*

I continued taking anti-anxiety meds as fear often tried to take control when the sun went down. I wrote out Scripture verses to help battle the dreaded F-word: FEAR. My favorite combat verse was *"For God has not given us a spirit of fear, but of power and of love and of a sound mind."* 2 Timothy 1:7 NKJV

This season of my life provided me with a level of true contentment I'd never known before. My job at the manufacturing plant turned into a valued career. I had just passed my five-year anniversary when I was named *Woman of the Year*. Right there on the certificate, it stated, as an employee, I was one of their greatest assets. They further declared I had held up the company's objective, which was to Honor God and Pursue Excellence.

What an unexpected tribute and cause for celebration! I am deeply humbled. I don't deserve this. I was simply doing my job, nothing special. Maybe that was

CHAPTER 40 ~ Interlude

the point. I am a champion, not a stupid nothing like when I received the Teacher of the Year award years ago. I was sure it was undeserved.

Grace and Teddy bought a nice gold frame. I hung my award on the wall as a reminder that I not only had value—I was valued. *I'm starting to believe it.* Although just a piece of paper, I treasured my award certificate.

Not a day went by that I didn't miss Comet, though. Frosty was slowing down, too, and his age showed during playtime. If cats have nine lives, I hoped Frosty had more time. *Is it time to increase our family before those lives run out?* That decision was made for me one day when a cardboard box containing four abandoned Siamese kittens was discovered in the back parking lot at work. The security guard who found them asked me if I'd be interested in adopting one or more. He knew cats were my thing, and it didn't take much convincing. That same day, I went home with two new furry family members and promptly named them Tweedledee and Tweedledum—like the twins in *Alice in Wonderland*.

How appropriate those names. I, Alice, was having quite an adventure in my own Wonderland. Not to mention I knew what it was like to fall down the rabbit hole. I hoped my story would have a "happily ever after ending."

But my interlude was about to come to an abrupt end.

Gains and Losses

He heals the brokenhearted and binds up their wounds.
Psalm 147:3

If my weight was an outward indication of my inward state of mind, it would be plain to see the mountain of challenges I wrestled with daily. Whoever said, "Just put the fork down," didn't have an eating issue. They enjoyed the gift of self-discipline. My strongest cravings came in my weakest moments. Helpless in such a place, I chose food as my comforter.

Eating soothed my anxiety so I could cope. A specialist in the medical field diagnosed me with a lazy metabolism. That fact, along with the emotional eating, exacerbated the numbers on the scale. I attempted to lose weight over the years through many dieting schemes—at least a dozen or more. The most challenging, yet successful, proved to be a liquid fast under the guidance of a professional monitor. *Eight hundred calories a day? You have got to be kidding!* I held on for seventeen weeks and dropped seventy pounds. But in a rush of weakness, I decided that I just couldn't take the limitations anymore. In no time at all, the weight piled back on and I zoomed to the 300-pound mark. *Morbidly Obese. Another label I hate!*

For months, my family doctor, Miss Lynn, pressed me to consider gastric bypass surgery as an option toward optimal health. I considered and prayed about the possibility but, it seemed like a cop-out. A shortcut because I didn't have what it took to do it the right way. *Is being fat a punishment? Something to be endured? Who is thinking this thought? Sounds like old-Alice thinking. This will not help me get well!*

I followed through with the surgery and dreamed of what a normal weight would look like on me. The surgery involved a huge amount of preparation. I scheduled twelve pre-op education classes

CHAPTER 41 ~ Gains and Losses

on nutrition and behavior modification and signed a contract committing to a year of follow-up to help stay the course.

When surgery day arrived, I entered the operating room prepared, hopeful for a positive outcome. The surgeon, Dr. Lemont, pronounced success. "The procedure went well," he said. "A textbook case." In addition to the six-inch vertical incision across my tummy, I had a small incision on my right side where a tube had been inserted.

On the second day of recovery, a nurse positioned me in a comfortable recliner for the afternoon and left the room. Unbeknownst to either of us, there was a jagged metal fragment sticking out of the bottom of the armrest. As I released the handle to the recline position, the shard caught the incision and tore my side open, leaving a bloody trail all over the chair. Because of the hefty dose of pain meds, I didn't immediately feel it. Coupled with my high tolerance for pain, I had no idea anything had happened until the bleeding became profuse from the six-inch wound. I sensed the wetness and reached my hands to that area to explore. I held my bloody hands in front of my face and screamed aloud.

Time stopped. Instantly, my panic transported me to another time and place where secret, unholy deeds caused blood to flow freely. I started to unravel. *No! No! No! This can't be happening. Help me Lord! Don't let me lose myself! Is this real? Had they found me at last?*

By the time the staff rushed in, the color of my gown had turned from blue to crimson. I slipped into a complete dissociative state as sedatives seeped into my veins. In the distance, I heard the staff questioning among themselves. They transferred me onto a stretcher and wheeled me away to be examined, stitched, and bandaged, I heard someone screaming. *Why are you screaming dear Alice? I warned you not to have this surgery. I told you your track record for things going right is lousy.* It was Jesse speaking, the Alter who knows everything.

I woke in my original room, got my bearings, and noticed a brand-new chair had replaced the relic that assaulted me. *Did this really happen or was it a nightmare?* The fresh bandages on my side proved I'd had no nightmare. My hospital stay was extended an extra three days beyond the usual for bariatric surgery.

A social worker apologized on behalf of the Board of Directors. *Really? So, you admit it's your fault that the Alter Alices appeared again?* The floor crew treated me like royalty. They made sure I had everything

CHAPTER 41 ~ Gains and Losses

I could want. You might have thought my name was Queen Alice. But I just wanted to go home.

Each visitor who came to see me, including my pastor, encouraged me to report my unexpected injury to the head of the hospital and perhaps beyond into the courtroom. But I didn't care what happened next due to physical weakness coupled with emotional instability. Iris, who would normally handle this situation, was shaken and retreated to the background. A lawsuit seemed like a good idea, yet without Iris in the lead it couldn't be managed.

It took four months for the chair wound to completely heal. It left a jagged scar and I hated it—a permanent reminder that the Alters could surface if prompted by a well-timed catalyst. I didn't hesitate to contact Dr. Wallace and schedule therapy. I needed his help and hoped he wouldn't be disappointed in my failure to keep all the Alices united. *Lord, I don't have the strength to go back to square one. I hope this only affected one or two of the Alters? Please put me together with your God glue.*

The only positive by-product of the hospital ordeal was weight loss. It disappeared very slowly—nothing came easy for me. In fact, Dr. Lemont confirmed that I had the slowest weight loss results of any of her patients. This statement confirmed what I knew to be true. I'm a slow loser with the key word being loser! She didn't understand that freaks just aren't the norm so normal results can't be expected.

At my eighteen-month surgery anniversary weigh-in, a total of one-hundred-and-one lost pounds were added to my medical history. I hadn't been that weight since my freshman year of college. The surgery kick-started my weight loss, but it wasn't a short-cut to achievement. Hard work, discipline, and good choices were the keys to my success—all while enduring therapy, attending church, and holding down a full-time job. I should have been over the moon with my new body, but my emotional struggles held me hostage.

Dr. Wallace encouraged me to continue writing in my journal to record my personal struggles. I was grateful I didn't dissociate into twenty-one parts as before, but fully understood that I couldn't handle life by myself. I welcomed the aid and support of the Alters who came forward.

So many tears are falling this morning Lord. My God, my God, have you forsaken me? I know you really haven't, but it sure feels that way. I need to hear your voice. I feel like Humpty Dumpty who fell off

CHAPTER 41 ~ Gains and Losses

a wall . . . broken into so many pieces that can't be put back together again. Lord, you remind me of your words in Jeremiah where you say, "I have a plan for you, for a hope and future." Please help me believe that. Work in me God whatever it is that you are teaching me and help me to learn it quickly. I want to be a doer of the Word, not just a hearer. Lord, even as I write, my thoughts are all over the place, but my prayer is always the same. Keep me as one mind, not divided. I want to be one.

Thank you for loving me in spite of myself.
Alice

Hello, God . . . are you there?

How long, O God, how long must I endure this hurt? I hurt so deep I cannot even articulate it. It seems my heart just groans. Words can't express my sorrow. I've lost my joy and my desire to live. I am going backwards. Every morning, it is a chore to wake up, well, not so much wake up, but get up and get ready for work.

You have been faithful each day to get me there and help me through the day. God, I am thankful I have a job, so I can take care of myself, pay my bills, and bless others. I'm working for you Lord, help me to do my best.

May I be found faithful.
Alice

Lord Jesus, I am so afraid!

So afraid to even pen my fears, let alone speak them out loud. I know my job is to heal and not go after the hospital or even those who hurt me so long ago.

It's hard to express my recent fears. I can't seem to get my thoughts, feelings, and questions out right now. In not doing so, I feel misunderstood. It is sad to be halfway through life and not be able to formulate my deepest hurts, needs, or even joys to anyone right now. Even the Alters aren't doing their job. Unless they are and I don't know about it. Confusion!

Alice and hopefully others

Oh Lord, my God—I am so broken.

I don't want to even fight this fight anymore. What is the purpose? Just when you think the hurt can't get any worse, it does. What am I doing wrong? Am I a mistake? Your Word says I am fearfully and wonderfully made. You are the life giver. Every breath comes from you.

CHAPTER 41 ~ Gains and Losses

Somehow God, give me hope, just for the next hour, then the next one. It's hard to think of a whole day ahead. My thoughts drift to those of death. What can I do but run to you?

God, I need you to feel close, held like a baby in your arms, hugged tight. I need to know you love me when it feels like the rest of the world doesn't. But, that's a lie from the enemy. I know I have people that love and care about me. I still feel fat and ugly, but that's a lie too, because the scale says otherwise. I will not believe the lie that I am broken beyond repair. I will persevere.

Even work currently is a struggle, so many demands that seem impossible to meet. Help me not to be afraid of whatever the future holds, because you are my future. I know you will take care of me. I know that is not a lie. Forgive my selfish whining ways. I need to reach out and get the focus off of me and my mess. As the New Year begins, fill the pages with selfless acts I have done on your behalf.

Believing for something new,
Alice

P.S. Lord, I just noticed that when you change the C in my name to a V, you get Alive. I am happy to be alive. Alice says thank you for that sign from above!

My daily refrain was *I can and will do this one day at a time, one hour at a time, or one baby step at a time.* God is a patient gentleman. At times, He walked in front of me, leading the way. Other times, He was a crutch to lean on. And often, He simply carried me through the day.

I faithfully showed up for my therapy sessions with Dr. Wallace and Susan. After an additional hundred plus sessions with Dr. Wallace, he expressed that he had personal news to share. He informed me that he would be retiring from practice. I sat there stunned as he encouraged me to continue with therapy. He reiterated that he was pleased with the progress that I made through the past two-and-a-half years, since the hospital incident. I promised I would continue. *Can I? How will I continue without Dr. Wallace's help? Did I lean on him too much Lord? Is that the lesson? I must trust you as the source, is that it? Help me to be whole once again.*

Dr. Wallace gave me a printed sheet of paper with the word TRUTH at the top as a reminder of some of our discussions.

CHAPTER 41 ~ Gains and Losses

TRUTH

- Iris is good and deserving of help.
- Alice, Lynda, Allison, Kris, and David are good and deserving of help.
- Any others who may be separate now are good and deserving of help.
- Being hurt doesn't make you bad.
- Being told you are bad doesn't make you bad.
- Being forced to do hurtful things doesn't make you bad.
- All (100%) of guilt belongs to the people who wanted bad things to happen and made it so.
- All pain and extreme sadness can lessen over time, with help, and hard work.
- If you stay safe and heal, LOVE can triumph and be the victor.
- He signed and dated the bottom. I will miss his kind, gentle ways.
- I have gained and lost much.
- I have lost and gained much.

New Friends

A friend loves at all times.
Proverbs 17:17a

It pleased me to learn that Victory Community Church appointed Rev. Jack Charles to the senior pastor position. A down-to-earth man, he always seemed genuinely interested and listened when you shared something important. He didn't preach deep theological messages with unpronounceable words that were hard to understand. He gave the straight up truth from the Word of God and taught how it could be applied to our lives in immediate, practical ways. His tender, caring heart put great importance on helping people to know and understand the love the Father has for them. He never hesitated to tell you Jesus is *the way, the truth, and the life*. "It's not about religion," he'd say, "it's about relationship. A Jesus connection is where it's at." And though sometimes his humor might run to the edge of inappropriate, he was humble enough to make himself the target.

Every time I interacted with Pastor Jack, I left the conversation encouraged. I appreciated his visits and prayers while I was hospitalized. I discerned his relational way wasn't an act. He truly loved and cared for everyone. Isaiah 61:1, "*. . .proclaiming the good news to the poor, binding up the brokenhearted and proclaiming freedom for the captives and releasing darkness from the prisoners;*" was a perfect description of Pastor Jack's heart for the people he led and served.

I told him my long-time therapist, Dr. Wallace, had retired and I needed a new counselor. I thought he might have a suggestion. *Could Pastor Jack be trusted with my whole story? Would that be stupid? He didn't seem judgmental at all. Would I shock him if I made a confession to him as I had with another staff member in the past?*

In the weeks that followed, I listened to my heart to see if I had peace about opening up to Pastor Jack. I was afraid to pray about it.

CHAPTER 42 ~ New Friends

What if God says, "Yes?" I'll be backed into a corner of obedience and I might be rejected. I don't ever want to feel rejection in God's house again. I had to consider my decision very carefully.

I consulted Grace. She thought the time had come for me to take a step of faith and counsel with Pastor Jack. "I believe he will allow you to teach in the Children's Ministry again," she said, "knowing forgiveness was nailed to the cross."

I wasn't ready to step out, but Grace's words gave me hope. I loved the thought that there might be a possibility for me to return to teaching in Children's Ministry. The church body reached out to me with acceptance. I freely took it to heart and especially enjoyed attending the monthly women's breakfast and Bible study. I hungered for more wisdom and counsel of the Lord.

During this time, Grace's daughter, Penny, came home after ten years on the mission field. She took a position at our church office overseeing the Mission's Department. A perfect fit. She worked on mission fundraisers and asked me to help at game booths, bake cookies, or handle ticket sales. I felt helpful. Penny had a way of getting me involved and I said "yes" to whatever she needed. While Penny lived in Africa, I not only supported her mission financially, but tried to encourage her through email. At some point, I started to sign my correspondence from "Aunt Alice." There were times I wished Penny was my daughter. I loved her as my own. She would always hold a special place in my heart.

It was easy for Penny, Grace, Teddy, and me to visit one another since we lived two miles apart. We had keys to each other's home—like a "home away from home." We helped each other with cat or dog sitting, projects, game nights, and book clubs, and enjoyed dinner and fellowship together once or twice a week. Since Grace's thumb never got any greener, I helped tend her flower gardens. She earned blue ribbons for cooking, and in exchange, taught me baking techniques. We combined our strengths and weaknesses and grew stronger for it. I treasured my life in fellowship with my dear friends.

Up to that point in my life, I had found contentment with my kitty cat family of three. Old age caught up with Frosty, and he died peacefully with his favorite rubber mouse by his side. I thought it might be nice to introduce another family member to Tweedledee and Tweedledum. They missed their sister. Whenever I visited Grace, Teddy, and Penny, I enjoyed energetic play with their spunky

CHAPTER 42 ~ New Friends

terrier, Moxie. My cats playfully batted around their catnip, but Moxie's interactive ball retrieval game was irresistible.

I confided in Penny that a puppy might be in my near future and asked her to go with me to the Puppy Barn. Just to look, of course. Ha! What a joke. You can't just go to look at puppies. Their delightful antics pulled us in right away. Penny pointed out an adorable litter of whippet and Jack Russell terrier mix puppies. I lowered my hand into the wire fenced space. A roly-poly, black and white puppy wobbled over to me and pushed up against my fingers. Penny and I looked at each other and laughed. A decision was made without an ounce of discussion.

I exited the store not only with this bundle of cuteness, but with several hundred dollars' worth of must-have supplies: a training crate, food, toys, and bedding. Penny later admitted she almost gave in to the urge to take a sister pup home. "It was close," she said, "but my Mom would disown me."

"You can visit any time and help with training," I said. "You'll get all the cuddles you can handle." I picked up the squirmy bundle of black and white wonderfulness and held him close, whispering, "I could eat you up! You look just like an Oreo, my favorite cookie."

Penny didn't like Oreo cookies, but she'd never be able to resist this kind of Oreo. He became a cherished family member. Just like Penny.

Freedom

*Yet to all who did receive him, to those who believed in his name,
he gave the right to become children of God.*
John 1:12

One Sunday after service, Pastor Jack invited me to follow him into his office. I sensed one of the Alters getting jittery about stepping into a pastor's office. He handed me a business card for a Christian therapist with experience in Dissociative Identity Disorder. "Give her a call and tell her I sent you," he said. "You'll find her very easy to talk to."

"Thank you," I said. Taking the card in my fingers, I read the name: *Yvonne Jordan, Christian Therapist, MA, LPC.*

"She loves the Lord," he continued, "and will pray with you at the start and close of each session. I believe she'd be a great fit for you, and you could do her counseling along with your art therapy."

I glanced at the card again and saw the words under her name: *My passion is to help the broken-hearted find hope and healing. Integrating spirit, mind, and body.*

Pastor Jack looked me in the eye. "And don't forget, Alice, my door is always open to you."

Not knowing what to say, I nodded my head. "Thank you."

As I headed to my car, unlocked the door, and sat behind the steering wheel, I paused to look over the card again and noticed a Scripture at the bottom. At first, I read it silently. Then, I repeated the words aloud several times: *"I will restore you to health and heal your wounds," declares the Lord."* Jeremiah 30:17

Recently we'd learned about God's perfect timing in Bible study. *Could this be one of those moments?* The verse printed in black and white became a catalyst towards my decision. *More than anything, Lord, I want . . . no . . . NEED my wounds to be healed.*

CHAPTER 43 ~ Freedom

I hesitated to start over with a new therapist. Just the thought of it stirred up all the messy details of my life. And threats to my life. I feared the Secret Society of the Serpent knowing my location. The shameful details of my life hung over me like a shadow. So, I just never followed through with finding a new therapist as I'd first intended. Although, I did continue with my art therapy. Not once had I thought to invite God, my Creator, into my therapy before. *Why hadn't I acknowledged His presence in therapy sooner? After all, He's been an ever-present close friend on my journey.*

In time, I made the initial phone call to Dr. Yvonne and began new therapy, inviting God into the process. We prayed before each session, and I was comforted that our talks centered on God. It was transformative. I could implicitly trust Him with my life. *Where would I be today if I hadn't called her? Thank you, Jesus!*

After several months of appointments, Yvonne suggested I invite one or two family members to several sessions. It was designed to be an opportunity for me to feel supported and for questions to be answered about my complex diagnosis. No way would I ask my real family, so I appealed to the family of my heart—Grace and Penny.

I'd come to a place of honest and open transparency in my relationship with them and was grateful for their support and personal validation. I never discussed my therapy sessions with them before, due to the possibility of retaliation from the Alters. But now, I trusted that God would protect me if I allowed them a more intimate place in my journey.

Dr. Yvonne and I embarked on an intensive discovery process. Therapy revealed seven Alters needed to blend together after the recent dissociation. Grace and Penny witnessed the therapist's brilliant method of integration with me in a few of the sessions. One thing set Dr. Yvonne's approach apart from all the other therapies and counsel I'd received over the years: The Gospel of Jesus Christ—His life, death, and resurrection—and the power of the Cross.

Since some of the Alters had never heard the Gospel message of Jesus Christ, nor had been given a chance to respond, Yvonne rightly concluded that we had no spiritual unity. She equipped me with an old-fashioned, well-worn children's book that presented a simple retelling of the Gospel. As I turned page after page, Yvonne saw my puzzled look. "Alice that was a gift from my grandmother. I could

CHAPTER 43 ~ Freedom

use a more contemporary version for this lesson, but the Gospel never changes. The words in these pages are as timeless and true today as when they were written over two thousand years ago."

This antique treasure retold the biblical account of the Gospel in straight-forward terms with simple, colorful illustrations. She instructed me to speak to the Alters, individually by name. "Read each of them the story," she advised. "The life-transforming message of redemption in the cross of Jesus Christ is vital for them all to hear. As the Alters understand and accept the Gospel, you'll discover the power to bring the freedom and spiritual wholeness you need to heal."

The Gospel wasn't new to me (Alice or Allison), since we'd heard the salvation message preached many times in church. Thumbing through the book brought back a vivid picture of the day I sat in the pew and surrendered my life to Jesus on a Good Friday long ago. The pastor had preached about Jesus coming for the 'one.' He said that Jesus came to earth, fully God and fully man, to show us how He wanted us to live in the Kingdom of God. He experienced every human emotion. That's how He knew exactly how I felt in my most painful moments. He knew what it felt like to be hurt, abused, betrayed. Although innocent, He was condemned to a horrible death by crucifixion taking on every sin ever committed past, present, and future. The blood from those nail-pierced hands and feet, along with the blood dripping down his brow from the crown of thorns, was a stark reminder that His shed blood was redemption for those sins.

Scripture tells us that after three days in a dark tomb, He rose up from the dead by His own power—a power greater than sin, death, and Satan. He was alive! He died so He could conquer death with life. And give us that same life—eternal life with Him. If we choose life in Him. If we believe in our hearts that Jesus died for our sins.

That life-changing Good Friday flashed in my mind's eye as though it were yesterday. The pastor, in that moment, appeared to look directly at me. *Yes, Jesus! You understand. You faced Satan just as I had to face him. But You didn't sin! Instead, You loved me so much that you took on Yourself my deserved punishment for all my wrong doing—all my sins. Even the ones I was forced to do against my will.*

The pastor invited people to pray at the altar with him. "Come forward if you want Jesus to take your burdens away today. Lay them at the foot of His cross. Invite Him into your life. Believe He is who

CHAPTER 43 ~ Freedom

He says He is. Confess to Him your sins, and He will make you brand new. He loves you so much and is waiting for you to respond to His love and the healing He has for your life."

I didn't walk to the front altar, but I bowed my head and heart and invited Jesus into my life right where I sat. I pictured myself dumping every hurt, every burden, and every dirty deed I was ever involved in at the foot of the cross.

"Alice, can you hear me?" questioned Yvonne.

Her voice gently nudged me back to the present moment. She smiled and continued, "It seems you spaced out there for a bit. Do you understand the purpose of this exercise?"

"Yes, I do," I said. "I know that even though I yielded my life over to Jesus, this may be a new concept to some of the Alters, especially those prone to self-hate and persecution. Those Alters would shut themselves off from Jesus entirely."

Yvonne helped me to better understand the Gospel at a level that I'd never grasped before. She explained that the only way to truly know God is through a living relationship with Him. "Open up your heart to Jesus and invite Him into every Part of your life. Jesus died for every Part, every Alter inside you."

I was riveted to Dr. Yvonne's words. They pierced me with renewed hope as I realized things about myself—and about God—that I'd never ventured to think.

"Alice," she continued, "it is important for you to understand about the redeeming blood of Jesus. God created man and woman—Adam and Eve—and breathed His Spirit into them. In man and animals, blood was the life force that flowed through them. But when Adam and Eve were tempted in the garden, they chose to sin against God. The penalty was the loss of intimacy with their holy God, toil and labor on the earth, and the ultimate condemnation to death. And that, not just for them, but for all who would be born after them. Even so, God loved His creation and promised to redeem mankind.

"But only something of like value could pay the price for the great value of human life lost to sin. The Bible tells us that life is in the blood. This is why God established the need for a blood sacrifice among His people to prepare them to receive, one day, the ultimate blood sacrifice of Himself in Jesus Christ.

"In the Old Testament, innocent animals, like pure and spotless lambs, were sacrificed to bridge the gap of sin between man and

CHAPTER 43 ~ Freedom

God. The lamb became a substitute to cover over someone's sins. This foreshadowed Jesus as the sacrificial Lamb of God, whose shed blood alone has the power to fully, once and for all, redeem the lives of all who believe. He covered our sins by breaking the power of evil and death through His death and shed blood. Here," she said, pointing to a verse in the book, "read this out loud."

It was a Bible verse. John 3:16. I was familiar with it, yet I seemed to hear it in a fresh way as I read it aloud: *"For God so loved the world that he gave his one and only Son, that whoever believes in him shall not perish but have eternal life."*

"Alice," she spoke slowly, as though each word was critical, "the reason this is so important for all the Alters to understand is that the rituals you unwillingly participated in during your childhood were a perversion of the holiness of the blood of Jesus and the sacrifice of His life on the cross. In Satanic rituals, the blood, which is a precious life force to the Father, Son, and Holy Spirit is perverted, twisted and defiles the sacred."

I nodded, "I understand. There is power and life in the blood of Jesus to rescue humanity from their sinful ways."

"Yes," Yvonne said, "and Satan, with all his demonic forces, uses the blood of innocents through ritual and sacrifice to exercise power and hold victims captive."

I looked her in the eyes with sudden clarity, "But Jesus is not dead! He rose from the dead! Because of that, He has the real power over sin, darkness, and death because of His life saving blood. That's why, in Jesus, Satan can't have power in my life anymore."

"Yes!" Yvonne said. "Jesus' death on the cross made it possible for us to exchange all the bad things we have done—and that have been done to us—for every good and perfect gift from the heart of God. Having all the Alters in spiritual agreement is the final choice to wholeness and complete freedom."

Like a bright light flipped on in my mind, I understood something I'd never really seen before in all my years of going to church. *I get it now, Lord! I get it! To accept Your grand and free invitation to receive Jesus as Lord of our lives—of MY life—or 'in charge' would unite all the Alters in mind AND spirit. This truly is the final step towards merging all the Alices. A living relationship, a faith-based life provides wholeness and healing! It's what I've longed for. Since You, Father God, Creator of all life, gave me life, You alone know how to mend my brokenness. I see it! The simple truth that Jesus, my Lord and my Savior, can bring beauty from ashes!*

CHAPTER 43 ~ Freedom

Over the following weeks of therapy, and my boldness in sharing the truth of the Gospel and Jesus' unconditional love for me—all of me—one by one, each Alter willingly submitted their life to Christ's authority. For the first time in all my years, there was complete wholeness in Christ—a oneness of mind, body, and spirit. The sense of living in freedom instead of fear opened a whole new world to me. Finally, I understood the truth behind 2 Corinthians 3:17: *"Now the Lord is the Spirit, and where the Spirit of the Lord is, there is freedom."*

Although years earlier, I had officially accepted Jesus Christ as my Savior and been born again of the Spirit, this newfound freedom felt like a re-birth—like a delayed reaction that came to fullness. Maybe I just went through the motions before with an incomplete understanding. Everything was different this time. *Thank you, God! You love me! You never gave up on me, even when I gave up on myself.*

My heart overflowed with appreciation for Yvonne's Godly wisdom, discernment, and keen insight in knowing how to bring about healing with spiritual integration. How thankful I was, too, for Pastor Jack who had invited me into his office that day and gave me Yvonne's card. God's perfect timing.

I learned what it meant to live in freedom. The dissonance of my life had tuned harmoniously into a beautiful symphony to the melodies of love, joy, and peace. The title of my masterpiece is *Freedom*. After hundreds of therapy sessions costing me thousands of dollars, I rejoiced that I had crossed the bridge over to the Promised Land of Freedom. As Jesus declared in the Gospel of Matthew 19:26: *"With man this is impossible, but with God, all things are possible!"*

Yes, they are, Lord! ALL things. And I can't wait to discover what else You have planned for my life!

Inner Healing

Lord my God, I called to you for help, and you healed me.
Psalm 30:2

When your life hits rock bottom, you've hit the best place to build a new foundation for your life. Matthew 7:24 says, *"Therefore, everyone who hears these words of mine and puts them into practice is like a wise man who built his house on the rock."* My heart's desire was to build my life on the solid foundation of Jesus Christ, the Rock.

The Bible came alive as never before in my renewed faith. I gained a deeper understanding of the words of Jesus and how they applied to my life. Sometimes, when I allowed my thoughts to take flight, unsettled questions about God niggled about in my mind. Not questions about the mysteries of life as many ask, but questions about my life specifically. *God, where were you when I was in that unholy place forced to participate in unspeakable acts?* I couldn't reconcile that a God who truly loved me would allow so many ungodly things to happen.

Grace and I planned a three-day weekend trip to the charming and gorgeous Shenandoah Valley in Virginia to visit her friend Rebecca. I met and interacted with Becky twice when she passed through our town on the way to visit her grandchildren in Massachusetts. I liked her friendly, outgoing demeanor. We shared a love of gardening and reading—my kind of friend.

We reserved a suite in a quaint rustic lodge along the Blue Ridge Parkway in the majestic Blue Ridge Mountains. We made plans to hike nature trails and enjoy the colorful fall foliage by day, and games, snacks, and girl time by the fireplace in our pajamas in the evening. Becky already knew bits and pieces of my history, but as we chatted through the day, I gave her a full account of how the Lord, by His grace, led me out of the pit of hell. We hadn't planned on

CHAPTER 44 ~ Inner Healing

tears on this trip, but many were shed in grief and loss for all I had endured as well as rejoicing for the healing God had brought!

Becky caught me off guard when she asked if any of my therapies had included Inner Healing. I didn't know what that meant. "Inner Healing?" I asked.

"Inner Healing," she explained, "is a unique counseling technique used to get to the root of anything hindering your personal relationship or connection with the Father, Son, or Holy Spirit. It's a journey you take with the Holy Spirit walking you through a time where there might be residue of an event or action that was resistant to coming to the light for total healing."

I'd never heard of such a thing. I truly believed I was well and whole and couldn't imagine any other healing that needed to take place. "How does it work?" I asked.

Becky could see I was a little confused and her warm smile put me at ease as she continued. "The enemy of our soul locks information in rooms or doors of our heart and tries to keep us bound there. It's about opening those doors and allowing God's Spirit in to cut off and close access to Satan. A choice is made to renounce any ties with the enemy of our soul. Inner Healing helps us remember past hurtful situations and visualize Jesus with us in those moments. It takes the focus off of us and keeps it on God, the author and finisher of our faith.

I paused for a moment to process the information and wondered how such a thing might apply to me. As if Becky could hear my thoughts, she said, "Alice, I think the Lord ordained our time together and desires to bring you into a greater understanding of deeply rooted experiences. With that, you will have greater peace and freedom. Pray and see what the Lord might be speaking to you about this. If you decide to move forward, I would be honored to do an Inner Healing session with you."

That night I wrote this in my journal:

> *Lord, thank You for this incredible and much needed vacation. It is easier to sense Your presence when I am out in Your beautiful and vast creation. It's glorious to be away from work and the associated stress. I am filled with gratitude for my mind to be as You designed it to be. I am a living miracle! I've decided tomorrow I am meeting with Becky for some Inner Healing. God, may You meet me there and help me to be open and receptive as I desire ALL that You have for me. I pray I will have a breakthrough, although I don't know what that*

CHAPTER 44 ~ Inner Healing

would even look like. I do know that I want every tie to the satanic world severed in the name of Jesus. Lord, if You sent me here for this reason, I am willing to trust you in this process. Help me! Help Becky! I love You, Lord, and praise your holy name.

Your friend and servant,
Alice Iris Fisher

P.S. Thank You for the blessing and opportunity to talk and share with my dear friend Grace . . . she always helps me understand things better and brings clarity to any situation. Somehow, she understands me better than others. What a treasure she is.

I looked forward to the following evening for my Inner Healing session. While Becky and I got comfortable in the Great Room of the suite, Grace cozied up in our shared bedroom to intercede on my behalf.

Here's my journal entry to record the events of that night:

Thank you, God, that I met with You last night and that further healing took place. I want to write down this final event to my healing so I won't forget it (not that I would). Becky prayed and simply asked by the power of the Holy Spirit to show me what You would like me to see and know.

I heard your gentle voice within me say "I am the vine and you are the branches." Then, in my mind's eye, I could see Jesus welcoming me with His open arms. He was waiting by a big tree, a tree full of life, but with broken branches on the ground underneath it. I knew I was one of those broken branches being stepped on and crushed into the ground. You, Jesus, came to me, hugged me, and asked me to go for a walk. You walked with me to the pond area that is behind our house. So many bad things happened at this place. We spent some time there, and You held me and caressed my cheeks, just like in the picture I remembered from Miss Mary Miller's classroom. While I cried, You cried with me. We cried over my babies. We went to the area where the "leftovers" of my babies were burned into ashes. There were plants growing there, tall Jack and the Beanstalk kind of plants, reaching all the way to Heaven! Together, our tears watered the ground. I know that my little ones are with You in Heaven and one day we will be reunited again. I sobbed until there were no more tears left.

Jesus held my hands and looked at me with love emanating from His piercing bright eyes. "Jesus, I do have a question that has been

CHAPTER 44 ~ Inner Healing

bothering me all these years. Where were You when my father and those evil people forced me to do things against my will? All those unholy acts which I know You don't condone. Why didn't You stop them? You see all things and know all things. Were You so busy with more important things than what was happening at Shivering Acres?"

"My child, my child, oh, how I dearly love you. It is a sin problem, Alice. Paradise was lost when sin entered the Garden of Eden. Our Father allows men free will—the ability to make their own choices, and they frequently don't choose life. You, my child, have chosen life. The enemy's time here is short; he seeks whom he may devour as he prowls around. His evil forces are opposed to the Father's original design. The Father loves you and cares which is why He sent me into the world. There will come a day very soon when Father, Holy Spirit, and I will wipe away every tear from the eyes of the suffering. There will be no more death, mourning, crying, or pain, for the old order of things will pass away. Alice, the world will be set right again. Now, as for where I was when you were enduring the torture and torment. My precious one, I was right there with you along with ministering angels. I wept for the evil inflicted upon you by those who chose evil. I knew your fragile mind couldn't withstand the continued assault of malevolence, so we fashioned a way for your mind to handle that which was thrust upon you. You are now healed, and His glory will be revealed in you for all to see."

This was a lot to absorb and work out deep within my heart and spirit. I didn't understand it all, but I instinctively knew it was the truth. The peace which the Bible talks about, the one which passes all human understanding, settled into the depths of my soul. Jesus continued to hold my hand and walked me back to the tree of life. As it came into view, individuals were crowded around the massive trunk. Some I knew because they were friends. Others represented future lives who will be touched by my journey of pain and faith. There were clusters of trembling living souls in the quaking tree branches. These were precious men, women, and children who were afraid of their tormentors and lacked freedom, just like I had. I need to help them! Lord, help me be an instrument of healing to those You will send me. This scene faded out, but it was so real; a colorful, beautiful vision alive with possibility.

Before we closed in prayer, Becky led me through a renouncing process where I had to verbally break and sever any soul ties of traditions, rituals, and belief systems. I wanted to establish a Godly

CHAPTER 44 ~ Inner Healing

legacy over my life, and I knew the importance of this as my early life was attached to satanic rituals and abuse. I wanted to be sure there was no evil DNA from that detested part of my life. We went through a comprehensive list of actions my monstrous father and his brothers of darkness had done to negate any effect on me. Some examples were demonic influences, witchcraft, unclean spirits, encounters with demons, occult practices, secret societies, childhood violence, mental bondages, incest, abortion, rejection, torture, ungodly rituals, blood rituals; anything that came against the will of a holy God.

After the words in Jesus' name and amen were spoken, Becky anointed me with a sweet-scented oil that she had purchased in the Holy Land the year before. Grace joined us, and we had a time of communion where we celebrated Christ's death on the cross and the blood He shed for us. This was the first time I ever took communion where it meant something special, and I believed Christ's sacrificial death was for me. The Holy Spirit flooded all the places where any darkness may have been trying to hide. I felt redeemed and set free by this gift of grace. I believe God ordained this special time for me, as I sought after it. It brought me to a greater place of understanding and freedom and for that I shall be forever grateful. I went to bed totally exhausted with the knowledge that Jesus had not deserted me in my time of greatest need and His promise that He will never leave me or forsake me is true!

Unfinished Business

*Be kind and compassionate to one another, forgiving each other,
just as in Christ, God forgave you.*
Ephesians 4:32

I lived with a newfound confidence. I'd viewed life in black and white, but now I saw everything in a brilliant kaleidoscope of color. The timing seemed right, so I took a leap of faith and made an appointment to speak with Pastor Jack. This time around, I could tell my story as a powerful testimony of God's transformation of my life. I clearly saw how Jesus and HIS story intertwined with mine. It proved easy to share. My journey was no longer a victim story, but a victory story. A story God had redeemed for His glory.

Pastor Jack put me at ease with his gentle voice. He exhibited all nine qualities of the fruit of the Holy Spirit: love, joy, peace, patience, kindness, goodness, faithfulness, gentleness, and self-control. If humor were a fruit, he would have an abundant crop. He always had a funny tale or joke in his back pocket.

I shared the painful experience of confiding in a former pastor and the pain that resulted. He shook his head with a genuine look of concern. "Alice," he said, "I am so sorry that happened to you. I want you to know that I am here to listen, not judge. How are you feeling now?"

"Thank you," I said. "It wasn't easy, but over time, I forgave Pastor X. It was necessary for my emotional healing. Now there's just a scar where there'd once been a deep wound."

Pastor Jack responded, "I will personally help you in your faith walk and in any other way I can. Christ died to set you free and there is now no guilt or condemnation." He picked up his worn, leather Bible and tenderly quoted 1 John 1:9: "*If we confess our sins, he is faithful and just and will forgive us our sins and purify us from all unrighteousness.*"

CHAPTER 45 ~ Unfinished Business

I breathed a sigh of relief. His words were a great comfort to me. Then he said something that made my heart sing.

"Alice, go ahead and fill out the Children's Ministry application and background check again. I would be pleased to personally approve it. In today's culture, children need someone with a heart like yours. You are an answer to prayer for our new after school and evening tutoring program. As I have said before, my door is always open to you, Alice. I know that, one day, you will share your story with the church and beyond as there is so much brokenness. The world needs what you have found in Christ."

Tears of joy. Unspeakable joy!

Happy days passed. Soon the Christmas season rolled around. My mother phoned and begged me to come for a visit. *Are you kidding me? Would I ever be ready?* I told her no, not now, maybe not ever! She knew exactly what I was saying and why. No explanations were needed! We never spoke about my childhood or acknowledged anything that could trigger a discussion about bygone issues. I suspected she knew all that went on at Shivering Acres. In my heart, I believe she stood idly by and allowed it to unfold. *Why? Why, Mom? I just don't understand. Why would you stay married to a monster?* I'm sure a permanent fear cord was firmly attached to her from my father, the master puppeteer.

In spite of everything, though, I loved my mom and worried for her. Most of all, I pitied her. She must have endured more than I will ever know. Until recently, concern for my own survival took precedence over thoughts of hers.

One day Sandy called. "You won't believe this Alice. Billy is engaged!" In a rush of words, she poured out the details with joyous enthusiasm. "Mom said Billy now has two years of sobriety under his belt. Two years! A miracle for sure! He met his fiancé, Renee, also a recovering addict, at a Celebrate Recovery meeting. And get this—they go to church together and have mentors! He's about to become a stepdad too! Renee has an eight-year-old daughter named Heather."

"That truly is amazing," I said, "but Sandy, you know I haven't connected with him in years. Do you think we'll get invited to the wedding? I don't know if I'd go even if I did. Maybe I should just call him and congratulate him. Do you have a valid phone number for him?" Sandy didn't, but promised she'd ask Mom and call me back. There were things I wanted—no needed—to say to Billy, and

CHAPTER 45 ~ Unfinished Business

I didn't want to save them for his wedding weekend. That's IF I was even invited.

Then, one sunny spring day, the postman delivered a thick envelope addressed with fancy calligraphy. *Could this be a wedding invitation?* I pulled the formal invite with raised letters out of the envelope. A small RSVP response and stamped, addressed envelope fell out with it. I read the wedding details in wonder. *So, it's true, my brother, William James Fisher ll is getting married to Renee Lynn Reynolds. Maybe he has turned his life around, after all.* I couldn't begrudge him any happiness he had found.

There were some things I needed to say to Billy, and I didn't want to wait until his wedding weekend. When I analyzed that thought, I realized I had already decided to connect with Billy, before the wedding, without seriously considering it. Just to be sure, I committed it to prayer. Butterflies stirred in my stomach at the thought that I might see my father or be in the same room with him. I knew Mom would finally get her wish for me to come visit. After I prayed, one thing I was very clear—do *not* stay at hell house!

Before mailing my RSVP, I gathered up an extra dose of courage and placed a call to Billy. He laughed when he realized it was me. "Alice, I'm so thankful you called." An awkward silence ensued before I heard sniffling on the other end of the line.

Billy was crying. After a few moments, he cleared his throat and continued. "Please listen without interrupting so I can get this all out. I've wanted to talk to you for quite a while. I need to ask you . . . to forgive me . . . for everything that happened in our childhood. The things we were made to do. The darkness. The evil. It wrecked me, and I'm sure it wrecked you, too. I've come to terms with it. Renee has helped me greatly. Jesus is my higher power, and I'm living for Him now. Not a dark destructive force." After another awkward pause, he continued in a broken voice between breathless sobs that could not be stifled. "I helped ruin your life. Please, please forgive me! I never stood up for myself and I'm ashamed about all the unspeakable things I did. I have no right to ask for forgiveness, but I am truly sorry. Forgive me. Will you forgive me? You can show me by coming to my wedding. Help me celebrate my new life."

I took a deep breath. "Billy, I have been praying for you and am happy to hear my prayers are answered. It took me years and years to overcome fear, hate, and the brokenness that resulted from our monstrous childhood. I have already forgiven you and am at a place

CHAPTER 45 ~ Unfinished Business

of contentment in my life. Jesus redeemed me, and I am walking in deeper faith now. No matter what happens from this point forward, I know that He loves me, and my eternity is secure with Him.

"Alice," he said, his voice sounding somewhat recovered, "thank you for your generous and much needed forgiveness. I really have to fight feelings of hatred toward dear old Dad. Every day. Renee insists he should be at the wedding, for Mom's sake. And she's not off the hook either. I know Dad made her life a living hell, too. I know one day he'll answer for his inhumane, evil ways."

We switched the conversation to wedding details. Billy's excitement was contagious. I smiled as I hit "end call." God had removed yet another heavy burden from the invisible luggage I carried around. The load, and my heart, felt lighter. I breathed a sigh of relief and circled Billy and Renee's wedding date on my calendar. I looked forward to the wedding and to meeting Billy's soon-to-be wife, and his new daughter, Heather. My immovable faith would be sufficient to carry me through any unexpected things I might encounter.

46

Forgiveness

When Jesus spoke again to the people, he said,
"I am the light of the world.
Whoever follows me will never walk in darkness,
but will have the light of life."
John 8:12

I embarked upon the wedding weekend festivities with the assurance that Jesus was by my side. Pastor Jack and the church intercessor team prayed for peace and protection over me. In the past, every time I made a trip back to my childhood home, I experienced a traumatic set-back at the hands of my father or dealt with triggered memories from all the suffering. Through years of determination, I'd moved forward to a good place and that's where I wanted to stay. No turning back!

What a delight to see Sandy, Michael, and the kids, now all grown, young adults. A sense of sorrow descended upon me. Regret. *Oh! I could have made more of an effort in their growing up years.* Birthday phone calls and Christmas packages didn't make up for attending events in real time.

Sammy, or Sam, as he insisted I call him, was a senior in college, majoring in Aeronautical Engineering. Rebecca had been recruited by colleges as a champion swimmer. I couldn't wait to connect with them again. The family visited me two years ago to tour the Amish countryside. *Where had the time gone?*

My mother could not fathom why I decided not to stay at the house along with Sandy and her family. "All of us should be together under one roof for this special occasion," she declared. But I established definitive boundaries and determined not to be coerced to cross them. Many times before, I'd fallen into that painful trap. I made reservations at a local country inn for the weekend. I enjoyed it as a beautiful, peaceful sanctuary to return to at the end of the day.

CHAPTER 46 ~ Forgiveness

We gathered for the wedding rehearsal on Friday evening. Since Billy and I talked on the phone several times since our big conversation, no awkwardness existed. Initiating hugs wasn't my thing, but Billy stepped up and gave me a big bear hug and whispered, "I'm glad you are here." He introduced me to his bride-to-be and her daughter. I liked them instantly and looked forward to getting to know them better.

The wedding ceremony took place outdoors surrounded by fragrant multi-colored flower gardens. Orange winged monarch butterflies flitted amongst the blossoms. Butterflies have a special meaning for me since I had fully integrated all my Alters. They represented new life, freedom, and rebirth in Christ. These fluttering beauties reminded me of God's presence as He watched over me, and kept me calm, since my father stood close by. He largely ignored me, not saying more than a brief hello. I stared at the back of his head. *Fine with me! Could it be that he senses something different about me? Something in direct conflict with his so-called controlling power? What a wasted life.*

We were to attend church the following day as a family, then meet back at the house for a roast beef dinner feast. I skipped church. *How can I sit near a person who perverted the sacred and made a mockery of everything Jesus said and did?* With my boundary in place, I informed Mom I would see everyone at the house in time for dinner.

Thoughts of Miss Mary Miller came to mind. *I wonder if the picture of Jesus surrounded by the children still hangs in her old Sunday School room.* I visualized the picture and hoped my childhood memory honored her at home in Heaven.

After breakfast Sunday morning, I grabbed my Bible and headed to a secluded garden bench at the back of the inn. *This is a perfect spot to read and pray!* The bright sunshine and the chorus of chirping birds provided a musical background for my quiet time with the Lord. Flipping through my Bible, my eyes fell on Deuteronomy 31:6: *"Be strong and courageous. Do not be afraid or terrified because of them, for the Lord your God goes with you; He will never leave you nor forsake you."*

Lord, if this is a message from you what does it mean? Bowing my head, I prayed for clarity. While communing with the Lord, an idea formed into a plan that could only have come from the Holy Spirit. Trust and a truckload of courage were required to carry out the inspired strategy.

CHAPTER 46 ~ Forgiveness

I drove to Shivering Acres earlier than planned. Church was still in session, but I had to act quickly. *Did that ritual chamber really exist or was it a figment of a fragmented mind?* The daylight gave me additional courage to face the truth of whatever was down there. My stomach lurched at the thought of what the darkness held.

I had written some verses in permanent ink on the inside back cover of my Bible. I read through them several times, hoping to fully store much needed courage:

> *For God has not given us a spirit of fear, but of power and of love and of a sound mind.*   2 Timothy 1:7 NKJV

> *But, if you do not forgive others their sins, your Father will not forgive your sins.*   Matthew 6:15

> *Put on the full armor of God, so that you can take your stand against the devil's schemes. For our struggle is not against flesh and blood, but against the rulers, against the authorities, against the powers of this dark world and against the spiritual forces of evil in the heavenly realms. Therefore, put on the full armor of God, so that when the day of evil comes, you may be able to stand your ground, and after you have done everything, to stand.*   Ephesians 6:10-13

> *Submit yourselves, then, to God. Resist the devil, and he will flee from you.*   James 4:7

> *Be kind and compassionate to one another, forgiving each other, just as in Christ, God forgave you.*   Ephesians 4:32

As I stepped out of my car, I resolved to follow the plan conceived in prayer. *Lord Jesus, help me!* A promise from Hebrews came to mind—*He will never leave me or forsake me. Thank you, Lord, I am not alone!* I operated on trust and faith in Jesus. If I didn't trust Him, I wouldn't be able to follow through. My emotions were as scattered as my mind once had been.

I entered the old stone portion of the house counting on the fact it was often left unlocked in the past. I carefully wound my way down the steep narrow staircase which led me to the dreaded ground cellar. Trembling, I clutched my Bible in my right hand while my left clung to an LED lantern I'd grabbed from my trunk. My sweater pocket hid the vial of scented oil from the Holy Land Becky had gifted me. *Why did I bring this? Lord guide my steps in this assignment.*

CHAPTER 46 ~ Forgiveness

Confidence rose as I recalled my prayers—invisible battle gear that didn't weigh me down—and fingered the oil vial in my pocket, a comforting companion.

Sweat moistened my hands. My legs felt like jelly. No turning back! I whispered, "Jesus, Jesus, Jesus, Jesus," and stepped forward into the darkness. My hands reached for the elusive, worn, thin string that lit the immediate area. In the light of the dim bulb, mice squeaked and scuffled for cover.

Peering into the darkness, I saw the outline of a doorway in the shadowy corner—right where I imagined it to be. The old, rusty latch felt cold to my touch. I sighed deep and lifted it, then swung the lamp in an arc around the room in the hope of spotting a light switch but couldn't see any. Panic and acrid bile rose in my throat.

The chamber sloped downward, smaller than I had imagined, but it was REAL! As the light illuminated the center of the room, I saw the most unholy stone structure. Shadowy images flashed across my mind's eye. *No! I won't think about all that happened here. How my childhood died on that cold, unyielding slab.* I shuddered and took baby steps toward it.

Ah! That's why I brought the oil.

Extracting the vial from my pocket, I flipped open the cap and doused that ungodly surface using every last drop. I imagined the clash in the spiritual realm at that precise moment. A battle raged around me in another dimension, but thankfully, I was blind to the demonic forces I had angered. My adrenaline raced.

I wanted to run out of that room of horrors, except—there was one more thing I had to do. I held my Bible high above my head like an Olympic torch and declared a verse from 1 Corinthians 15:57: *But thanks be to God! He gives us the victory through our Lord Jesus Christ.*

A warm glow filled my heart as I decreed the Word of God over the room. It was a stark contrast to the damp chill in the secret chamber of horrors. I walked out of the room and loudly proclaimed, "Thank you Father that no weapon formed against me shall prosper. It is finished!"

In my rush to escape, I didn't close the door to the evil room or remember to pull the string to return all to darkness. It didn't occur to me that, in doing so, I left clues behind that someone had invaded their territory. My heart beat wildly within—*thump, thump, thump*—as I stumbled up the stairs toward the fresh air and sunshine. I stepped

CHAPTER 46 ~ Forgiveness

out of hidden darkness into the bright light of day and came face to face with the Monster. He walked briskly toward me.

"What have you done, Alice?" Gruff, angry words spit at me from his twisted red face.

I surprised myself and boldly shouted in immediate response, "What have I done, Monster? It is what you have done! There is nothing you can do to hurt me anymore. You and your brothers of darkness have no control or hold over me. Evil never wins." I paused for an instant, then blurted out, "In the name of Jesus Christ—I forgive you, Dad!"

He seemed frozen in place and time. The only way I could tell that my words had any effect on him were his beady-black eyes—otherworldly. They stared straight into my soul. I don't know who, or what, was looking at me, but it wasn't my father.

My father.

I had made a conscious choice to forgive him, for my own benefit. I would not call him "monster" again. In fact, this was the first time I called him "Dad." A title more about what might have been, than what was. I jumped into my car, drove away, and didn't bother to look back.

Victory

Rebirth

Gratitude

*And whatever you do, whether in word or deed,
do it all in the name of the Lord Jesus,
giving thanks to God the Father through him.*
Colossians 3:17

My life overflowed with joy and thanksgiving on a daily basis, so I started a Gratitude Journal.

I am thankful for . . .

1. No injuries from my recent car accident
2. A shiny new blue car
3. Pastor Jack's teaching on dreams…need to revive some old ones
4. Chatting with my best friend, Grace
5. Walks with my furry buddy, Oreo
6. My job, even with its frustrations and challenges
7. A warm place to live and work in cold, wintry weather
8. Friendly and caring church people at Victory Community Church
9. Tutoring and the extra income it provides to bless others
10. A good night's sleep
11. Helping to plan a surprise birthday party for Penny
12. Encouraging phone calls and emails from friends
13. Great praise and worship at VCC
14. Jesus and the victorious freedom He has brought to my life

I established a new habit to write at least three things in my Gratitude Journal every day. I'd take nothing for granted, like in the past, because I'd learned the lesson of the precious nature of a well-balanced life. When the page turned for the New Year, I aimed for intentional Acts of Kindness and recorded one act a day. Giving of

CHAPTER 47 ~ Gratitude

myself to others was a small way to celebrate my life, be thankful for my life, and spread happiness around.

In Acts 20:35, Jesus said: *"It is more blessed to give than receive."* I had a new mission! *What would the world look like if each person did just one act of kindness every day?*

I was determined to do my part and kept a record in my journal:

1. Baked cookies for refreshment time at church
2. Sent handmade card to Grace telling her I appreciate her friendship and support
3. Gave each lady in my work department small tubes of hand cream
4. Helped clean out a house for an elderly lady at church
5. Donated to fund for a family who lost their home in a house fire
6. Sponsored a teen for the all-night Youth Party at church
7. Cleaned the snow off of every car at church during service
8. Bought donuts for the men at the addiction recovery house
9. Made lasagna for Sunday lunch fundraiser at church
10. Bought prizes for game night for the Youth Ministry
11. Gave a favorite book to a friend
12. Treated book group to breakfast
13. Hosted neighborhood Christmas luncheon
14. Made a gift appreciation basket for the neighbors for no special reason

Along with intentional Random Acts of Kindness, I thought about Pastor Jack's challenge to resurrect a dream or visualize a new one. It was time to make my first Bucket List of things I hoped to do in my life. *Lord, help me to dream and believe big*!

So, of course, I recorded My Dream List:

1. Travel—Alaska, Hawaii, Disney World, Washington State, and Germany
2. Refinish Oma Elise's antique secretary desk
3. Dig a garden plot in the back yard and plant vegetables
4. Write my story to help others who are broken and need hope
5. Go on another cruise with Grace
6. Learn how to quilt

CHAPTER 47 ~ Gratitude

7. Make a will
8. Take prayer walks around town
9. Raise money and walk in a fundraiser for literacy or for a disease
10. Read at least fifty books a year. Buy them, read, and give away

So many incredible options were before me. Since counseling concluded, I had the time and money to accomplish goals beyond myself. I cherished this new season of contentment as peace filled my heart and home. Life wasn't perfect, but like Goldilocks, everything seemed "just right."

I read a line in Ann Voskamp's book, *A Thousand Gifts*, that spoke to my heart. She wrote: *"You don't get to make up most of your story. You get to make peace with it. You don't get to demand your life, like a given. You get to accept your life, like a gift. Beginnings and middles, they are only yours to embrace, to unwrap, like a gift. But you get the endings. You always get the endings. You get the endings and you get to make them a gift back to the Giver."*

For eighteen months, I enjoyed a season of serenity before the fight of my life began.

Part 3
THE FINAL BATTLE

"I imagined if I could see into the spiritual realm, there was surely a battle raging all around me."

The Diagnosis

So do not fear, for I am with you; do not be dismayed for I am your God. I will strengthen you and help you; I will uphold you with my righteous right hand.
Isaiah 41:10

It started in the fall, my favorite season. Whenever I walked up the stairs, I experienced shortness of breath. That might have made sense if I had been a smoker, but I was not. Walking Oreo and mowing the lawn had always been easy-breezy, but the day I realized such simple chores were a struggle, I began to wonder why.

As weeks passed, muscle weakness developed in my legs. At times, they were hard to lift for even the smallest step. My family physician recommended an appointment with a neurologist, Dr. Firth, to possibly diagnose the unusual symptoms. He scheduled me for stat tests: electro-diagnostics, a nerve biopsy, and a lumbar puncture. Initially, only my legs were affected, but after several months, my arms weakened to the point of not being able to carry a small bag of groceries or my small purse. After all I had been through in my lifetime, I leaned into my faith to avoid a stroll down Fear Avenue.

Test results concluded that I had CIDP or Chronic Inflammatory Demyelinating Polyneuropathy. *With a name that long, this can't be good.* The specialist described it as an autoimmune disorder where the myelin or covering of the nerves were being destroyed. Concern turned into anxiousness as I wondered how I would continue to work in such a weakened condition.

Doctors tried a few different experimental treatments, including IVIG (Intravenous Immunoglobulin Therapy) which used a mixture of antibodies. The torturous, weekly treatment lasted six long hours. I prayed through each session: *Lord, lead me, guide me, help me, heal me, HEAR me! I know You are there, I'm standing on Your Word and promises.*

CHAPTER 48 ~ The Diagnosis

Healing didn't arrive as I'd hoped over the next many months that year, and I fought disappointment. I became more debilitated and continued to lose muscle in my upper and lower extremities. My breathing function plummeted. During an exam at the doctor's office, I struggled to get up on the exam table, so he ordered further tests to be completed in six different appointments. That wore me out!

Three separate times I fell when my legs simply collapsed underneath of me. *What is happening to me? I'm scared!* One fall happened while mowing the lawn, one when I stepped into the car, and one at home in the bathroom—just like the commercial, *I've fallen down and I can't get up!* I looked in the mirror and didn't recognize myself anymore. Like a heavyweight prize fighter after a loss, black and blue hues surrounded my eyes and purple bruises covered my legs and arms.

My journal entry for September 27th:

> *It's been quite a week and I can honestly say I am glad this one will soon be "in the books." On Monday I had another round of EMG/NCV tests. These are tests that measure nerve and muscle responses to electrical stimulation. I was a human pin cushion again that day...lots of needle pokes in my legs, arms, hands, feet, face, and so on. Nerve damage and muscle weakness were confirmed. What is all of this? CIPD was my original diagnosis, but that has now been ruled out, so no more infusions—for which I am thankful. Today I had another lumbar puncture (spinal tap) and it took two doctors three tries to "strike gold." The results of these tests and the spinal fluid will be available next week and I am told there will be a definitive diagnosis. It will be good to know what we are dealing with here. I have been praying for Godly wisdom for the doctors.*
>
> *The one bright spot just ahead is the cruise Grace and I are taking to Bermuda in two weeks. I'm looking forward to a week away with lots of R&R (Rest & Relaxation).*

Four days later, on October 1st, the official diagnosis arrived: ALS, or Amyotrophic Lateral Sclerosis, sometimes referred to as Lou Gehrig's disease. Most patients die within three to five years from respiratory failure. I had just received a death sentence.

The Lasts

I can do all this through him who gives me strength.
Philippians 4:13

I read through the ALS brochure the doctor had given me and tried to calculate how soon the grim reaper would arrive. I read the same words over and over again, secretly hoping each time, they would say something different.

Note to Self: *The words blur when you cry and read at the same time:*

"ALS is a rapidly progressive disease that attacks the nerve cells responsible for controlling muscles. There is gradual degeneration and eventual death of the motor neurons. [*Sigh.*] When that happens, they will no longer be able to send messages to the muscles. [*Ugh! It's already happening!*] Eventually, individuals lose their strength and the ability to move their arms, legs, and body. When muscles in the diaphragm and chest wall fail, individuals [*Meaning me!*] will lose the ability to breathe without ventilation support. [*I can't imagine this actually happening to me!*] Most people die from respiratory failure within three to five years from the onset of symptoms."

I'm already well over a year into this! My Lord, My God! Death is looming!

Uncontrollable tears poured from my eyes and strained my breath with heaving sobs. I gathered myself together and continued reading:

"An estimated six-thousand people [*Lucky me!*] are diagnosed yearly. There are twenty-thousand people living with the disease at any given time. [*Aren't I special?*] The average age is fifty-five. [*Is this joke? I just turned 55 on my last birthday. I should have skipped this year!*] Military combat veterans are twice as likely to be diagnosed as non-vets due to Post Traumatic Stress Disorder."

CHAPTER 49 ~ The Lasts

This made sense. Although not a vet, I had been in combat my whole life.

It took days to come to grasp the reality of the diagnosis, though I had yet to fully accept it. But, just getting through the day, every day, proved the existence of the situation: the need for a cane to walk so I did not fall down, the struggle to lift my arm to get my cereal bowl out of the cabinet, or the effort necessary to get up off the toilet were difficult reminders of my reality.

My calendar filled with appointments. I scheduled one with the Greater Philadelphia Chapter of ALS to provide patient support and services, as my doctor suggested. My neurologist referred me to the University of Pennsylvania where I scheduled an appointment with an ALS specialist. And, not to be forgotten, I needed to inform Pastor Jack and seek his counsel and support. He told me his door would always be open to me. *Oh, God! I need Pastor Jack's door wide open to me, now!*

But before any of that, Grace and I would still take our scheduled cruise to Bermuda. More than ever, I welcomed this trip even though my mobility would be a challenge. *Bermuda might be my last big adventure—ever!* The cruise served as a diversion from the mountain of decision making and consultations that would await me when the ship docked after our journey. I had to establish a new normal, but for one week, I would pretend nothing had changed in my life; that my world didn't just flip upside down.

On October 5th, friends from work drove me and Grace to the New York Port where we embarked on our seven-day trip. I rented a motorized scooter in which to gallivant around, on and off the ship. It was a small consolation, with my documents labeled "handicapped," that I didn't have to wait in lines and got preferential treatment in the dining room. I'd have traded that perk for a healthy diagnosis. Even so, nothing was going to keep me from enjoying a vacation I had looked forward to all year.

I found many new things to add to my gratitude journal, starting with our spacious handicapped-equipped room outfitted with extra plugs to keep all my devices, including my BiPAP breathing machine, functioning.

Grace always had some special plan up her sleeve to surprise me. She had collected notes and cards of encouragement for me from my co-workers, church friends, and neighbors who knew of my struggle over the past months. Every morning she placed a stack of

CHAPTER 49 ~ The Lasts

mail on my pillow. Tears flowed as I read them each day with messages of love, support, and prayers. What comforting thoughts they expressed, even though not everyone knew about the official ALS diagnosis. *When they found out, would they pity me? I didn't want pity from anyone!*

One evening, we dressed up for the Captain's dinner and took a "friend photo" in our fancy clothes, though we wore casual outfits for everything else. Grace helped me out of the scooter and we sat down for our bestie portraits. After the shutter snapped, I tried to stand up but couldn't do it. Two nearby ship stewards came to my rescue. *This is embarrassing. Help to stand up? Lord, help me not to cry!* I glanced up at Grace and saw tears in her eyes. This wasn't easy for either of us.

From this point forward, I started thinking about everything in *lasts*: my *last* cruise, my *last* vacation, my *last* big trip with my best friend, my *last* time to dig my toes in the sand, and my *last* time to wade in the ocean. I had a memorable first, though, among the many lasts on the trip. While Grace did a below deck walking tour, I treated myself to my first full-body massage. If I had known how awesome it was to be pampered, I would have indulged sooner. Money well spent.

One night, after we finished our daily devotions, Grace tearfully told me how much I meant to her and how she would support me to the end, whatever that looked like. She stated emphatically, "I know you value your independence, but promise me you will allow me and others to help you." She knew me so well. I nodded my head, unable to speak. My life goal was not to be a botheration to anyone for any reason. I needed the Lord's help to adjust my thinking on this asking-for-help thing.

That night, we joked about the mansions the Lord was preparing for each of us, and we hoped we would be next-door neighbors. What a relief to laugh and talk about what was destined to be, my short future. From that point on, we vowed to make new memories to hold onto until we docked in the New York harbor.

Another last that was important to me before I could no longer drive was to contact Dr. Wallace, my psychologist, and Susan, my art therapist. I knew it might be a bit unconventional to contact former counselors and invite them to meet you at a restaurant, but convention went out the window with my diagnosis. Although nervous, I was eager to see them in a much different capacity.

CHAPTER 49 ~ The Lasts

They graciously accepted my invitation. First and foremost, I wanted to give them the news of my recent diagnosis. I saw our meeting as my last opportunity to see them and tell them how much I appreciated their support through the years.

It proved to be a pleasant and satisfying evening where we caught up on each other's lives, but my sad news changed the atmosphere. As I sat across from the amazing professionals whom I held in great honor for the part they played in my life, I saw how they didn't have immediate words to respond to my news.

"Did you ever ask, 'Why me?' " Dr. Wallace asked.

I responded, "Why not me?" I wanted God's glory displayed through this disease but didn't, at that moment, have the proper words to explain my feelings. I couldn't put a voice to it. I was thankful to be in the presence of two individuals who had seen the worst of me without judgment. We said our last goodbyes and, as I drove away, tears welled up in my eyes, blurring my vision in the overflow. *God, please bless these helpers, who so blessed me—with every good and perfect gift from above.*

Random Thoughts

May the God of all hope fill you with joy and peace as you trust in him so that you may overflow with hope by the power of the Holy Spirit.
Romans 15:13

Journal Entry:

It has been so difficult the last week or so to stay positive, but thankfully it's just been Oreo, Tweedledee, and me, so most of my despair has gone unnoticed. It seems like every day, there is something else I cannot do. Oh, God, please help me focus on what I can do. Maybe, it's the letdown of coming back after such a special vacation, the last day of my job on the 19th, the loss of Tweedledum, and the finality of ALS all happening in rapid succession . . . not in that order, but happening nonetheless. I am so emotional. I can't seem to speak without tears.

The falls are happening more frequently, and the last one was extra scary. What would I have done if Jared, the IT guy from church hadn't come when he did to fix my computer? I could have lain in that pool of blood for who knows how long? I am grateful that there are no broken bones, just cuts, scrapes and multi-colored bruises. I have a fountain of tears and a mountain of fears. Help me Jesus!

Fear!

i fear the change that is occurring in me, i can't stop it
i fear i will fall too hard
i fear i will mess up
i fear asking for help
i fear for my sanity
i fear being all alone
i fear falling asleep at night and not waking up
i fear my family is forever broken

CHAPTER 50 ~ Random Thoughts

i fear the sound of footsteps coming closer in the night
i fear i don't belong
i fear i will give up
i fear i will never stop crying
i fear i will never catch my breath again
i fear my past will haunt me once again
i fear running out of money
i fear being vulnerable all over again
i fear losing my independence
i fear my driving days are done
i fear steps are insurmountable
i fear i'll come undone
i fear i'll never stop fearing, but fear isn't from you, Lord

I needed a different type of counseling now. Dealing with the finality of my life and the loss of my independence were mountains to conquer. The ALS Association assigned me a counselor named Glorie-Ann. She worked strictly with ALS and hospice patients. She was trained to help patients manage their emotions and grief, two tremendous by-products of this disease. We developed an instant rapport. She, too, was a cat lover. I felt safe with her and poured out my emotions during each visit. She understood everything I shared. She'd heard it all before from other patients. I looked forward to her bi-weekly visits, grateful to unburden the tangled emotions ALS brought into my life.

Pastor Jack stopped by as often as his schedule allowed. His funny stories and amusing anecdotes were welcomed. His goal every visit was to make me smile, and I didn't let him down. He prayed, encouraged, and dispensed the elements of communion with me. I loved the sacredness of communion now that I fully understood the atoning blood of Christ versus the perversion of the blood used in Satanic rituals.

On one visit I asked, "When Jesus takes me home, would you conduct my Life Celebration Service?"

I saw tears gather in his eyes as he said, "It would be my great honor."

"Pastor Jack," I continued, "I'm not afraid of death, but the process of dying with ALS and struggling to breathe frightens me."

"That's a natural response," he said. "Fear tries to take control. Trust the Holy Spirit to remind you of His promises." Then he gave

CHAPTER 50 ~ Random Thoughts

me a list of things I could count on God to do for me as He walked with me through my valley season:

1. A sufficient and great grace
2. An unfailing love
3. A hope that doesn't disappoint
4. A secured eternity with my heavenly Father
5. A joy unspeakable
6. A praying High Priest
7. A Savior who lives
8. A Holy Spirit who comforts
9. A peace that passes our human understanding
10. An atoning blood that cleanses
11. A book full of His promises

I never blamed God for my diagnosis and anger toward Him never surfaced. Like Job in the Old Testament, no matter what I faced, I wouldn't blame God. I had questions. Some would never get answered, like the "why" of it all. God brought me through the fires of hell in my past. I had every expectation that He would help me through this difficult, unknown season. I trusted that He was with me every step of the way. It might look different than what I imagined, but it would be okay. Jesus promised me that.

In John 10:10, it says there is an enemy of our soul: ". . . *the thief comes only to steal, kill, and destroy." The devil is the one to blame. But he won't win. Evil never wins. My God is bigger and stronger and will see me through to the gates of Heaven.*

I clung to the verse from James 1:12: *"Blessed is the one who perseveres under trial because, having stood the test, that person will receive the crown of life that the Lord has promised to those who love Him."*

Somehow, I needed to wrap my head around my diagnosis and figure out what this meant for my life and the time I had left on earth. I had to figure out the next steps. *What will I do with all my possessions? My house?*

I asked Grace and Penny to come over one afternoon for a prayer session about this very thing. After we said "Amen," I made an honest assessment of what I needed, and Penny wrote it down in my journal:

> *i need help and need to ask and accept it when offered*
> *i need help washing my hair*

CHAPTER 50 ~ Random Thoughts

i need help pulling up my covers at night
i need help getting dressed sometimes
i need help cutting Twee's claws
i need help breathing
i need to be needed
i need to give to others
i need to be organized
i need to speak up
i need to be understood
i need a bed that is the right height
i need to forgive myself
i need to be zapped with energy
i need to finish my will
i need to sell my car
i need to get over my sadness
i need to stay connected
i need daily encouragement
i need to love and be loved
i need to fear less
i need to give myself permission to feel what I feel
i need hugs
i need to plan things to look forward to
i need to stay in my own home
i need to remember that heaven is my real home
i need a heavenly or eternal perspective
i need to remember God is with me

The next day after work, Penny stopped by with a white grocery bag stashed full of my favorite cookies—Oreos. She frequently swung by after work and helped with the yard, walked Oreo, cleaned Twee's litter box, and tidied up the house. I welcomed her drop by visits. She had refrigerator rights, a true symbol of family.

She handed me the cookies with a serious look on her face and sat down. "Aunt Alice, this past week I fasted and prayed about how I could help you on this difficult journey. I know your heart's desire is to stay home with Oreo and Twee by your side. That is only possible if you have 24/7, around the clock care. Because of my love for you, I would like to provide that care for you. If you'll have me, I'll give immediate notice at the church, move into the guest room, and be your caregiver, plus whatever else needs to be done. Mom agrees that with me as your advocate and manager in all the aspects

CHAPTER 50 ~ Random Thoughts

of your care, it will be less worrisome for all of us. So, what do you think?" She said this quickly, breathlessly blurting out a flood of words.

What do I think? I didn't have to think. Or pray. God provided my heart's desire in a way I could not have imagined. No words formed on my lips as I sobbed in joyful relief. I nodded my head to affirm my answer—a wonderful, super-sized YES!

Life Sentence

Now to Him who is able to do immeasurably more than all we ask or imagine, according to his power that is at work within us.
Ephesians 3:20

When Penny moved in, it made life easier to manage on a daily basis. It was a blessing to have someone to talk to anytime day or night. Though it had been only three months since the official ALS diagnosis, I was into the second year of the disease due to the initial misdiagnosis. My time was short.

All the doctors, nurses, and therapists at the impressive ALS Clinic were caring and helpful. My heart overflowed with thankfulness at the compassionate care I received there.

Even so, as the days passed my mobility declined to where I rarely walked unassisted. I became dependent on my walker, wheelchair and, occasionally, my cane. The ALS Association loaned me a power wheelchair which allowed me to get outside more often. The first thing I did when that chair arrived was take Oreo for a ride. He sat proudly on my lap as we scooted here and there in the sunshine.

I found it difficult to give up driving. Losing my independence was a difficult step in the progress of the disease, though I tried to accept it with grace. My home was fitted out with several pieces of new equipment for invalid care. A hospital bed was delivered which made it easier to get in and out of bed. Sleeping on an incline helped my breathing, a difficult chore when lying down. A power-lift recliner chair gave me a comfortable place to sit during the day and lift to a standing position. My legs had little strength left to stand. Oreo liked it when I sat in the recliner and jumped on my lap to comfort me. The wheelchair was too high for him to jump up on me there. Twee sought chair time, too, and got very vocal about it when

CHAPTER 51 ~ Life Sentence

she felt she'd missed her turn. We all tried to figure out new ways of doing things.

But the best news came when the date was set for my custom-built power wheelchair to be delivered. I waited six weeks after being measured and fitted for it. Teddy built a wheelchair ramp at the front door so I could zoom out and enjoy a sense of independence when I needed some fresh air.

Before I lost more arm strength, I sorted through all my accumulated paperwork from the past fifty-five years of my life. Penny and Grace helped me decide what was needed. It was hard to let go of certain things. *Come on, Alice, you know you can't hold on to everything. You can't really hold onto anything. You can't take it with you.*

"I want to donate my art therapy books," I said. "I'd like four of them to go to Susan. Maybe she can use them as examples for other struggling complex patients in her practice."

"That's a great idea," agreed Grace. "What about the others?"

The two other art books had darker images of my childhood. I entrusted them into Grace's safekeeping, along with my personal journals.

"And we should plan a big estate sale in the spring." I said.

"That will be a big project," said Penny.

"I know." I said, as I looked around the room at all my possessions. "What to sell, what to give away, what to donate, and what to discard." It was hard to not be sentimental about things. It was all just stuff. But it was my stuff. *Everything that makes my house a home is all around me.* I admit, it took me a little while to make peace with the idea of doling out all my treasures. "Oh, well," I concluded, "they say there are no U-hauls going to Heaven—and I'm Heaven-bound!"

Penny and I shared a devotional time every morning which included Scripture reading, journaling, and prayer. One day, after prayer, I was feeling sorry for myself that I'd been given a death sentence. But as I waded into a pity pond, a new stream of thought flashed in my mind and I shook off despair in renewed hope: *What if? What if I flip it around? What if I make this a LIFE sentence? What if I dedicate whatever time I have left to the plans and purposes of God and make each day a blessing! A gift back to Him?*

Joy welled up from deep within me, like a fresh spring of rejuvenating water. For the first time since the diagnosis, I didn't want to waste another minute thinking about death. *I know where my*

CHAPTER 51 ~ Life Sentence

ultimate destination is going to be. Most people don't get the opportunity to know when the end is near. I can tie up all the loose ends of my life. I can make decisions in advance about my money, my possessions, my funeral, who I can bless, and how I can help others who are suffering. Yes, I'm going to make every day count for the Kingdom! I'll make the time I have left a season filled with Acts of Kindness on steroids! It will be my gift back to the Giver of my life.

When my heavenly Father healed my mind and emotions, I said I could face anything if He was beside me. ALS was my anything and I determined to face it with faith, dignity, and in ways that would honor the life He gave me. *Yes, Lord, life has been more than crappy at times. But my mind is whole now, and I have the ability to bless others with my belongings and money in the bank. I declare this ALS,* **A L***ife* **S***entence. I know You will continue to guide me through the treacherous waters of this cursed disease.*

I didn't know how long was left of my appointed time on earth, but I had a renewed purpose to make my life count.

If You Choose, God Will Use

In the same way, let your light shine before others, that they may see your good deeds and glorify your Father in heaven.
Matthew 5:16

I had never joined in group activities with ease. But ALS ushered me, not by choice, into a very unique group fellowship of sorts—the fellowship of suffering that the Apostle Paul talked about in Philippians 3:10 NKJV: *". . . that I might know Him and the power of His resurrection and the fellowship of His suffering; being conformed to His death."*

That verse took on a whole new meaning to me in light of my ALS. Being in "the fellowship of His suffering," I desired to suffer well. My Savior had gone before me and made the way. I had to trust that His grace would be sufficient for me, and He would lead me through whatever dark valleys lay before me.

Every day when I awoke, I'd pray, "Lord, I'm still here. Thank You for Your portion of grace to help me suffer well so I can love and bless those around me."

One day, I was inspired to go up and down every street in my town, of almost ten-thousand residents, and pray for all who lived there. The weather was expected to turn cold soon so I started immediately, grateful for the mobility my motorized chair afforded me. The project would serve two purposes: I'd get out into the fresh air, where I felt truly alive, and I'd be doing something personal to uplift my town—a new spin on the commandment to love thy neighbor! It took twenty-one days to complete my prayer project, an act that brought me great joy and diverted my focus from the things I couldn't do.

By the time spring rolled around, Grace and Penny had successfully planned a two-day estate sale. We went through all the contents of my house, attic to basement. One of Grace's superpowers was her ability to organize well. She put price tags on all the collectibles and anything of real value.

CHAPTER 52 ~ If You Choose, God Will Use

On the day of the sale, I struggled with a roller coaster of emotions. *I knew this day would come. I've been planning it all winter. But is my stuff good enough that someone else would want it? Is it priced right? All. My. Stuff.*

I learned through therapy that every time negative thoughts flashed across the screen of my mind, I should change the channel. After the first hour of the sale, as I surveyed the bits and pieces of my life on full display, a playlist of negativity rolled through my thoughts. It was scary and sad to watch strangers carry off the contents of my home and the treasures of my heart. *No, stop! Don't take that! I bake pumpkin bread in that pan every year. Wait—I'm never going to bake again!*

I needed to change the channel. *I don't need these things anymore. I really don't. God has something greater for me. My future is far, far better than stuff. It's of eternal value.*

After a little change-the-channel self-talk, I went out front into the center of the sale on the lawn and thanked each buyer for giving their purchases a good home.

"Why are you selling all these things?" a lady asked.

"I'm getting ready to move," I said. I neglected to tell her that Heaven would be my new home.

My hospital bed and medical equipment did not fit in my bedroom located at the back corner of the house. But Penny rearranged everything to fit perfectly in the Florida room where the large windows allowed the warm sunlight to stream through and brighten each day. From my hospital bed, I could look out the windows, bask in the light, and see everything going on in my neighborhood. I watched the established patterns of people coming and going to their respective jobs. I knew when to expect the mailman. I knew the time by when the different dogs were taken for their walks throughout the day. My view into the outside world helped me feel connected and less isolated.

There was a rash of burglaries throughout our immediate and extended neighborhood. They occurred during the day when the burglar thought no one was at home. The police patrol cars passed by at two-hour intervals.

One day, I was getting bathed in my room with the blinds drawn when we heard the front doorknob being turned as if to see if it was unlocked. Oreo heard it, too, and yapped in his piercing "someone is at the door" bark. The visiting nurse peeked out the window and

CHAPTER 52 ~ If You Choose, God Will Use

saw someone run down the street. She described him as a white male in his early twenties, about six-feet tall, and wearing a black hooded sweatshirt,

The next day, I sat up in my bed and looked out the windows at a couple of squirrels chasing each other up and down a tree. My attention was caught by someone fitting the description of the burglar, hanging out by the stop sign across the street. The way he furtively looked from side to side with an air of secrecy made me suspicious. I picked up my cell phone and pressed the 9-1-1 buttons. By the time the police arrived, the suspect had fled the scene, but I was able to give a more detailed description of him.

A few hours later, the police came to the house again with an update. They were able to successfully apprehend the perpetrator based on my report. The police thanked me over and over again for taking action. They called me a crime stopper, and I received the label with pride.

I learned that God could use me even when I was confined to a hospital bed, as long as I was willing to be used. *I'm not completely helpless, God! What else can You do through me?*

Tantrums

Therefore we do not lose heart. Though outwardly we are wasting away, yet inwardly we are being renewed day by day.
2 Corinthians 4:16

My visits to the ALS Clinic took place every two months at the hospital in Philadelphia. The main purpose was to measure my progress. Some of the details they check are my breathing ability, body strength, and weight. Thankfully, my weight stayed the same over the months since my last check-up.

But my strength was failing at a rapid rate. Items I could pick up one day, I could not pick up the next day. Everyday activities became more and more of a challenge. Simple tasks like pulling the covers over me in bed, opening a door, turning a light switch on or off, seemed monumental. I never thought a towel would be too heavy to pick up or lifting a cup of water to my mouth would be so difficult. Just to brush my teeth used every ounce of energy. And worst of all, I could barely pet Twee and Oreo.

Eventually, when a doctor asked me to take a deep breath, I couldn't do it. My breathing capacity when sitting was 23% and only 12% when I'd lie down. The numbers continued to drop significantly over the next months until I could no longer get in or out of bed without assistance.

I fell several times, one of which resulted in a visit to the emergency room. Fortunately, I came away with no broken bones, only cuts, scrapes, bruises, and a big lump of discouragement. While I desperately wanted to maintain my independence, I had to face the fact that I was totally dependent on others. *Isn't that how life starts? Babies can't do anything on their own and are dependent on others. And if I'm honest, I sometimes throw tantrums like a toddler because—this just isn't fair!!!*

It was humbling to rely on others to bathe, dress, and take care of my bathroom needs, but I could still feed myself if the food was

CHAPTER 53 ~ Tantrums

cut up into bite size pieces. Although my body was on a steady decline, my mind remained the same. I lost the use of my left arm and hand, leaving a little strength in my right arm and hand allowing me to press the buttons on my cell phone—my lifeline to the outside world.

I tried to see things from a different perspective. Instead of mowing the lawn, I enjoyed the smell of fresh cut grass. Instead of being able to swim or stick my toes in the water, I relished the sound of children as they splashed and frolicked in the pool. Instead of being able to walk my dog on a leash, I cherished the wheelchair rides we had together with him sitting on my lap. And even though I couldn't write anymore, Penny became my personal scribe which allowed me to continue the record of my life in my journal. I poured out the words from deep inside me and, she wrote them down:

> *Another accident today; that's the third time I fell in the last few days. Today, it happened in church—so embarrassing. All of these falls are taking a toll on me physically. They hurt and I have so many bruises. They're affecting me emotionally as well. I am having a hard time separating the past and the present. Seeing all of these bruises and scrapes on my body reminds me all too much of my past abuse. I hate all of these reminders. I silently cry out to God, Please God, don't let me split again because of this nasty disease. I want my mind to remain whole.*

I want out
out of this failing body
with its weakening muscles and extreme fatigue.
Seems like hourly, daily
there's something else I can't do.
To walk across the room
to rise from a chair
seems like training for a marathon.
The falls and struggle to recover
take their toll and leave me
gasping for breath.
Should I just give up
and throw in the towel
or keep on fighting
until the end?

CHAPTER 53 ~ Tantrums

The joke is on me, and suddenly I am moved to smile because I can't even pick up the towel to throw it back in. I feel another pity party in my near future. I have to remember it's OK to whine, scream, shout, and cry. I'm not a curser, so that isn't in the line-up. I take a few minutes and have a great whine fest. I am unable to stomp my feet or pick something up and throw it. I visualize that I can. In my mind's eye I just threw a plate of spaghetti at the wall and what a fine mess that made. I am picturing Oreo and Twee running toward an unexpected meal. OK, that was satisfying; I can now change the channel.

When I changed the channel in my mind to a different way of thinking, I grew more aware of all God's blessings in my life. First and foremost, I was thankful that Penny looked after me from sun-up to sun-down and all the dark hours in between. Every evening I'd thank God for His grace and Penny's help to get me through another day. *How many days do I have left, Lord? I really want each day to be a gift back to You, the Giver of Life. A day without a tantrum.*

Winning

I press on toward the goal to win the prize for which God has called me heavenward in Christ Jesus.
Philippians 3:14

Unless God gave me a miracle equal to the raising of Lazarus from the dead, my time on earth would be short.

One beautiful sunny day, I prayed and contemplated on the positive statements I could make about living with ALS. *What does winning with ALS mean to me? What does it look like?*

With Penny's help, I journaled my answers:

- *winning means finishing strong*
- *winning means staying the course*
- *winning means laughing along the way*
- *winning is putting a smile on someone else's face*
- *winning is blessing someone*
- *winning is finding creative ways to move forward*
- *winning is celebrating the simple and smallest of victories*
- *winning is making it to the bathroom on time*
- *winning is enjoying a game of cards*
- *winning is reading or listening to a good book*
- *winning is connecting with an old friend*
- *winning is no alarm clock in the morning*
- *winning is "walking" the dog*
- *winning is still being able to call Twee to my side*
- *winning is holding on with one hand and reaching out with the other*
- *winning is having things in order for those I leave behind*
- *winning is having a why to live for*
- *winning is getting through one day without crying*

CHAPTER 54 ~ Winning

- *winning is to understand that winning isn't everything, but the trying gives me purpose*

With ALS, there were always more questions to ask. Sometimes the answers produced tears, and other times, fear and doubt accompanied the hard, honest facts.

I challenged myself to think of positive ways the disease impacted my life. First and foremost, ALS increased my prayer and devotional life. Jesus was either all or nothing at all. Indeed, I found Him to be my all, and more. When I meditated upon that truth, I could smile and be at rest in my soul.

On the other hand, I regretted that it took a life-threatening disease to make me realize that I could have had deeper intimacy with Jesus all along if I hadn't been so busy just trying to survive. I had squeezed Jesus in when it was convenient. My great regret is knowing that a trusting, loving relationship with Jesus was available to me all through my years and I didn't fully embrace it until ALS. For those who might read my story, I pray they learn this powerful lesson from my experience. Jesus is *"a friend who sticks closer than a brother."* Proverbs 18:24

Winning means I had the opportunity to meet a whole new group of people. My bi-weekly attendance at the ALS support group proved to me that I was not alone in my struggles. The dedicated hospice staff workers, and those who volunteered in and out of my home on a daily basis, I came to call my friends. The awkwardness I used to wrestle with in forming new friendships quickly faded. I had to get right down to the business of living in trust and connection with others. I was grateful for all the committed doctors, nurses, and technicians that served me every time ALS required me to have a check-up. They were the best of the best.

Winning tasted delicious, too! My church community brought me yummy meals three or four times a week—a definite positive. The fact that I didn't know people well or not at all didn't stop them from blessing me. Neighbors I barely saw before stopped by just to say "hello." Such visits allowed me the opportunity to know them on a deeper level and pray with them. Joel, Henry, Maggie, and Ellie, four beautiful kids who live on my street popped in weekly to see how I was doing. They often read stories to me from their library books—a blessing that wouldn't have happened before ALS.

CHAPTER 54 ~ Winning

Penny's best friend, Katie and her three children, Calvin (9), Caroline (8), and David (6), visited often with offers to serve and help in any capacity. Their arrival brought me joy with an energetic burst through the doorway. Time spent with that bunch was always a win. They infused their surroundings with joy and loved to play with Oreo and Twee—when they cooperated. Frequently, the kids sprawled on the floor and surrounded my bed playing with the different games and puzzles I'd stored in the closet. It brought me great joy to hear their laughter. Even their sibling bickering delighted me.

Being in their presence made me long for what I missed in my childhood and caused me to think about my own siblings, Sandy and Billy. I wished they lived closer and could visit more often. I missed my nieces and nephew very much. But God was gracious and filled the family void in my life with Katie and her three kids who loved me and hugged me and affectionately called me "Aunt Alice." Just like Penny does. This is another glimpse of what winning looks like. So. Much. Win.

I also considered it a big win to appreciate the things in life I had once taken for granted: a comfortable home, bright sunshine, fat pens to help me write, cards with words of encouragement, food in the fridge, caring friends, electric blankets, cups with straws, and most of all—the simple act of breathing.

I received VIP invitations to ALS events—more big wins. I loved ALS night at the Philadelphia Phillies. I was a super fan since I'd lived in my first apartment in the city so many years ago. Penny accompanied me to the stadium, and I got to meet all the players before the game in a special meet and greet event. What fun it was to have my picture taken with my favorite players, along with the official team mascot, that silly Phillie Phanatic! Then, we felt like celebrities when the pictures were published in our local newspaper.

Winning was about the many opportunities that came my way through the ALS Ice Bucket Challenge. People were asked to dump a bucket of ice water over their head and film it to post as a video on social media. Then, they had to nominate three others to take the challenge or make a donation to ALS. The idea was to raise awareness and research dollars. Until the challenge went viral, most people didn't know what ALS was other than its alternate name of Lou Gehrig's Disease. Most were unaware of the effects of the disease as it progressed. I found myself in situations where I could

CHAPTER 54 ~ Winning

explain how ALS changed people's lives, slowly breaking them down until their body just stopped working. Often, my story was the first time a listener had ever heard of it. Winning was knowing ALS exists—and helping others to know, too. Many of my former co-workers, friends, and family members took the Ice Bucket Challenge. Every time someone posted a video in my honor, I was triple blessed: for the honor, for how it made me laugh, and for the increased donations of research dollars.

Winning with ALS was about being informed. Winning was caring. It was not giving up, but spurring others on in their struggles with a positive attitude in the middle of the battle of a lifetime.

55

Almost Home

My flesh and my heart may fail, but God is the strength of my heart and my portion forever.
Psalm 73:26

The shadow of death loomed over me. If you are attuned to your "knower," you can sense it. The holidays were fast approaching, and I prayed I would be allowed one more Thanksgiving and one more Christmas—my favorite holiday. More than receiving, I loved the challenge of finding the perfect gift for others. Penny dutifully stood by my bed, either turning the pages of the catalog or scrolling the iPad screen for me. I wanted to have one more holiday buying spree.

I indulged in a carefree attitude about my money because, very soon, it no longer would be designated for the mortgage, electric, cable, and other homeowner necessities. So, as I perused gift shopping options, I pulled out all the stops and didn't concern myself with the price tags. *I will be a blessing to others until the end.*

Penny phoned my sister, my brother, and their families, along with my mom and dad, and extended an invitation to what she called a *Thanksmas* dinner. We planned to celebrate both holidays at once, in case the angel escorts arrived before Christmas.

Grace took over the details of the menu, and Penny decorated the Christmas tree on November 15th with all my favorite Disney ornaments. The total invitations extended for this celebration would be fourteen: Sandy, Michael, Sam, Rebecca, Billy, Renee, Heather, Grace, Teddy, Penny, Harvey Mason and his new wife, Julianne, all planned to attend. Mom and Dad declined due to health reasons and the travel distance. Mom wanted to come, but it was Dad's decision to stay home. Sandy invited Mom to travel with them, but I knew Mom would not leave Dad behind, nor would he want her to go without him. *What is the real reason behind his no-show response? Coming here means he wouldn't be in control. That makes sense.*

CHAPTER 55 ~ Almost Home

This was the first time my family would be guests in my home—and possibly the last according to the ALS timetable. Though we did live some distance apart, there always seemed to be excuses for my siblings not to visit me. Perhaps I was too much a reminder of our childhood trauma. I couldn't say for sure and would never ask such a question of them.

I examined my heart over this matter. *Am I happy or sad that my parents are not coming? Am I foolish and selfish for wanting ALL my family here, the ones of my origin and the ones of my heart, all in the same room at the same time? This is probably the last opportunity for us to be together and, once again, it's dear old Dad who messed up the plan. Will he come up with an excuse not to show up at my Life Celebration Service, too? No matter. I will not have my joy stolen from me. This is my last big family celebration. God will help me with all the details. I can count on Him.*

I just hoped I would be well enough to enjoy the celebration.

Every day I woke up thankful for a new day. I felt like a little kid who hoped Santa had her name on the Nice List. I counted down the days until *Thanksmas* finally arrived.

All of the out of town guests settled in the day before at a nearby Bed and Breakfast. They stopped by the house to drop off their gift packages and food and to say a quick "hello" before bed. It was so good to see them. I could tell by the look in their eyes how shocked they were by my physical appearance. It must have been different for them to hear about my sickness on the phone, as opposed to seeing the full effects of the ravaging disease in person. With all the equipment surrounding my bed, it was difficult for anyone to get close. I received lots of air kisses, toe squeezes, and hand holds. Oreo didn't mind all the attention he got either. Twee hid under the bed, not quite used to all the chattering voices and feet standing close to her tail. The excitement for all the festivities awaiting us the next day, and the nagging thought that I might not wake up for it at all, made it difficult to sleep without medication.

In God's goodness to me, I opened my eyes the next day truly thankful that my time had not run out during the night. *Thanksmas* gave me the gift of seeing everyone one more time and celebrating our Savior's birth—a perfect, winning combination!

The regular table wasn't big enough for everyone to gather around. It took two additional card tables and four TV trays to seat everyone and hold all the food. Although Mom wasn't in attendance, she sent along her traditional cranberry orange chutney—my holiday

CHAPTER 55 ~ Almost Home

favorite. Mr. Mason, (I could never get used to calling him Harvey), and his wife, Julianne, provided the golden-brown turkey. We were thankful for that since our oven overflowed with a baked spiral ham, whipped sweet potatoes, au gratin potatoes, and roasted Brussels sprouts. Creamed corn, gravy, homemade rolls, and stuffing rounded out the bountiful meal. Sandy baked six kinds of Christmas cookies—all Oma's recipes that had been passed down to us. It was hard to choose from snickerdoodles, iced sugar cookies, shortbread stars, chocolate, chocolate chip, thumbprint, and date pinwheels. Mom also sent a tin that once held fruitcake, now filled with her classic peanut butter fudge. Cream cheese pumpkin roll, pumpkin and pecan pies, and pumpkin cheesecake added to the dessert selections. I wondered if Jesus felt like this at His last supper. I wanted three things: time to slow down, a God moment with each person, and a taste of everything.

After I was rolled into place, sitting up in my wheelchair, we started our Thanksgiving dinner with the customary expression of thanks by everyone at the table. I think holiday hijinks were afoot as each person honored me, sharing a special memory or quality about me they were thankful for. My heart felt like it might burst within me by the time everyone took a turn. It choked me up to hear such loving, generous words directed at me. I couldn't speak more than a whisper and said, "Thanks, everyone."

Teddy said grace in thanksgiving to God, we passed around all the food, and dug in. My full heart left no room for embarrassment because I had to wear an adult bib. After our scrumptious and plentiful feast, we agreed to open gifts and have dessert. With seams busted and bellies stuffed like the turkey prior to dinner, we successfully completed the "thanks" portion of the day. Time for Christmas fun!

Michael read the Christmas story from the book of Luke in the Bible to focus everyone on the real reason for celebration. Each word was like water to my soul, especially since it would be my last Christmas. Soon, I would meet the Savior of the world—the One who assigned my every breath. *I'm going to meet Jesus face to face!* My heart soared, but I had to stay grounded in the moment. Each one, precious to me.

Christmas joy filled the room as my family and friends received and opened their gifts from me. Penny ordered them. Grace wrapped them. Teddy tagged them. In the past, people accused me

CHAPTER 55 ~ Almost Home

of going overboard when it came to buying gifts. But that year, the word extravagant might best describe my shopping plan. Bits of colorful wrapping paper tossed to and fro as I watched each face open their individual gifts like a free for all. I loved the moment when they spied the treasure chosen just for them under the wrapping. When I saw their face light up with a bright smile, I knew I got it right!

After all the gifts were opened, examined, and held up for everyone to admire, Penny reached into the side of the tree and pulled out an envelope. "Alice, this one's for you!"

"What?" I said, "For me? I didn't expect a gift. I mean—you all just being here is my gift." Still, Penny pressed the envelope into my hand with a knowing smile. "Oh, seriously, Penny. I mean, what do you buy someone who is dying and celebrating her last Christmas?"

Sam offered to help me open the envelope and pulled out what looked like a gift certificate. He looked at me silently, as if to ask if he should continue. I nodded my head. He started to read. "Alice, you are courageously fighting a battle. You have been such an inspiration to each of us and we know you will have the ultimate victory when you cross Heaven's threshold. We wanted to honor your life in a special way. We all contributed money to an international agency that will purchase four goats, four sheep, one cow, and a dozen baby chicks for a village in Africa in your honor. These precious gifts will provide food, milk, and wool to a needy family. The animal droppings—or poop if you prefer—are an added bonus as they provide fertilizer for crops."

Our hearts touched, we had teary eyes until Sam extemporaneously tossed the word "poop" in there. The room erupted in laughter at the idea of poop as a gift by-product. The generosity of my loved ones overwhelmed me. I soaked in the faces of each dear, dear soul that surrounded me. *God, bless them!*

Penny suggested I take my afternoon nap. It was necessary, but I didn't want to miss a single moment of the gathering. Grace promised she would take notes on everything that happened while I slept. A few did the dishes, some opted for card games, and others Mexican train dominoes. I fell asleep to the beautiful sound of background voices, domino tiles clicking, and my nephew accusing someone of cheating.

I woke up to the sound of Mr. Mason's guitar playing, *O Come All Ye Faithful*. The day's activities wore me out, and I was too weak

CHAPTER 55 ~ Almost Home

to sit up in the wheelchair again as I had hoped. So, everyone squeezed into my room and gathered around. I had slept longer than expected. In fact, I missed out on dessert time entirely. Truth be told, I couldn't eat another bite. *I'll have dessert tomorrow, maybe even as a main course!*

For the next thirty minutes, we sang Christmas carols and ended with *Silent Night*, my favorite. *I don't want this day to end. It's a perfect day! What does my family think of it all? A day mixed with the joyful sounds of laughter and tears that refuse to remain unshed. Oh, loved ones, I hope next year this day is a precious memory for you who I leave behind.*

By 8:00 p.m. I could no longer keep my eyes open, as much as I wanted to. My spirit was certainly willing, but my flesh was indeed weak. Billy led us in a prayer for traveling mercies and blessing before everyone prepared to leave. Mr. Mason, Julianne, Grace and Teddy went their respective ways and allowed my family to be the last to say goodnight. But we all knew it was more than good night. It was really good-bye. The forever kind.

Penny hovered in the background in case she was required for my personal needs. Oreo and Twee snuggled into their usual nighttime spots. My family had planned to hit the road early the next morning after breakfast. I had reached the moment in time that would be the final farewell. The last goodbye. At least in person on the earth.

What an awkward time, more so for them than me. Not that I didn't care, but I was so tired, my mind about to shut down, and my emotions had shifted into neutral. I sensed that Sandy was getting ready to do the ugly cry. Michael had his arm around her as she leaned over the bedrail. "I love you Alice, see you later." The interpretation of later meant, I'll see you in Heaven. I knew what she meant. No more needed to be said. Each one took a turn to say their last goodbye. I hoped they could see in my eyes what my mouth couldn't say with a breathing mask attached to it.

Finally, the day ended and quiet returned. Penny, Oreo, and Twee sat alone with me, silent but for the ebb and flow of my breathing machine. *The Lord has been good to me. I feel loved and appreciated. This is what being content feels like. All is right in my world and I am truly blessed. If you come for me tonight, Lord, I am ready.*

Reflections

For God so loved the world that he gave his one and only Son, that whoever believes in him shall not perish but have eternal life.
John 3:16

I felt a little down after the big *Thankmas* celebration, which I'd looked so forward to with great expectation, was over. Not that I didn't have anything else to look forward to. Heaven was just around the corner with its golden streets and mansions. I heard the clock tick as it counted down to the appointed day and time. Jesus faintly called my name. *Is this the last day, Lord? Heaven sounds . . . well . . . heavenly! It's the dying part I'm not too fond of. But ready or not, it is inevitable for all of us. I am truly ready for Moving Day and hope it comes quickly. I want to fall asleep and wake up in Heaven. Everyone who comes through the doors to see me is on high alert. They know, too. Soon—very soon.*

I had a pleasant dream one night where I saw glowing figures dressed in white in the front yard trying to peek in the windows. *Lord, is my dream meant as a prophetic message? Perhaps they are angelic beings waiting to escort me on my final journey.*

I've checked all the boxes from the original list Penny and I had made a year ago. Grace had informed me last Sunday that all the letters were ready for delivery. Over the last few months, I'd painstakingly dictated twenty-six letters and asked Grace to distribute them after I permanently moved. Along with the letters, I carefully selected gifts and Grace beautifully wrapped them for me with much love. Project Blessing was complete and ready to go when I was gone.

Grace didn't know that Katie helped me prepare a very special letter for her, too. It was a difficult one to write, to tell my best friend how thankful I was that God allowed our paths to cross all those years ago. Grace liked to be in control and always wanted to be in

CHAPTER 56 ~ Reflections

the know, but my secret letter would be my last big surprise for her—the letter and a final gift—my cherished butterfly ring.

Dictating all those letters took a long time and expended a lot of my energy. But it was important that my family, closest friends, and caregivers knew beyond a shadow of a doubt how much I loved and appreciated them. I wanted them to understand how much I appreciated their help which allowed me to live a gracious life up to the end. I trusted Grace and Penny, women of their word, to deliver my last gifts.

Without Penny, I'd have been in a nursing home surrounded by strangers. My prayer was to die comfortably in my home with Oreo and Twee by my side, encircled by loved ones. *How do you begin to thank someone for helping you die well while navigating the treacherous waters of ALS?*

Since I couldn't do anything but lie in bed and be still, I needed to take an inventory of my life and meditate on all the Father, Son, and Holy Spirit had done for me. It was a group effort.

If I viewed my days through a panoramic lens, I would clearly see the many Parts of Alice and that long journey to wholeness as preeminent. God gave me many miracles along the way, but I count the restoration miracle of my life in pieces to wholeness first and foremost! Yes, it took hard work. But He gave me every good and perfect gift from above to help make it happen. He aligned and connected all the helpers in my life. God designed us to live in community—a hard lesson I often fought, but I had to learn. The stalwart independence I tenaciously clung to was a facade. Despite that, He faithfully sent rescuers in the flesh to help at specific moments in time—some just in time—to save me from death and destruction. No doubt, there were angelic encounters I was not aware of that protected me from falling into perilous situations as I journeyed through life. The darkness and despair in my life was so thick at times. He called me out of the densest darkness into His glorious and beautiful light. I couldn't be more grateful. *Ah, yes! Such darkness I have known! I wonder if God ever needed night vision goggles to locate me.* Such a silly thought made me smile.

God invaded my heart. His love seeped into all the gaps while it saturated me with His peace over and over again. My problems and challenges were bigger than me, but not bigger than Him. All my failures never separated me from His love. He was an ever-present God. When trust was absent and worry out of control, He took the

CHAPTER 56 ~ Reflections

reins of my life and the driver's seat. He knew how to navigate all the obstacles, distractions, and potholes of life. I needed to buckle up and enjoy the glorious adventure. It took years of therapy to understand that God knew what He was doing and was always at work doing it.

The familiar words from The Lord's Prayer, *"Give us this our daily bread"* took on a whole new meaning. We were designed to live our lives one day at a time, trusting Him to give us what we need for the day; especially our daily measure of grace. I didn't need convincing, like so many do, that we have an enemy of our soul and he is a dirty rotten thief; always trying to steal our dignity and crumble our defenses with his wicked ways and lies.

> *Lord, I thank You that Your Word, the Bible is a beautiful roadmap for our lives, if only we take precious time to read it, study it, and hide it in our heart. I'm sorry I got such a late start in really digging deep. Your Word is a powerful weapon against Satan and his demonic army. It took too many years until I paused and prayed daily to put on the armor of God. I now know prayer is the most powerful weapon of all. I have learned through Your teachings I can overcome evil by the blood of the lamb, Jesus, and the word of my testimony.*
>
> *Lord, as I continue to reflect, I am reminded of the Bible story where You went into the temple, so angry, turning over the tables of the moneychangers who used Your house for reasons other than prayer. That is what You did for me Jesus. You were angry at those who victimized me and You overturned and drove out my fears, worries, shame, disgrace, and humiliation, and made me a vessel of honor. You have known the worst, but always sought to give me the best.*
>
> *I am so thankful that You helped me shine for You in these last days. You helped me be a good example, even in the midst of suffering. You have shown me that if I have a willing spirit, I can still be used even when I am physically down. I love You more each day and suspect we will meet face to face very soon.*

When I opened my eyes each day, the first thing I'd see were the messages of encouragement in the cards people sent me on display. Penny strung them up all around my room like a garland of love decorating my life. She also hung butterflies on fishing wire from the ceiling—an army of them in yellow, blue, purple, and pink, with sheer, gauzy wings. When the heater fan kicked on, they came alive

CHAPTER 56 ~ Reflections

and flitted around, a reminder of new beginnings—creatures of beauty that were once bound by a tightly wrapped cocoon.

Just like me. Bound up in my sin, my depression, my self-injury, my suicidal thoughts, and my hopelessness.

Then, by faith, I made the leap into eternity by inviting God into my mess. Into my brokenness. Into my sin-stained madness. Suddenly, everything changed! Bit by bit, I worked my way out of my self-imposed cocoon until one day—I felt a new me emerging. Just like a butterfly.

My body may have been grounded, but my spirit flew high. Freedom was available for me all along. I just didn't believe I was worthy enough. What a lie! The cross at Calvary declared that I am worth it! If only I had trusted sooner.

Father, forgive me for all the times I doubted you. I know you are always at work, busy putting the pieces of my life into place to be revealed at just the right time. As long as I have a breath left in me, I will declare you as King of Kings and Lord of Lords, the Author and Finisher of my faith. I pray the darkness of my past can light someone's future. May it be so in Jesus' name.

Epilogue

*Jesus said to her, "I am the resurrection and the life.
The one who believes in me will live, even though they die."*
John 11:25

Alice Iris Fisher's prayer was answered on December 31st when she passed into glory, dying peacefully in her sleep, surrounded by her precious pets, Oreo and Twee.

Several weeks have now passed, but I remember that day so clearly. It was almost midnight when Penny phoned me. I thought she called to wish me a Happy New Year as the clock was about to strike midnight in a few minutes. The first thing I heard was Penny's sobs on the line and immediately knew my best friend was in the arms of Jesus.

Alice fought valiantly and courageously to the very end. Those of us who stood by her bedside in vigil did not expect that day to be the day. Her condition didn't seem to have worsened. In fact, she was rather perky. She smiled and laughed with a calm demeanor, not agitated as she sometimes behaved. When I left her earlier that evening, there wasn't anything to be alarmed about. When Teddy and I were about to leave, she asked me to get her an Oreo cookie. My last words to her were, "I love you and don't choke on that cookie."

I was thankful that Penny sat in the recliner next to her bed, waiting for the ball to drop to usher in the New Year on TV when Alice slipped into the Lord's arms. Teddy and I arrived at the house as soon as she called and were greeted by Pastor Jack and the Masons, Alice's wonderful neighbors. An almost tangible peace permeated the atmosphere of the room where she lay. Our spirits sensed a sweet serenity, perfectly reflected in the expression on Alice's face. Oreo and Twee snuggled dutifully by her side as we prayed and thanked God for the remarkable individual who had

CHAPTER 57 ~ Epilogue

taken up a permanent place of residence in our hearts. It was a joy to know her and, in time, I knew I would be able to celebrate the depth of that joy.

Penny and I carried out Alice's requests, just as she desired. She had chosen to be cremated, but before that took place, there was one more gift she'd left to the world. Alice unselfishly donated her brain and spinal cord to further ALS research and help find a cure to the dreadful disease.

I believe that death is only the intermission that precedes the main and glorious act of our lives. In Christ, the rest of the story has no ending. There is no final curtain that will come down. Death is not the final act, but the beginning of realized hope and a reward far greater than the applause of man.

Alice is home. She truly did have a "happily ever after."

She requested that I scatter her ashes in a beautiful flower garden. "Where?" I asked.

She smiled and said, "Look for the butterflies."

I found the butterflies, Alice.
Rest in His arms, my friend.
Grace

In Alice's Own Words

In Alice's Own Words *are selections from readings shared at her Life Celebration Service. It was Alice's wish that her story give all the glory to God and point readers to the love of her life and Savior of her soul, Jesus Christ.*

ON GOD'S LOVE
God says in Psalms 147:11: *"The LORD delights in those who fear him, who put their hope in his unfailing love."*

> **Alice prayed:** Thank You, Lord, for Your love for me, every moment of every day. Thank You for reminding me that nothing can separate me from Your love. Even my weaknesses and failures cannot separate me from You and Your great love. How awesome that is! Thank You for Your everlasting love and that You have never stopped loving me and You never will.

God says in Romans 8:38-39: *"For I am convinced that neither death nor life, neither angels nor demons, neither the present nor the future, nor any powers, neither height nor depth, nor anything else in all creation, will be able to separate us from the love of God that is in Christ Jesus our Lord."*

> **Alice prayed:** Lord Jesus, I do need Your help. My trials are too big for me to handle alone. I am so glad You care for me, love me, and that You promise You will never forsake me. Thank You that I am Yours no matter what and that I will always be Yours. You never let go of my hand.

God says in Psalms 139:1-12: *"You have searched me, Lord*
 and you know me.
You know when I sit and when I rise;
 you perceive my thoughts from afar.
You discern my going out and my lying down;
 you are familiar with all my ways.

CHAPTER 58 ~ In Alice's Own Words

Before a word is on my tongue
   you, Lord, know it completely.
You hem me in behind and before,
   and you lay your hand upon me.
Such knowledge is too wonderful for me,
   too lofty for me to attain.
Where can I go from your Spirit?
   Where can I flee from your presence?
If I go up to the heavens, you are there;
   if I make my bed in the depths, you are there.
If I rise on the wings of the dawn,
   if I settle on the far side of the sea,
Even there your hand will guide me,
   your right hand will hold me fast;
If I say, "Surely the darkness will hide me
   and the light become night around me,"
Even the darkness will not be dark to you;
   the night will shine like the day,
   for darkness is as light to you.

Alice prays: Lord, Your love wraps around me like a warm fuzzy blanket. I sense Your overwhelming love for me. I will read these verses again and rejoice that You know me and are with me, I can rest in that truth.

ON GOD'S WAYS

God says in Isaiah 55:8-9: *"For my thoughts are not your thoughts, neither are your ways my ways," declares the LORD. "As the heavens are higher than the earth, so are my ways higher than your ways and my thoughts than your thoughts."*

Alice Prayed: Lord, I know Your ways are better than mine and I do choose to trust You. Lord You know my fears, my struggles, my sorrows, and I lay them at your feet. Help me to leave them there. I wish for joy on this journey. One step at a time—even that seems hard right now! But I know You are with me, Lord! Where You lead me, I will follow even if it is somewhere I don't want to go. I'm trusting You because You know better than I do.

CHAPTER 58 ~ In Alice's Own Words

God says in Jeremiah 29:11: *"For I know the plans I have for you," declares the* LORD, *"plans to prosper you and not to harm you, plans to give you hope and a future."*

> **Alice prayed**: *Don't Worry, Be Happy!* That is the title of a song. Lord—help me make it my mantra, that I don't worry, but be happy in knowing You lead me in paths of righteousness. You know everything the future holds and will not disappoint.

God says in 2 Corinthians 4:16-18: *"Therefore we do not lose heart. Though outwardly we are wasting away, yet inwardly we are being renewed day by day. For our light and momentary troubles are achieving for us an eternal glory that far outweighs them all. So we fix our eyes not on what is seen, but on what is unseen, since what is seen is temporary, but what is unseen is eternal."*

> **Alice Prayed**: Depression is an all-consuming flood that sweeps you away and seems to carry you downstream so fast that you can't keep your head above the raging waters. Lord, You know I am hanging on, clinging to You during this storm. Help me to hang on even when the desire to let go is so strong. Be my ever-present help . . . every day, every hour, every minute. You are my Hope, my Light, and my Salvation.

ON GOD'S PEACE

God says in Psalms 42:1-3, 5: *"As the deer pants for streams of water, so my soul pants for you, my God. My soul thirsts for God, for the living God. When can I go and meet with God? My tears have been my food day and night, while people say to me all day long, "Where is your God?" Why, my soul, are so downcast? Why so disturbed within me? Put your hope in God, for I will yet praise him, my Savior and my God."*

> **Alice prayed**: Trust versus worry. Peace versus out of control. Oh God, let me give the reins over to You and let You be in the driver's seat because You know the road ahead—every hill, valley, twist, turn, pot hole, and You know how to navigate all of it. I trust You, Lord.

CHAPTER 58 ~ In Alice's Own Words

God says in Philippians 4:7: *"And the peace of God, which transcends all understanding, will guard your hearts and your minds in Christ Jesus."*

> **Alice prayed:** Thank You, Lord, for the difficult situations in my life so that I can learn of Your peace. Your peace will outweigh the difficult trials. Please fill me with Your peace—the peace that passes all understanding. Let me not be anxious about whatever is before me but let me treasure Your peace.

God says in John 14:27: *Jesus said, "Peace I leave with you; my peace I give you. I do not give to you as the world gives. Do not let your hearts be troubled and do not be afraid."*

> **Alice Noted:** God's peace is like a helicopter; it's not going to land unless the landing pad is clear. Our minds need to stop swirling around and our hearts need to be free from debris and clutter so God's peace can land.

A Personal Invitation to the Reader from Alice

If my faith journey has brought hope into your life and you would like to know that your final destination is Heaven, this invitation is for you. If you have already invited Jesus into your life as Savior and Lord, I would want you to dig deeper and live your life knowing He loves you unconditionally. This is a truth I didn't fully grasp until my final diagnosis.

When Jesus was asked by His disciples how we know the way to the Father, he answered, *"I am the way and the truth and the life. No one comes to the Father except through me."* John 14:6

The Bible, further states in Romans 10:9-10, *"if you declare with your mouth, Jesus is Lord, and believe in your heart that God raised him from the dead, you will be saved from the clutches of hell. For it is with your heart that you believe and are justified, and it is with your mouth that you profess your faith and are saved."*

> Going to Heaven is as simple as the ABC's.
> A. **Admit** you are a sinner. *"All have sinned and fall short of the glory of God."* (Romans 3:23
> B. **Believe** that Jesus died on the cross and rose again for your sins. *"Believe in the Lord Jesus Christ and you will be saved."* Acts 16:31

CHAPTER 58 ~ In Alice's Own Words

C. **Confess** your sins. *"If we confess our sins, He is faithful and just to forgive our sins."* 1John 1:9

If you are ready to make this profession of your faith, I invite you to pray the following prayer:

Heavenly Father,
I know that I am a sinner and that I cannot save myself. I have tried that, and it didn't work. I gratefully receive your gift of eternal life through my faith in You. I am ready to trust You as my Lord and Savior. Thank You, Jesus, for coming to earth. I believe You are the Son of God who died on the cross for my sins and rose on the third day. Thank You for forgiving my sins and giving me the gift of eternal life. I believe You are the way the truth and life. I invite You into my heart this day, to be my Savior. May I always live for You. Amen.

Part 4
REFLECTIONS

"Alice wanted her truth written so it might offer help and comfort to those who might need it."

Dr. G. Wallace, Ph.D.
Alice's Psychologist

In Part 4, individuals like me, whom you met in this book as part of Alice's true story, share thoughts about their interactions, experiences with, and views of Alice. It is like the old story of the elephant and the four blind men, each of whom described the elephant as the part they happened to be touching. Alice touched each of us in different ways. I knew more about her inner life than did her friends. But they knew more about other sides of her that I had no opportunity to observe and experience.

I am a retired clinical psychologist and spent over ten years and over 500 sessions of individual psychotherapy with Alice. To honor this remarkable human being, I will attempt to paint a bit of a picture, from my point of view, of what she bravely wrestled with, how she used her mind to survive, what psychotherapy was for her, and my experience of offering her help. Her personal history was extremely complex, as was her psychotherapy, and it would take a long book to describe it all in detail, so I will try to give a meaningful overview.

In her mid-twenties, Alice became severely depressed, made a suicide attempt, and spent weeks in a psychiatric hospital without much outpatient follow-up. Years later, she again spent time in a psychiatric hospital with little outpatient follow-up. She reported a history of childhood abuse, and it was determined that she had more than one "part" to her mind. She suffered with Multiple Personality Disorder, now renamed Dissociative Identity Disorder.

Alice grew unhappy in her job at that time and felt unsafe living near her childhood home where she'd endured so much trauma. She decided she needed a fresh start and moved to my area to take a new job. Soon, she had to enter a major psychiatric hospital, where she spent five weeks and received excellent care. Part of that care involved sessions with Susan, an art therapist, who was known to me. Upon discharge, Alice continued her art therapy on an outpatient basis and was referred to me, since I had experience with people who struggled with Dissociative Disorders.

In our first meeting, she was open and cooperative, yet moderately anxious and showed signs of depression, though not suicidal. There was no sign of psychosis, and she was clearly of above average intelligence. I could tell she was uncomfortable seeing a male therapist, but since she had been specifically referred to me by Susan, her female art therapist, she was willing to endure me.

Alice reported a history of childhood abuse within her family, and amnesias about many things. Fragmentary childhood memories suddenly came to her and in our first session she reported finding objects in her vagina, with no knowledge of how they got there. She recalled that objects were often placed inside her during childhood abuse, and that sometimes she herself would place them there to hurt those who would rape her.

At the end of our first session she chose to continue to see me for psychotherapy. This was to be a therapy trial to determine if she was comfortable working with me. If not, we would find another therapist with whom she could be comfortable. The right relationship was critical to her benefitting from therapy.

Over time, she decided to continue her therapy with me twice a week, and see Susan, her art therapist, on a weekly basis. This arrangement was helpful to her progress with double support, two modes of therapy, and a relationship with both a male and a female.

Susan and I had phone contact on a weekly basis, with Alice's permission, and were always on the same wavelength regarding what was going on in Alice's therapy and our mutual approaches. We enjoyed a rare synergy, unlike anything I had ever experienced prior in my profession, much to Alice's advantage. Given the nature of the abuse that Alice described over time, the collaboration helped us deal with our personal emotions in light of the unspeakable horrors in her story.

I divided Alice's psychotherapy into two time frames. She saw me over a seven and one-half year period, for a total of over 400 sessions before she terminated therapy with me, by mutual agreement. She had done so well. We worked through the memories of her childhood, gradually integrated all of her 21 separate parts into one mind and celebrated as she took off 70 pounds. She felt ready to live her life, and I agreed.

However, after almost four years, she returned to therapy due to a traumatic incident from medical error when she had bariatric surgery for her ongoing weight challenges and began to dissociate again. Additional medical problems and stress at work exacerbated her troubles. I continued to see her once a week, for two and one-half years and one hundred sessions. At that point I delivered the painful news that I would be retiring from practice. Though the news upset her, she accepted it with grace and class and wished me well in my retirement. She continued to see Susan, who occasionally updated me on Alice's progress.

Alice's abuse in her home began around age three or four. Her mother did not seem to be an active abuser, although she did say things that got Alice in trouble with her father. I thought her mother to be a passive, virtual non-person; timid, overwhelmed, and either a childhood abuse survivor herself or had been so abused by her husband that she was practically non-functional. She made no attempt to protect Alice and knew that severe abuse occurred since the father made no secret of his actions.

His emotional abuse of Alice was severe, verbally assaulting her with names like ugly, retard, and worthless. He beat her and made her do things like lick the kitchen floor with her tongue if he didn't think she had cleaned it properly. Sometimes he made her eat feces as a punishment and put tape over her mouth so she couldn't spit it out. He killed family pets in her presence and raped her vaginally, orally, and anally, and required her to perform oral sex upon him. He inserted objects into her vagina and anus.

As the years passed, her brother abused her in many of the same ways. It was not clear to what extent the father abused his son, but the boy knew what happened within his family and followed his father's lead. It was also unclear as to the extent of abuse Alice's sister endured. She may have been dissociative herself. The sister chose to not pursue psychological help and claimed to not remember much of her childhood.

But the abuse that Alice reported goes even further. As a young teenager she became pregnant twice, probably from the father, but given the amount of sexual abuse that was going on it would be hard to tell. Her father participated in a local cult with a Satanic orientation. Sometimes these cult meetings occurred in the woods, other times in the basement of the home, where Alice was publicly abused in varied ways. Other children were also abused, and Alice witnessed at least one of them being killed. Worst of all, Alice also birthed an infant, whom she was forced to kill by knife in the presence of the cult members. She had given names to these infants. Her sadness and shame at participation in the act was profound.

The above description of the father raises the issue of what he was exactly. One could accurately call him a sadistic sociopath, a person without any sense of shame or guilt. It would be hard to know if he was just born that way, or whether he himself had been a victim of profound child abuse. Most people who have been abused do not go on to abuse others, but the research indicates that among those who do abuse, most have been abused themselves. This description of the father seems sterile and clinical, yet from Alice's perspective, she was living with a monster. Her brother became another monster, and the members of the cult were monsters, too.

Alice's history was one of the two worst personal histories I had heard in treating many hundreds of clients in my career. Many people reading her history might find it too terrible to believe. Perhaps she was psychotic and delusional. Perhaps she just had an over-active imagination. Perhaps she was just conjuring all this up to get attention. Surely no one could believe that such things could really happen.

My experience as a psychologist over the decades proves to me that people do unspeakable, horrible things to other human beings. I have no reason to doubt Alice's story, any more than I would doubt the stories of other clients I have worked with. She possessed all the symptoms of a person profoundly traumatized—anxiety, depression, severe and irrational shame, suicidal behavior, bodily self-harm, eating disorders, bodily elimination fears, fear of sexuality, and flashbacks.

Given the problems she had in living daily life, her psychological symptoms, and the way she presented herself in therapy with me, the whole picture and story made psychological sense. My worldview is pretty simple: People experience life on a continuum. Some people live incredibly blessed lives with little or no trauma. Most of us are pretty much in the middle, some good things happen and some bad things. Others are profoundly unfortunate and experience massive amounts of horrendous things, which sometimes kill them.

For those who still tend to doubt that such horrible things could befall someone, I suggest a read through a world history book to learn what some human beings have done to other human beings *in public* over the last 10,000 years of civilization. Then consider why such similar atrocities couldn't happen in private. In fact, given current events, a world history book isn't even necessary to realize what some people are capable of doing. Just read a newspaper.

How She Coped

Dissociative Identity Disorder (DID) is a psychiatric diagnosis that describes a particular way of coping with extreme, chronic trauma that starts in childhood. It can be seen as a form of Post-Traumatic Stress Disorder, well known in our culture due to military personnel who developed it in war, and to the increasing awareness of the number of women who have been physically and sexually assaulted.

DID develops in early childhood, almost always prior to the age of ten. Children who develop DID somehow stumble onto the psychological defense mechanism which leaves them with multiple identities. When being abused, they manage to create a special ego-state (personality state or alter) which experiences the abuse. The end result is that the rest of the mind doesn't feel that the abuse happened to it but happened to someone else.

The second aspect of DID is that amnesias are created, wherein much or the entire remaining mind no longer remembers what happened. In this sense, DID is a double coping strategy—it didn't happen to me, and also it didn't even happen (that is, can't be recalled).

The two most famous cases of DID in our culture were described in the books *Sybil* and *The Three Faces of Eve*. Each of these cases became well-known, and movies were made about them. However, they were highly atypical in that the two individuals in the stories were quite dramatic in their personal styles. Research has shown that over 95% of people with DID are quiet and reserved in their everyday manner. For them, DID is a disorder of hiddenness—hidden from others, and in many ways, from themselves.

The various parts of the mind which develop as a result of trauma have been called alters, personalities, parts, ego-states, resources, among others. Each serves a purpose.

For example, some parts may hold the knowledge and experience of specific forms of abuse, for example, emotional, physical, or sexual. Other parts may be the reservoir of specific emotions, such as anger, terror, depression, shame, and sometimes even hope and optimism. Others may be relatively unemotional, just holding the memories without any emotion about them. The average person with DID has about ten parts, but the number can range from just one or two to dozens.

Some parts are complicated and can serve a range of functions. These are the ones that most resemble a whole person. Others can be limited, for example, just holding one specific memory. The ages of parts can range from infantile states to someone very old, even older than the biological age of the person themselves. About half of persons with DID have at least one opposite sex part. Alice had several. For example, a female might create a male part to somehow make themselves feel stronger, or less sexually vulnerable, or to represent the hope that if they had been male, they might have been loved. Alice had 21 separate alters.

The presence of all these parts could certainly lead to a confusing pattern of behavior. A part might "take over" control of the body and act in ways dramatically different from the person's usual style. The person might appear extremely angry, or sad, or fearful or ashamed. Some parts may never take over control of the body, but just exert inner influences upon the other alters. Each part may know about all, some, or none of the other parts, depending upon the inner amnesias.

Inner relationships can develop. For example, the child alters may be in one location in the mind. An extremely angry alter might be quite alone and isolated. Some alters may protect other alters. Others may abuse different alters, resulting in internal civil wars. It can begin to look like an extremely cooperative inner family, or an extremely dysfunctional inner family, or indeed, both.

The above description just skims the surface of the amount of inner complexity that a person with DID possesses and experiences. But one must be aware that the overall goal of their complex inner life is to endure and survive, even though it may not seem that way.

There are no "bad parts." A deep understanding of each part leads to an appreciation that they each have a function to help with physical and emotional survival.

People with DID are not as different from ourselves as one might think. In a real sense, we are all multiple. We are in different ego-states over time as we go about living our everyday lives. We are in different ego-states, or frame of mind, when we are at work, with a child, with a spouse, when giving a speech, when praying, or at a party. Our thoughts, behaviors, and emotions are quite different from situation to situation.

But we have something that people with DID cannot afford to have—continuity of identity. No matter what we do or feel, we usually own it all as "me." *Yes, I did that, and that, and then that.* And we also have something else that people with DID cannot afford to have—continuity of memory. We mostly remember all of what we have done and experienced.

People with DID are not crazy, even though their behavior and emotions can be intense and strange at times. The structure of their minds is driven by profound and chronic trauma during early childhood, and it's important to recognize and respect their tremendous accomplishment of survival. Many have quarreled with the name Dissociative Identity "Disorder," and prefer to call it a "response" instead. The thought is that a disorder minimizes the creativity and resourcefulness of the individual.

A common question should be addressed at this point: *Why didn't Alice just tell someone outside the family what was going on?*

People who hear a story like Alice's from a safe, adult, non-abused point of view, are often prone to ask that question. As humans, we are wired to be attached to our parents, just as little ducklings follow their mothers around on land or in the water. Alice wanted to see her parents as good and loving, no matter what. She was also outwardly brain-washed to think and feel that she was bad, that if something hurt, it was her fault and she deserved it. She was shamed into great depths. In fact, even if she had not been overtly shamed by her parents, she would have, and did, shame herself. This was her way to maintain an attachment to her parents whom she desired to see as good.

Alice lived in terror on a daily basis. She saw animals and pets brutally killed. She witnessed people murdered. She knew her own life was not guaranteed. She wouldn't take the risk of telling anybody what was really going on.

Alice's Psychotherapy

Psychotherapy with Alice was both terrifying and necessary. For whatever and unknowable reason, Alice possessed a high level of innate resilience—perhaps her innate nature or her soul. Her strong will and determination drove her to get well and live her own life unpolluted or determined by her past.

For Alice, or any other person with DID, psychotherapy was a terrifying thing. It required trust in another human being. For Alice, this was hard since her own family had failed her so miserably. I would act warm and kind to her, but would she take the risk to open up to me, and to herself, when she feared, if not expected, that I would betray her at any moment?

To continue therapy, session by session, was to face that fear once or twice a week for years. It took her that long to, gradually, not be terrified of her own therapist.

Another source of terror Alice lived with was the thought of telling somebody outside the family what she lived through. Throughout her childhood, it was made clear that to speak of what went on in the family was to invite death. Younger parts of her believed that her father knew everything at all times, and that he would somehow know if she told.

Facing the horror of her memories, locked away in the depths of her mind, terrorized her too. At some level, her overall mind knew that great pain lay buried deep within. To face the horrors of what she had experienced, seen with her eyes, and was forced to do, caused her torment. A terrible memory could surface in her awareness at any time. As she discussed her life with me in therapy, flashbacks were likely. Something that happened in her everyday life might trigger a memory, or a memory might surface for no known reason at all. This source of terror caused her much fear. Certain memories rose up in her consciousness, and her general sense of shame would magnify to an unbearable level.

Despite all her fears of therapy, she persisted, and attended over 500 sessions of individual therapy with me alone, and hundreds more with her art therapist. Often, with great hesitancy, she bravely chose to endure fear and let some part of her mind take over her body and talk to me directly, telling its story.

Earlier in her life she chose to stay in school, complete high school, get a college degree, and get a job working with young people. That she was able to complete this level of schooling, given her background, defies explanation. Alice made many quality choices:

- She chose to make friends and attend church.

- She chose to attend therapy with her art therapist and endure the terror of opening up her secrets with yet another person.
- She chose to take risks and change jobs, several times.
- She chose to exercise and try to control her weight.
- She chose to have bariatric surgery when her attempts to lose weight did not work satisfactorily.
- She and others in her mind chose to write me Christmas and birthday cards full of profound thanks for my help.
- She chose to laugh with me from time to time when something funny happened.

Alice's faith was important to her, but she chose to continue in therapy with me knowing that I am not a religious person. It didn't bother her, and she didn't hold it against me. Over time she chose to let my respect and care for her into her heart and help wash away layers of shame. After seven and a half years, she experienced a tremendous amount of healing with no evidence of inner dividedness. She chose to stop therapy and go about living her life. Then, when she suffered medical trauma and fell apart again, she chose to return to therapy and pick up the pieces.

For Alice, therapy was about terror and courage.

On Being Alice's Therapist

The way I felt about and reacted to my relationship with Alice and my attempts to help her were complicated and often intense. It was a great responsibility to be in a deep, emotional relationship with someone who was so wounded, needy, and fragile. I listened more than usual and weighed the words I'd speak and when I'd speak them, carefully. I worked to wordlessly communicate that I took her seriously, did not judge her negatively, and cared about her welfare. I didn't want her to feel rushed in the process or think I had expectations for her to just "get over it." I wanted to hear her entire story, no matter how many years it took.

As interested as I was to help Alice heal from the traumas of her childhood, I had to be mindful that she was an adult with a life that included problems at work, problems in relationships with others, and, at times, serious health problems. We couldn't and didn't always talk about the past. Often the present took priority.

REFLECTIONS ~ Dr. G. Wallace, Ph. D.

As time passed and more horrendous details of her childhood were revealed, I had my own emotional responses to deal with: anger and disgust at her abusers, continual reminders that not everyone is good at some level, and great sadness over the things had happened to her.

Alice often felt suicidal, and a few times she made suicidal gestures, though not deadly attempts. I worried that if therapy failed or went awry, our whole endeavor could end in a final tragedy for her, as well as a personal and professional tragedy for me. Sometimes, I had to make decisions about whether to trust her positive outlook believing she would be okay, or whether to discern if she was too overwhelmed and needed a time of respite and stabilization in a hospital. Fortunately, my weekly conversations with her art therapist were helpful, as we bounced ideas off each other and gave each other emotional support. We felt less alone as we teamed up to help Alice.

Another aspect of Alice's background involved the presence of, not only noisy trauma, but quiet trauma. Noisy trauma might be defined as the horrible things that happen to a person. Quiet trauma is the absence of what should happen in a person's life—the presence of loving and protective parents and relatives, and the support of friends and others.

To the best of my knowledge, Alice had massive quiet trauma in her childhood and early adolescence. There was one teacher who, though supportive of Alice, had no idea of her real story. But that was about it.

Quiet trauma is as destructive as noisy trauma, if not more so. Quiet trauma leaves you alone, hopeless, and ashamed.

As therapy continued, I felt it a private honor and privilege to help such a kind and courageous human being. The experience humbled me. Even though I was the professional with all the supposed knowledge about trauma, and DID in particular, she was the person who chose to endure and survive. I don't think I would have had the courage and strength to survive what she experienced. I'll never know for sure, and maybe I underestimate myself, but I simply can't imagine it. In a way, I was in the strange position of trying to help someone stronger than I thought I was.

After I retired, I kept in touch with Susan, Alice's art therapist, to keep up with her progress. I did not keep in touch with Alice directly. That would be inappropriate according to professional ethics. Alice needed to make a complete transfer of all her therapy to her art therapist, without the ghost of me hanging around in the background.

I stepped outside that ethics box when Alice was diagnosed with ALS. The three of us, Alice, Susan, and I, met at a restaurant for lunch in a reunion of sorts. Amazingly, Alice was not depressed or tearful on the occasion. We had a pleasant lunch together.

Toward the end of our visit I turned to her and said, "Alice, with everything that has happened to you in your life, and now you face ALS, do you ever ask yourself, why me?"

Without hesitation she replied, "No. I just figure, why not me?"

That statement was pregnant with meaning for me. Alice moved beyond irrational shame. Beyond anger. She would no longer tell herself that she was bad and deserved punishment. She understood that bad things do happen to people through no fault of their own. Alice was not an angry person by nature, and she didn't rail against her fate. She was scared of her medical future and dreaded becoming a burden to her dear friends. Also, I believe she was sad to have her life cut short just as she had begun to live more fully than ever.

I saw her again when I was invited to her birthday party. Susan was ill and unable to attend. It was a Hawaiian themed party with many in costumes and a good time was had by all—especially Alice. I saw it as further affirmation that Alice knew she deserved a birthday party and to be surrounded by those who valued her. Friends are the family you choose.

Alice wanted her truth written in book form so it might offer help and comfort to those who need it. Those to whom bad things happen through no fault of their own—her life story as a gift to the world. But I would caution any reader to not compare themselves unfavorably to Alice and her determination and courage. Alice was a highly unusual person. If you think you can't quite measure up to her capacity for resilience, welcome to the club. Take whatever good thing you can glean from her story with a hopeful heart and encouragement to carry on.

Thank you, Alice, for all you have given to those of us who knew you, each in a special and different way.

Susan

Alice's Art Therapist

Alice entered the evaluation room with a downward gaze and poor eye contact. She was neatly dressed, soft spoken, appeared depressed, and reported difficulty with concentration on the job and "fuzzy feelings" in her head. Though she cordially responded to the intake questions without hesitation, it was what she didn't say that resonated with me when our meeting ended. The presence of "something else" within the interview room raised a red flag for me. Her initial drawing confirmed my suspicion. She sketched a head with wobbly eyes, tongue sticking out, and fingers that looked like guns pointed at the crown of the figure's head. She titled her drawing, "I'm so confused!" and denied suicidal ideation—though it seemed clear this was on her mind.

Alice seemed to lack words when it came to talking about the onset of symptoms leading to her recent hospitalization, but she did express an interest in art. I enrolled her in my art therapy group. Aware of her catastrophic despair, I noticed variances in her art renderings that were unusual. At times she seemed disconnected from the content of the many drawings she created. She rarely interacted with others in group and appeared guarded, disclosing little about herself during each session. Her creative gifts were quickly apparent though and gleaned attention from group members, which seemed to further shut her down.

Alice and I spoke about meeting individually in addition to group art therapy, which might allow me to gain a clearer diagnostic picture. During a full-scale art therapy evaluation consisting of six drawings, her artwork revealed a myriad of developmental stages, artistic variances and conflicting narratives that led me to consider a diagnosis of Dissociative Identity Disorder (DID)—formerly called Multiple Personality Disorder (MPD). I requested a psychiatric evaluation by an in-house psychiatrist who specialized in complex dissociation, and the diagnosis of DID was confirmed. This was no surprise to me as her art renderings suggested long standing underlying childhood trauma and dissociation.

Prior to her discharge, Alice and I set aside a lengthy individual session to review the artwork she had created throughout the hospital admission. There were numerous drawings reflecting the terror that she felt inside, along with disjointed human figures that were either floating on the page space or trapped. There was a paucity of color in many pictures, though others exploded with jarring colors and jagged edges. An array of heads was banded together in numerous drawings while on other pages a repetition of forms seemed to replicate the presence of a "group of many" within her head. She expressed shame, disgust, rage, and despair at the revelation of multiple selves. She was unwilling to corroborate the diagnosis, and yet didn't quite refute it.

Once discharged from the hospital, Alice returned to work and continued in outpatient therapy. She agreed to work with me and a team of providers including a psychiatrist and a psychologist, all of whom had extensive experience in treating complex trauma and dissociation.

The journey was excruciating at times, as we all met younger and older Alice–parts who independently offered vignettes of extreme abuse. Each held a fragment of Alice's personal narrative, some elements more jolting than others but all reflective of a life of horrific pain starting prior to the age of three. There were very young parts, latency age selves, adolescents, and adults, who described themselves as distinctly different from one another—many unaware that there was a system of selves within one body.

Amnestic elements are common in DID, as the burden of awareness prompts wishes for death in most individuals. The reality is too much to bear and therefore the core self disappears, protected by a system that trusts few yet longs to be safely embraced.

Alice's artwork exposed the darkest of these narratives, interspersed with occasional images illustrating the kindness she felt from a teacher or other "safe" adults in her life. Her past was shocking, at times painful to hear, even for a therapist. What she reportedly endured was unconscionable, yet she was capable of love. She often shared visual journal entries related to her church life and the comfort she received from several friends there. Her kittens were like children to her, and she often drew about them as well.

Most significantly though, was her willingness to trust the process with me and allow the parts within to come forward and reveal their memories through a vehicle that did not include talking or telling. Art bypassed the threats of former abusers who had warned her against sharing her experiences. The images stood on their own merit without words.

Despite the distinctive chatter in her head, Alice created a bridge that was acceptable to most parts within through her art. Her visual metaphors provided passage to a chaotic inner world that we spent years deciphering and working to piece together in peace. Throughout our work together, which lasted over a decade, Alice's images became her preferred way to chronicle her heinous story. She was a prolific artist and often worked on pictures independently between sessions to present them at our weekly meetings. She also kept written journals that became instrumental in decoding the images she created.

Alice was able to fully integrate prior to her death from a serious medical illness. In her later years she experienced much joy and accepted her fate, fearlessly willing to meet her Maker in Heaven.

I am grateful for all Alice taught me and that she allowed me to help her find her voice and guide her journey to wholeness through art. Through visual metaphor, she created, destroyed, and recreated her life—a reward for both of us. I am a better therapist as a result of our therapeutic relationship and ultimately, our friendship in the end.

Pastor Jack Charles

Alice's Pastor

I met Alice when she began to attend the church I pastor close to where she lived. She visited one day with a friend but chose to sit alone toward the back during Sunday morning service. I found her to be always pleasant, yet quiet, perhaps a little withdrawn, and easy to talk to if I initiated the conversation. Initially, we discussed news, sports, and weather types of things and did not venture into any deep conversations.

When Alice and I first met, she worked at a large industrial corporation and had done so for many years. She proved herself to be a faithful, hard worker, and valuable asset to the company, advancing her career through the years.

I observed her to be likeable and a safe person to those in need; a diligent worker at her responsibilities, not overly talkative, pleasant and kind to anyone she met.

As time progressed, I had the opportunity to know her more intimately when she sought counsel from me about troubled areas of her life. I had no idea, nor could I have imagined, what I would learn of her experiences. Alice was a survivor in the truest sense of the word. Regardless of the challenges, she overcame a tremendous amount of trial and suffering and could extend unlimited amounts of grace to others.

When we began deeper one-on-one discussions, I was stunned to learn of the years of horrific abuse she endured at the hands of those she trusted. It was inconceivable abuse that damaged her soul in unimaginable ways. As we explored her life, it was evident that she had much to process and work through, but she was persistent. Even though she had the right to be bitter and angry about her past, she did not seek revenge. She just wanted to heal and live her life. I remember being quietly amazed that, in spite of her difficult life experiences, she composed herself with extraordinary dignity and integrity. She thought about others more than herself.

She continued on her healing journey and connected with an incredible counseling situation that helped unwrap her past and lead her to find wholeness. It was a paradox that at the time she truly found her inner healing, her physical body began to break down. She ultimately received a diagnosis of ALS; commonly known as Lou Gehrig's disease.

Her soul and body had endured so much anguish that it finally started to shut down. Ironically, her spirit life and relationship with Christ deepened and grew stronger. Alice was never afraid to share her faith, which took on a far more profound meaning in her life. She was a woman of prayer, kind, generous, and giving to the very end. The more her disease worsened, the deeper her roots went down into Christ.

I visited Alice regularly at her home to encourage her, share communion, and pray, but found that it was she who always had something of value to share with me. In the throes of a dying body, I saw Alice allow the life of Christ to overcome any residue left of a broken life. Even though she never experienced physical healing, her heart and soul were restored daily.

Each time I visited her, in spite of all the necessary hospital equipment to keep her alive, she was at peace. She received constant comfort from her loving dog, Oreo. He was her delightful companion to the end and never wavered in his love, taking up residence on her bed. Her kindness and gentle touch had always reassured Oreo he was in a safe place with someone who loved him dearly. I witnessed the authentic love that Alice expressed towards others, both human and those of the furry variety. As her body began to deteriorate, Oreo's sense of being in proximity to her became stronger and stronger. It was beautiful to observe this devotion.

God's love, meaning, and purpose rooted deeper in her heart daily. She prayed fervently and, even as she became more helpless physically, she became a stronger advocate for other victims of the disease. Alice's strength grew from the inside out and it was miraculous to observe the process unfold.

Everyone, including Alice, knew that her time on earth was coming to an end. Even though there was great sadness, there was also a true peace and comfort present because of her strength and unwavering faith. There were many things to fear, but she found refuge in Christ and in the Word and filled her room with worship and praise music. Her house overflowed with friends and family who loved her and believed with her that she was stepping into eternity with her Savior.

I vividly remember the day I walked into her house and saw her lying in bed minutes after she passed into glory. I felt a tangible peace in the room. Not like the peace that the world gives, but the peace that only God can give. When we recognize that God judges us in a completely different way than the world does, we see and understand the things in life that truly matter. Alice lived that truth out, especially during the last season of her life.

Her death brought sadness to all those who loved her. Death brought the end of a beautiful restored life on this earth, but it is not the end for those who believe in Christ as their Savior. It is the beginning.

Alice looked forward to Heaven where there would be no more pain, sickness, or disease. The grace I saw and experienced through connection to her life and death greatly impacted me.

I had the honor of officiating at Alice's funeral—a joyous celebration of her life. Many friends and family comforted each other with rejoicing. We shared how Alice touched our lives and encouraged each other with stories of her trust in God through all her challenges. God redeemed the suffering of a soul named Alice, that multiplied into blessings for everyone fortunate enough to know her.

Katie

Close Family Friend

When looking at a piece of coal one might miss the treasure that lies within. Through time and pressure, a diamond emerges, and its brilliance is realized. So, too, at first glance, Alice, unassuming and quiet, might not have struck those around her with excitement and pizzazz. However, the beauty and treasure that authentically exuded from her were profound.

I met Alice through my best friend, Penny. She lived with Alice as her caregiver, so it was a natural intersection that our paths would cross as I came and went with my friend.

My birthday arrived shortly after we met. To my surprise, she made me a full-sized poster board filled with a witty birthday sentiment and sprinkled with various candy bars. The creative thoughtfulness of her gift to someone she had just met touched me. I learned that her thoughtful ways were far reaching and am convinced that only God knows the true impact of her generosity.

Alice always looked for ways to bless and give to others. It was not uncommon to mention in conversation something you saw in a store or an item you desired, only to have Alice bring it to you. When my youngest son, David, was two, he liked to put things in holes or hide things. One day, I shared that the two beaters for my electric mixer were missing. We laughed as we knew David probably hid them somewhere, and at some unforeseen time in the future, I'd find them in a random place. The next time I saw Alice, she presented me with a new mixer she "just happened" to find on her latest run to Walmart.

In the beginning, I thought she did those things for acceptance. While appreciated, I never wanted her to feel my acceptance of her hinged on gifts. But as I got to know Alice better, I realized her generosity, while often exhibited in store bought things, extended to her time, listening ear, wisdom and huge heart. Generous Alice was just Alice.

She was very gentle and had a smile that could light up a room. Her presence was very inviting—especially for children. Every time we came to visit, my two boys, David and Calvin, sat on Alice's lap and she read them the book, *Caps for Sale*. There was no shortage of laughter as the storyline flowed, telling of monkeys who stole caps from a peddler. She played memory games and, like a favorite aunt or grandma, always served snacks to enjoy. Alice had a way of making my daughter, Caroline, and my two sons feel welcomed and valued in her home.

After Alice was diagnosed with ALS, it wasn't long before she started walking with a cane and ultimately needed a power wheelchair for mobility. Even with each debilitating progression of the disease, Alice still wanted my kids to continue their visits. She never wanted them to be afraid of her disability or scared to interact with her. Even as Alice's ability to move decreased, Caroline, Calvin, and David loved to be with her. Because of the power wheelchair, we would go shopping, take trips to places like the aquarium or zoo, and even walk to the local park together. Near Alice's house was a nature reserve which was a favorite place to go and see wildlife, bugs, and butterflies. Alice, who was once a teacher, came to life as we explored, and the kids asked questions and showed her their findings. Because of her traumatic upbringing, she saw children as precious; to be cherished and loved. She treated my children that way and left a profound impression on them.

As a mother, I am deeply grateful for the investment Alice made in Calvin, David, and Caroline's lives. However, her love and generosity extended to me as well. In the last year of her life, my family was in a major transition. My husband had accepted a job in another state, so my kids and I had to wait to move until our house sold. I spent a lot of time at Alice's home while we waited. In the morning, after I dropped the kids at school, I dropped in on Alice and shared the reading of a daily devotional comprised of an inspirational passage along with Bible verses. Alice's heart of faith and unwavering commitment to Jesus was evident. While her body deteriorated, her heart glowed with life. We prayed, and her prayers were always focused on others. She was a faithful prayer warrior for her neighbors and friends.

REFLECTIONS ~ Katie

When Penny had places to go, or went away for vacation, I stayed with Alice. We joked that I was the second string! It was a privilege to be trusted enough to care for her.

While I attended to her physical needs, we shared great conversations. She told me about her college years, teaching, and traveling. I was in awe of Alice's self-awareness and her courage to contend for wholeness. She was a great listener with valuable insight and normally had a great attitude. But there were some days of discouragement. The reality of not being able to move was difficult. Her mind and heart were fully alive, yet her body was not able to function. Admirably, Alice did not stay in a place of discouragement long but always came back to a place of thanksgiving and praise.

I had a front row view of the transforming power of love through Alice's life in her final days. Alice learned how to receive through a lifetime of crucibles that produced blessing and treasured friendships. Alice never lost her giving spirit and enriched all who knew her. People from her church brought meals, read books to her, and stopped by just to visit. Home health aides, hospice workers, and other healthcare professionals ministered to Alice in a home of peace and joy in the midst of a terrible disease. Alice genuinely cared for anyone who crossed the threshold of her home and made it her mission to be a blessing to them. But what blessed me most was to see how Alice had learned to receive the care and love of others returned to her.

I am grateful for the years I knew Alice. Her story is of heroic proportion. She lived through a level of suffering no human should endure. Yet God's grace kept her alive and wove even the most painful episodes into a redeemed thread of beauty in her life.

I miss her smile and funny quips when we played games. I know she would be so proud of each of my kids. Each day I choose to be thankful for the time we had together and know, one day, I will see her again. Until then, I am reminded that God's grace is sufficient because Alice was living proof.

Penny
Alice's Caregiver

I called her Aunt Alice and knew her as an extremely generous woman with a giving heart. She gave of her time, money, resources, and herself to those around her with great pleasure and joy. Often, she'd do things anonymously because she never wanted the attention or the praise for her good deeds. She had a way of listening to a person's preferences and then surprise them with the desired thing mentioned—whether want or need—but never expected to receive.

After her initial ALS diagnosis, Alice came to grips with the need for additional help, and we brainstormed about her options. One day, in prayer, I asked the Lord for the best solution for Alice and clearly heard Him say, "Penny, why don't you do it?" Initially, I dismissed the thought as not being from the Lord. I served on staff at Victory Community Church and my plate was already full.

But then I felt a strong stirring in my heart, "Why not? What would be a greater privilege than serving Aunt Alice and taking care of her during this last season of her life?" I was the answer to our prayers! When I spoke to Alice about this, she agreed without reservation.

I moved in with Aunt Alice and assumed full responsibility for her care, in the full knowledge it would not be an easy task for either of us. However, I did not anticipate that the arrangement would become a mutual blessing for both of us and a time in my life that I wouldn't trade for anything. I'm grateful and honored that Alice allowed me to care for her in such a personal way. We lived through the struggles and victories, tears and laughter, bad days and good days, all of which revealed a beautiful display of God's sustaining grace in the process.

At first, Aunt Alice was very vocal about her independence and enlisted me to help her do what she wanted to do. Every day, if the weather was amenable, she wanted to ride her wheelchair around the town and get some fresh air. When she started to come home with bags from Walmart, almost four miles away, I gently let her know that I didn't think it was a good idea for her to travel the distance. She agreed but continued her Walmart runs anyway.

One day, my phone rang, and the caller ID said "Alice." I panicked as I answered. Alice's voice came on the line and told me not to worry. She was in her wheelchair and stuck in the sand on a trail at the local nature reserve. A rescue operation was in order!

Unfortunately, Alice wasn't very good with her right or left directions. She'd simply say "turn your way" or "turn my way." This wasn't useful as she tried to tell me how to get to where she was. I called the local police to help find her.

Meanwhile, the maintenance man at the nature reserve looked for her on his golf cart. When we finally found her, the men helped hoist her and her 500 lb. wheelchair back onto the path. She just sat there as happy as a clam and commented that maybe she should stick to the path. That was Aunt Alice—always an adventurer!

Soon after that little episode, she fell again and lost the mobility in her legs—a devastating blow to her independence. She would be confined to her hospital bed and needed someone's help with everything. This was a game-changer for Aunt Alice, not just affecting her physically, but mentally, and emotionally as well. She was no longer able to use the bedside commode for toileting or a sponge bath. Overnight, she went from going to the bathroom independently to diapers. Although we knew that would eventually happen, it proved difficult for us to navigate when the day came upon us. But we worked through the new challenge together.

As Alice's caregiver, I desired to maintain her dignity in the daily work of changing diapers, dealing with rashes, cleaning up accidents and giving bird baths. I discovered how to approach these intimate things and allow her to feel valued and cared for as opposed to feeling like an inanimate object. I didn't always get it right.

Sometimes tired or frustrated, I'd just go through the motions. At first, Aunt Alice didn't comment. In time, she voiced her concern that she didn't feel like she was being treated with respect. Once, while Katie helped me with her, she told us to stop treating her like a piece of meat! We apologized that we rushed to get her changed into comfortable pajamas and into bed after a long day shopping.

Not long after she was bed ridden, we decided it was time to make the transition to hospice care. I always thought of hospice in a negative way. To me it meant, "Let's just keep her comfortable because death is just around the corner." Hospice didn't appeal to Aunt Alice either, but we both saw the benefits outweighed the stigmas.

With hospice came a home health aide five days a week, a nurse two days a week, a licensed reflexologist who gave her a foot massage weekly, all supplies and medication delivered to the house, very useful and practical equipment, and 24/7 access to a hospice nurse. It was like we hit the jackpot with the specialized things that she needed to continue living, as opposed to dying. It was a huge benefit to have someone help with her baths and get her dressed during the week. Aunt Alice's hospice team quickly became like family to us for the eighteen months she received their services. It certainly changed my perspective of hospice care, emphasis on *care*.

One useful and practical piece of equipment we had access to was a Hoyer lift—an assistive device that uses hydraulic power to transfer someone from the bed to a chair or wheelchair. It was a life-saver for us because it allowed Aunt Alice to gain some independence by using her wheelchair. She was so happy and overjoyed to be on the streets of our neighborhood again.

But the streets weren't enough for her. She wanted to go shopping and attend local ALS meetings. Renting a handicapped accessible van was expensive. We were blessed to learn that someone anonymously donated a used, serviceable handicapped van to our church. We rejoiced at the goodness of the Lord—a clear answer to prayer. Aunt Alice could hardly contain her excitement; was on board and ready to roll, so to speak!

Aunt Alice suffered many losses during her battle with ALS that we grieved along the way. When she lost the use of her legs, she could no longer get up on her own, use the bathroom, take a shower or walk. Weakness and loss of movement in her arms and hands meant she could not answer email, text, touch base with friends on Facebook, surf the web, or play Candy Crush—her favorite. I was happy to help her with any of these things, but it wasn't the same.

Soon it became too tiring to even focus on or to read social media or emails. And she couldn't feed herself anymore; another big bridge that we had to cross. I learned to feed her when she was hungry, to help her drink when thirsty, put medicine in her mouth so she could swallow it, help blow her nose, and more.

As a caregiver, I tried to anticipate her needs to save her from asking. I worried she'd interpret my actions as dictating to her what she wanted and didn't want.

Breathing, for an ALS patient, moves from an involuntary action that you don't ever think about to something that you are consciously aware of all the time.

Aunt Alice's fear of suffocation came because she couldn't breathe sometimes. The majority of ALS patients die because of carbon monoxide poisoning built up in the lungs because the lungs lose the muscle capacity to inhale and exhale. Early on, she used a BiPAP machine at night while she slept. The BiPAP pushed air into her lungs and then helped to suck the poisonous carbon monoxide air out. As time went on, she needed the BiPAP during the day at different times when she felt like she couldn't catch her breath. Shortly after I started to care for her, she needed her BiPAP machine 24/7 as her lung muscles began to deteriorate.

On several occasions, her face mask came loose, or the machine malfunctioned and caused Aunt Alice much anxiety. At night, I heard her voice shout my name from the baby monitor next to my bed. I ran into her room and re-sealed the mask so she could breathe again. Sometimes it was difficult for her to fall back to sleep for fear it would happen again. I'd spend the rest of the night in the recliner chair next to her bed, so she would know she was not alone. These were scary moments for us, but we were grateful for the BiPAP lifesaver machine.

With the ownership of a van at our disposal, Aunt Alice wanted to go shopping on a whim which became a big contention between us. There was a lot of preparation involved in a trip to the store or anywhere, for that matter. Not only did it take about two hours to get her bathed and dressed and in her chair, but it took an hour to get her out of her chair, changed, and in bed upon our return. The battery for her portable BiPAP machine needed to be charged and ready to help her breathe while we shopped. We had to plan the event. It could not be a spontaneous action.

Because Aunt Alice's safety was of utmost importance, I wasn't willing to risk going out if she didn't feel well, have the proper rest, or if the weather wasn't cooperative. There were times that I had to say "no" and she didn't like that at all. It was always a delicate balance for us to come to an understanding. I wasn't trying to tell her what she could and couldn't do, but that I was concerned for her health and safety. Each episode reminded Aunt Alice of her loss of independence and freedom, which up to this point had never been challenged.

These moments reminded me of how someone with ALS is a person with thoughts, feelings, desires, and people still able to make their own choices. It is easy to compartmentalize the physical/medical aspect of caregiving and to attend to needs in a clinical way. However, a singular care level does not take into account how the deadly disease affects the person mentally, emotionally, and spiritually. Soul-care was harder to manage than physical care, which is why we were grateful to have a wonderful support system through hospice, the Greater Philadelphia ALS Chapter, friends, family, our church, and neighbors.

Aunt Alice had amazing support from the ALS chapter with comprehensive help to manage her physical, mental, and emotional needs. It was important for her to connect to others who also suffered from ALS. We made it a priority to attend the monthly ALS support group. The meetings were bittersweet for both of us. It was helpful to share and discuss different ALS challenges with others who understood yet disheartening to see the decline in those on the same journey. It sobered me to know that I sat across from ALS patients who would not be around in five years—maybe not even for the next meeting.

Usually, I tried to go shopping after the meetings to help take our minds and hearts off the stark reality of the situation. Aunt Alice and I grew close to several ALS families and stayed in contact, even after she wasn't strong enough to attend the meetings anymore.

Although her body grew weaker, her mind and spirit grew stronger. Knowing Aunt Alice's history with Dissociative Identity Disorder (DID) and her incredible and courageous journey to become integrated, it astonished me to witness how she finally became mentally and emotionally whole even as her body broke down. It didn't seem fair that after a remarkable victory in a difficult fight, she immediately catapulted into another devastating situation. Only her strong faith allowed her to surrender and embrace the next season ahead of her. I watched her respond to her situation with grace. She never questioned God, but accepted everything, in the knowledge that God always had a purpose and plan and didn't want her to suffer.

Although ALS dramatically speeds up the process of death, Aunt Alice chose to see this last season of her life as a "LIFE sentence," not a "death sentence." As a result, I was careful about the people, things, and influences I allowed into our home. I wanted her to be surrounded by those who loved and encouraged her—not those who would deny the truth of the situation. People who would help bring faith, hope, and positivity to her days.

I was also mindful about what we watched on TV or what kind of audiobooks we listened to. We were both sensitive to the reality of her impending death and didn't need to focus on doom and gloom when we had a choice.

Because it was never easy for Aunt Alice to make friends or trust others, she was more comfortable to give of herself than receive. The irony is that, in the last years of her life, she was able to experience the beauty of receiving an overwhelming outpouring of love from Victory Community Church, friends, neighbors, and countless others, without being able to do anything in return.

Many invaluable people were part of Aunt Alice's "life" support. They brought meals, sat by her bedside, held her hand and talked with her, stayed with her so I could go grocery shopping or have coffee with a friend, gave her massages, volunteered to read to her, helped with chores around the house, sent cards with words of encouragement, cried and laughed with us, did daily devotions and prayed with us, and most importantly, they just loved Aunt Alice unconditionally.

Caregiving is not for the faint of heart and it certainly is a 24/7 job. It is physically, mentally, and emotionally demanding. Every day is a different day with new challenges and responsibility to manage schedules, medications, visitors, meetings, doctors' appointments, and unexpected things along the way. There were many months I slept in her room on an air mattress because she was afraid and didn't want to be alone. Every night I set my alarm for 2:00 a.m. to give her medication. It was tiring and required me to be attentive and alert—and I'd do it all over again. I count it as one of my greatest joys that Aunt Alice allowed me to care for her so intimately. We both considered it precious shared time.

Although some patients with ALS lose their ability to speak, Aunt Alice never experienced this which allowed her to verbally communicate until the very end. She and I had an open-door policy that allowed us to honestly discuss anything freely without judgment or defense.

There was no topic off limits, and I appreciated some of the rich and insightful discussions we had. She was just as concerned for how caretaking took its toll on me, as I was concerned about how the disease affected her. Aunt Alice was a wonderful storyteller and I wanted to listen to all that she had to say. As time went on, her voice grew weaker and speaking became more tiring for her. We learned to appreciate these times of quietness and silence. We understood that you can still communicate without using any words.

Oreo and Twee were great comfort companions for Aunt Alice. They each had their spot on the bed next to her and wouldn't leave her side. You could hear Twee purring from down the hall and, because Oreo didn't want to be left out, he started his own form of purring. It was a hard day when Oreo could no longer sleep with her because he was too heavy for her to move when he snuggled on her legs. He became my furry companion at bedtime but couldn't wait until the morning when he jumped on the bed and smothered Aunt Alice with kisses. Both Twee and Oreo loved when company came because they got extra attention and love. Aunt Alice loved her furry companions and they loved her.

There were many days I thought it would be Aunt Alice's last, and I called those close to us to prepare them. Then she would surprise us and miraculously get better. It was confounding to all of us, even the hospice nurses. Every night before bed, when I prayed with her, we talked through the events of the day and made sure we made things right with one another if there were disagreements or hurts. We both knew that it might possibly be her last night. It was important to us that we maintained a sense of peace in our hearts and toward one another.

When "moving day" finally came, it surprised me because Aunt Alice was having a good day. There was nothing in her demeanor or even her physical state that gave any indication that the end was near. I had plans to meet Katie for coffee that afternoon, so our neighbors, the Masons, came over to stay with her. When I left, everything seemed in order. I gave Aunt Alice a hug and told her I loved her, and she replied in kind. I had no idea that this would be her last day or I never would have gone out.

Since it was New Year's Eve, my parents and Katie, her husband, and crew were coming over for a light dinner and prayers for the

New Year. I checked in with the Masons and, since Aunt Alice was having a good day, I did a little grocery shopping before going home.

Although Aunt Alice seemed weak and didn't have much of an appetite, she seemed very with it as we enjoyed our dinner. After clean up, we put on glitzy beaded necklaces and paper New Year's hats—a tiara for Aunt Alice. We crowned her Princess Braveheart. We enjoyed a beautiful time of prayer and lively discussion about what we wanted to change in the New Year, as well thoughts on where we might like to travel. She listened intently to the conversations and contributed by telling us all the things she was anticipating once she moved and was a resident of Heaven. We laughed when she asked, "Do you think the zip code in heaven is 77777?"

Unbeknownst to us, that was to be our last big laugh together as a family.

Mom and Katie helped me get Aunt Alice ready for bed before everyone left for home. Mom asked Aunt Alice if there was anything else she could do for her and, surprisingly, she asked her for an Oreo cookie. I wondered why she didn't ask me. Maybe she thought Mom was an easy target when it came to cookies and chocolate.

Once everyone left and it was quiet, Aunt Alice settled down peacefully, although her breathing was shallow. The machine worked extra hard. Just after 11:00 p.m., as I watched the news before the midnight ball drop, I noticed that her breathing slowed down considerably. I kept a watchful eye on her, checking all the equipment and noticed her breathing continued to be very shallow. I called Lori, a neighbor, friend, and registered nurse, and she rushed over. Once she arrived, everything happened in a hazy slow motion. Lori affirmed that Aunt Alice was no longer breathing, but that she still had a strong heartbeat. I called 9-1-1, and then my parents, and my friend Katie to alert them to the fact that the end was in sight and to please pray while they dressed and drove back to the house.

They arrived at the house with two police cars and an ambulance parked out front. Minutes before, Harvey and Julianne Mason, and Pastor Jack arrived, to add their love and support. As Mom, Dad, and Katie walked in, I calmly asked the EMT responders if there was anything else they could do for Aunt Alice in light of her Do Not Resuscitate order. They said "no." As they left, I thanked them for responding so quickly.

All of us gathered around Aunt Alice for a beautiful heavenly send off. We spoke words of encouragement to her and hoped the words would break through to her spirit if she could no longer hear us. We sang over her and prayed until her heart stopped beating. It was one of the most peaceful times that I've ever experienced. There was no fear or anxiety, just a holy hush that all of us sensed. It was like I could feel Jesus and the angels coming to get her and could hear him say, "Well done, good and faithful, Alice."

There was no way to know how it would be in the end, but I didn't envision it to be so serene. At first, I was upset that I wasn't there earlier in the day but remembered that people sometimes wait for the caregiver to leave before they fully let go. Her homegoing happened as it was meant to, and I was grateful that Aunt Alice had people with her who dearly loved her when she breathed her last breath. It saddened me greatly, but at the same time it was well with my soul. I thanked the Lord she no longer suffered in her mind or body.

Grief is a process. It takes time. I wasn't overwhelmed with grief on Aunt Alice's moving day or the days and weeks that followed because I grieved the loss along the way with her. It didn't make me miss her any less or take the sting of her death away, but it gave me perspective. Even while Aunt Alice worked through her last days, we grieved together so she could live. Her life taught me what it means to choose celebration over cynicism, light over darkness, faith over fear, tenderness over toughness, compassion over cruelty, helping over hurting, generosity over greed, and last but not least, life over death.

Grace

Alice's Best Friend

I remember the first time I met Alice some twenty years ago. How could I have known that first encounter would be the beginning of a long and treasured friendship?

Alice showed up at the weight loss group I led. Since she hadn't signed up, I figured she may have been on the fence about her commitment. My first impression of her was that of a quiet, unassuming young woman, uncomfortable in her surroundings. I admired her courage to come to a group where she didn't know anyone. I suspected some inner turmoil on her part when I asked everyone to join hands in a prayer circle to end our first session of the God-centered weight loss program.

After I stated my request, Alice bolted for the doorway without saying goodbye. I thought it odd and, much to my surprise, as I completed the final clean up alone, she walked back into the classroom and cautiously approached me. She didn't make eye contact and apologized for her abrupt exit. I could tell she was nervous as she further explained that she wasn't comfortable getting into a circle due to a cult practice she was forced to participate in as a child.

Her confession caught me off guard, but I managed to say, "We will change the format around next week. I hope you'll come back." She nodded and quickly retreated from the room.

Alice did come back the next week and continued to do so until the course ended. Along with greater conversations, I developed greater insights. I sensed trust was hard won with Alice but felt I had made inroads in that area. After the twelve-week program ended, I invited her to dinner at my home, and she accepted. This was the first of many shared meals with me, my husband, and daughter.

Soon after, there was a reciprocal dinner at her apartment where she served pineapple pork, one of her favorites. My husband and I were introduced to her precious furry family members. As I looked around at her teddy bear collection and Disney paraphernalia, I sensed a fun, inner child hid inside whom I had yet to see.

In time, we discovered that we had much in common. In addition to our weight struggles, we both enjoyed simple country décor, trips to the Amish country, walking, hiking, crafts, games, and puzzles.

I often metaphorically compared Alice to a puzzle. When you open a puzzle box, you are challenged to connect the 500 or more pieces inside. The goal is to achieve the finished picture on the front of the box.

The day I met Alice, she gave me a personalized puzzle box with her life story pictured on the front, but no pieces inside. From time to time, she gave me a glimpse into her childhood or life in general. In doing so, she handed me some pieces from her puzzle box. They were given at random and as time went by, the puzzle pieces formed a detailed picture of her life.

Several years into our friendship, we took one of our much-loved trips to the Amish countryside, and stayed at our favorite bed and breakfast, the Rose Cottage. Before exploring the artsy boutiques and shops, we took advantage of some peaceful moments in the beautiful fragrant rose garden tucked behind the main building. It was a perfect fall day with a slight breeze and the temperature hovering around seventy-five degrees.

As we sat peacefully on the handcrafted wooden garden bench in conversation, Alice jumped up and said "Hang on, I want to show you something. I'll be right back." She proceeded to the trunk of her car and came back minutes later with two bulky, heavy scrapbooks filled with original art that she created during her art therapy sessions. She nervously handed them to me saying, "These will tell you a story that I am unable to speak about." Before I opened the books, a colorful butterfly flitted by; a symbol that would prove to be very significant in the future.

I knew from previous conversations that she had been abused verbally and sexually as a child, but I was not prepared for the visualization of events from her past. Page after colorful page showed the darker side of her victimization. One page, in particular, took my breath away. Alice had sketched the interior of her house showing all the rooms, including the secret one in the basement. I stared at the drawing trying to wrap my mind around the detail of what appeared to be a satanic ritual. In the center was an altar with a child lying horizontally and a hooded figure dressed in black on top of her. Others dressed in black wearing pointed hoods surrounded the altar. There were lit candles placed all around. I was mesmerized by this drawing. I couldn't stop staring at that altar. I instinctively knew it was Alice lying there and horrible unspeakable acts were happening to her. I got chills and shivered, even though the sun shone brightly.

Goosebumps appeared on my arms as I sensed the evil in the image. I was speechless. Tears welled up and spilled over. I said something like "Alice, tell me this isn't you pictured here."

Alice said, "That wasn't the only time. Turn the page and see what happened to me as a result of that."

I cautiously turned the page. There was a pencil drawing of a head. I knew it was a girl by the earrings. Depicted inside her mind were seventeen different faces. There were baby faces, little girl faces, boy faces, silly and sad faces, faces of various ages, and one faceless girl with pigtails.

It took a few minutes for my mind to comprehend what I had seen. All the different faces, or personalities, lived within Alice as a result of the hideous vile scene on the previous page. Alice quietly stated, "Now you know my deepest secret. I have not shared this with anyone outside of therapy."

That day, Alice gave me several large puzzle pieces. I got quite a picture of her tormented life, and a deeper understanding came into focus. From that time forward, Alice gave me master key access into her world and the freedom to ask questions. I often hesitated to ask anything because I didn't want to trigger a flashback or self-destructive behavior.

I had read about Dissociative Identity Disorder, formerly known as Multiple Personality Disorder, but never encountered anyone with that diagnosis. Alice did not want me to pity her or feel sorry for her in any way. She wanted to be treated normally as with any other relationship. The knowledge of what she endured freaked me out at first. I read up on DID and tried to grasp the facts surrounding the label. I prayed for understanding and acceptance. I sought professional counsel so I could better understand how to navigate pitfalls associated with the revelations about Alice's life. I didn't want Alice to think I judged her in any way because of what happened to her or what she was forced to participate in against her will. The knowledge of deeper details in Alice's story stirred up hidden emotions of my own childhood sexual abuse. I felt like my mind and emotions were on a bullet train speeding on to an unknown destination.

After Godly counsel and prayer, I concluded that nothing was really different except I now had a deeper understanding of *what* caused her brokenness and *why* life was such a struggle for her. Alice was my friend—a friend who needed unconditional love and acceptance, not judgment. About a month after I learned the secret, I couldn't help crying every time I saw her. In my mind's eye, I saw that helpless girl lying on that cold unfriendly slab and tears flowed. Along with the tears, compassion rose up. It took a great deal of courage for her to trust me with this hidden part of her life.

Over the months and years, in between shared vacations, fun events, long walks, book exchanges, crafts nights, church, and life in general, Alice handed me many more pieces of the puzzle. I rarely asked for a puzzle piece but was grateful when she freely gave them to me. Each piece brought more understanding about her childhood, her family and her experiences with self-injury, therapy, and psychiatric hospital stays.

Visits to her home of origin triggered breakdowns or trauma of some sort. I visited her when she stayed as a patient in a psych ward and tried to act brave. It was a challenge to engage with someone whose hope leaked out from so many wounds. I feared I'd say the wrong thing. I hoped that being a good listener would be enough.

One time, Alice asked me to drive her to a psychiatric hospital for a few weeks stay on the advice of her therapist. Every time I left her in these situations, I cried all the way home. I felt sorry for her and wondered why certain individuals in this world were subjected to so much heartache. But Alice was a champion, a warrior, and, in my estimation, a true heroine.

When Alice counseled with Yvonne Jordan, Penny and I were invited to several sessions to participate in her therapy. We observed Yvonne call on a variety of Alice's personalities and ask them questions. Up to this point neither Penny nor I had witnessed any other personalities surface. "What if an unknown or hostile Part manifests itself?" I asked.

In the following weeks, as Alice continued to unravel before her last in-patient treatment, I'd sit on the sofa in her home and have normal conversations. One day, I said something that triggered one of the antagonistic Parts. Alice stopped talking. In the quietness of the moment, she sat still in her chair. It was Alice—but it wasn't. Chills crept up my spine as fear gripped me. I didn't recognize the person staring back at me! Her glazed-over eyes were black darts, shooting out hatred. Her body language changed as she shifted position. Whoever it was, they didn't like me.

The Holy Spirit reminded me of Yvonne's answer to my question the day we witnessed such an episode in her office. "If that ever happens," she said, "simply ask to speak to Alice."

I held my position and called out in a panicked tone, "I'd like to speak to Alice!" In the blink of an eye, I witnessed in wonderment as Hate-filled Alice transformed back into my friend Alice. She spoke as though nothing had happened. I took a breath and continued with our conversation as if nothing happened.

Later that night, I sensed directed-hate and wondered which of her Alters was jealous of my relationship with Alice. I prayed through the situation and was grateful I never had the experience again. There may have been times when Alice flowed in and out, shifting with her co-manager Parts. But she did it so smoothly that I never noticed.

Alice told me time and again, that her faith is what carried her forward. I remember her saying, "Hope is a knot at the end of the rope. When you reach the bottom, it is there for you to grab and hold onto." I frequently encouraged her to write her journey and publish it to help others who needed hope in the midst of despair.

Alice's story is a powerful testimony to the resilience of the human experience when you put God in charge. She said she was too ashamed and embarrassed to write the details of her life. As her mind began to heal and unify into oneness, she shared little bits of her story with other trusted individuals. On a mission trip to Africa, I watched her bravely share a portion of her testimony with women prisoners.

Her biggest fear in sharing about the darker parts of her life was that she wouldn't be believed, she would be rejected, and she would be treated differently. Alice still feared the long arm of the cult. *They* certainly didn't want word getting out about who they were and what deeds of darkness they carried out.

After Alice received her ALS diagnosis, she made the brave decision to think of her last days as a *life* sentence rather than a *death* sentence. She asked me if I would consider writing her life story after she passed on to her eternal home. I immediately responded, "Of course, but what about your family? I don't want to hurt anyone."

"This is my truth," she said. "My journey and my story. If another perspective exists, they are free to write about it. I trust, with God's help, you will do what I never had the courage to do. Grace, do you know that my very name means truthful? For once in my life, I want the truth of my story out there."

Although it was Alice who asked me to write her story, I believe it was a God assignment and one I humbly agreed to do. Alice believed that if her journey from darkness into the light could help even one person, it would be worth it. She wanted everyone to know that her life wasn't an easy one, but Jesus, her Savior, made it easier with His daily deliveries of grace. When hope was low, she dug into her Bible where she had underlined key verses. She viewed Psalms in particular as a spiritual prescription and understood that there was a Kingdom purpose to her life—to her suffering. She didn't have all the answers on this side of heaven and was okay with that.

I moved in with Alice and my daughter Penny for about two weeks with the purpose of interviewing her for the book you are now reading. She was on hospice care and pretty weak at the time, confined to her hospital bed. She told me more random bits and pieces of her life but wasn't able to do it on a timeline. As chance thoughts flowed, I listened and took pages and pages of notes. She told me where her private journals were and trusted me to use them to help make sense of her story. The journals were a real gift, filled with her inner most thoughts and emotions. They were difficult to read with so many dark and gloomy thoughts. She didn't candy coat anything and was transparent and honest in her writing.

A great listener, even when she knew her time on earth was short, she wanted to know what was going on in everyone's life so she could be a part of their sacred space. It was a privilege to be a part of her life. What an incredible human being! It was a personal goal of mine to make her smile or laugh and, funny or not, she always laughed at my stupid puns and jokes.

Alice was a great personal encourager who sent handmade cards with beautifully written notes to people. When writing was no longer possible, she had someone write notes for her. Her concern for those around her was more important than anything to do with herself. Alice and love were synonymous. Up until her last breath, she radiated love.

My life is so much richer having known Alice; whose very name *means one of integrity; truthful.* She lived a life of integrity and desired that her story be one of truth. She knew her Savior brought victory over sin and darkness in her life and looked forward to seeing Jesus face to face.

Because she knew ALS would bring an untimely end to her life, she wanted to be involved with every detail including planning the celebration of her life service after she was gone. She chose a butterfly theme to represent that, after death, she would fly free without the weight of this world upon her and all would be redeemed. Papers in the shape of a butterfly, filled with Forget Me Not seeds, were to be handed out at her service. She was afraid that she would be forgotten. I reassured her that she had left a deep imprint on my heart and in the hearts of many.

I had the honor of speaking at her Life Celebration Service and shared the puzzle analogy for her life. I spoke about how a puzzle is made by finding all the border pieces to build the frame. The puzzle frame in Alice's life was her faith. No matter how dark, scary, or uncertain things were, she never lost sight of her faith. Inside that frame, she felt safe, secure and comforted that God's promises were not only true, but for her.

With her premature death, I had the last piece of her life puzzle. As it went in place, we could see a clear and beautiful picture of how God took her brokenness, depression, and shame out of darkness into His light where she could experience victorious living.

Each of us who knew her represented an important puzzle piece for Alice. Connected and linked together, we made a treasured life puzzle of her. We each played a different role and she was grateful and appreciative for all the people who intersected with her life.

With a smile, Alice told me that when she arrived in Heaven, she would reserve the mansion next to hers for me. I know if I could peek into her Heavenly home, I would see her completed life puzzle mounted in a gold frame. The gold plate above where it hangs would read, "Well done my good and faithful servant."

Part 5
APPENDIX

"The world is a needy place, lost, and broken – in need of you, Jesus." ~Alice

Group Discussion Questions
Reader's Guide

1. What intrigued you about the opening chapter? Have you known anyone with a secret or double life? How difficult do you think it would be to maintain this type of lifestyle?
2. Have you ever encountered or read about a cult group of this nature? What surprised you the most?
3. Is it possible to tell if someone is a true Christian? What does the verse, *"Thus, by their fruit you will recognize them."* (Matthew 7:20), mean to you?
4. What can we do to keep from being deceived? Is it enough to know Scriptures such as Colossians 2:8? *"See to it that no one takes you captive through hollow and deceptive philosophy, which depends on human tradition and the elemental spiritual forces of this world rather than on Christ."*
5. Alice was born into the cult and had few choices—or did she? What do you think?
6. What do you know about the subject of generational curses? Do you think these evil practices were handed down through the family lineage?
7. Was Alice's mother a victim or a bystander who knew, but didn't act?
8. Alice seems to have been singled out for abuse in her family and at school. Do people tend to oppress those they perceive as weak or different?
9. Miss Mary Miller helped Alice in various ways and showed her much kindness. Do you think Miss Miller suspected abuse? Could she have done more?
10. Miss Miller taught Alice about Jesus when she was at a young age and gave her the thread of hope she clung to throughout her life. What would have happened to Alice without her faith in God?

Group Discussion Questions

11. Reading about Alice's abuse is difficult. Have you ever suspected someone you know was/is being abused? How did/should you handle it?
12. Why didn't her brother protect her more? Do you think her Oma and Opa knew the truth?
13. Name some ways Alice coped throughout and after the ritualistic abuse.
14. Do you believe secret societies exist?
15. Did you imagine the depths of evil she was subjected to? In what ways were you rooting for Alice?
16. It took great courage for Alice to drive away and not look back. Have you ever made a difficult decision in fear, but knew it was right for you?
17. In Chapter 13, Alice shares a prayer. How did the prayer affect you?
18. Did you ever befriend someone who was "different?"
19. Why do you think Alice went home for Christmas break while at college?
20. Alice started to suspect there was more going on than meets the eye. Have you ever felt like there were more parts to you than you present to the world?
21. Have you ever wanted to escape a situation so badly, and felt there was no hope left, that you contemplated suicide?
22. Dissociative Identity Disorder (DID)—was this a mental health diagnosis you were aware of?
23. Why was it important for Alice to know about the other parts of herself?
24. Have you ever had an immediate answer to prayer like Alice finding the note under her pillow in the psychiatric ward?
25. Alice's breakdown and suicide attempt seemed a turning point in her life. Do you see it that way? Why?
26. Art Therapy is a brilliant concept toward healing. Have you ever expressed yourself through a creative medium? What did that look like for you?
27. Alice confided her deepest secret to Grace. Have you ever shared a secret about something you did or that happened to you and risked rejection?
28. Contrast the reactions/responses of Grace and Pastor X when her secrets were shared.

Group Discussion Questions

29. When Dr. Wallace retired, he gave Alice a list of truth reminders. What are some truth statements that you are committed to live by?
30. How did you respond when Alice was tasked to invite the individual alters to receive Christ and bring unity and wholeness?
31. God's perfect plan is for us to have a personal relationship with Him through the Father, Son, and Holy Spirit. Have you invited Jesus into your life like Alice did?
32. It is important that we try not to live life isolated, but as a part of a network or community, and encourage one another along the way. Do you have a support system?
33. Have you ever heard of "inner healing" or experienced it? If so, was it helpful?
34. Alice allowed Billy back into her life. Did you have any concerns for her in doing so?
35. Pastor Jack and Pastor X had two different approaches after Alice confessed her unwilling participation in the rituals. What approach would you have taken?
36. Why do you think Alice refused to stay at a hotel through the years, but kept going back to her childhood home?
37. It took great courage to seek out the ritual chamber one final time. What was she trying to prove? In what way(s) was this experience healing for her?
38. Alice's Gratitude Journal and Acts of Kindness List were inspiring. What are you grateful for? What acts of kindness can you incorporate into your life?
39. When Alice received her diagnosis, she decided to turn a death sentence into a *life* sentence. How did this impact you? Do you have a personal bucket list? Name one thing on it.
40. Alice said, "We can't control a lot of things in our lives, but the way we handle them can be a gift back to the Giver of life." How does this impact your thinking about the rest of your life?
41. Do you think the ALS diagnosis was unfair after all Alice had been through? Do you ever wonder why some people have more misfortune than others? Does it cause you to wonder how you would handle such a diagnosis?

Group Discussion Questions

42. How can God's glory be displayed in this tragic situation? Did Alice's life cause you to be more aware of the suffering around you?
43. At some point in our lives, we are all in need of comfort. Did you find solace in the list of God's promises that Pastor Jack gave Alice? Name a time when you could have used that list in your own life.
44. Is there an advantage in being prepared for death?
45. Despite the challenges her disease brought, Alice was creative with what she could still do to bless others. An example of that was her praying for all the residents in her town. What can you begin to do to each day to be a blessing to others in your sphere of influence?
46. What were your thoughts when Alice realized that she could have had a more intimate relationship with Jesus all along? If you were to embrace that truth, what changes do you need to make?
47. Alice counted her blessings and wrote letters of gratitude to be given out after her death. How did that act affect you? Make a list of everyone you are thankful for and consider writing them a note of gratitude.
48. What is your idea of the perfect way to die? If it were today, are you ready?
49. What do you hope will be spoken about you after you leave this earth?
50. What effect did Alice's life story have on you and your faith?

Resource Guide

Disclaimer: This list is by no means a comprehensive guide. The author does not guarantee positive outcomes with the hotlines listed. If you are in a crisis of any type, call 911, seek help immediately, and get to a safe place.

Abortion/Pregnancy
- **National Right to Life:** nrlc.org, 800-848-5683
- **National Safe Haven Alliance:** nationalsafehavenalliance.org, 888-510-BABY. Call this number if you want to surrender your baby or are pregnant and have questions about how the "Safely Surrendered Baby" laws in your state can help you. There are "safe surrender" sites in many locations—usually any hospital, fire station, or lifeguard station where you can safely hand over your baby with no questions asked. There are laws in place to protect your privacy and ensure that your baby is not abandoned in an unsafe place when you are in crisis.
- **After Abortion Help:** hopeafterabortion.com, Project Rachel

ALS (amyotrophic lateral sclerosis)
- Contact ALS.org for symptoms, facts, and local chapters

Anxiety/Depression
- **Anxiety and Depression Association of America (ADAA):** adaa.org, 240-485-1001, a non-profit organization providing information on prevention, treatment, and symptoms of anxiety, depression, and related conditions.

Biblical Counseling-Find a Counselor
- **AACC:** American Association of Christian Counselors, AACC.net, 800-526-8673
- **ABC:** Association of Biblical Counselors, Christiancounseling.com, 877-222-4551
- **CCEF:** Christian Counseling & Educational Foundation, CCEF.org, 215-884-7676

Child/Youth Abuse
- **National Child Abuse Hotline:** Call or text 800-422-4453 for help if you have been abused, suspect a child or teenager is being sexually abused, or if you are an abuser. Chat live with a counselor at childhelphotline.org
- **National Center for Missing and Exploited Children:** missingkids.org, 800-843-5678, Use also to communicate information to the authorities about child pornography or child sex trafficking.
- **On-line Sexual Abuse and Child Sexual Abuse Material** (Child Pornography): 800-843-5678
- **CyberTipline:** www.missingkids.org/gethelpnow/cybertipline; accepts reports of online enticement of children for sexual acts, extra-familial child sexual molestation, child pornography, child sex trafficking & tourism, and unsolicited obscene materials sent to a child.
- **National Youth Crisis Hotlines:** teencentral.com/help/

Depression
- **Depression Hotline:** 630-482-9696
- **Depression and Bipolar Support Alliance (DBSA):** dbsalliance.org, 800-826-3632

Domestic Violence
- **The National Domestic Violence Hotline:** thehotline.org, 800-799-7233

Eating Disorders
- **National Center of Excellence for Eating Disorders (NCEED):** nceedus.org, 800-931-2237

- **National Eating Disorders Association:** nationaleatingdisorders.org, 800-931-2237

Human Trafficking
- **National Human Trafficking Hotline:** humantraffickinghotline.org, 888-373-7888 or text HELP to 233733.

Mental Health including info on Dissociative Identity Disorder (DID)
- **National Institute of Mental Health (NIMH):** nimh.nih.gov, 866-615-6464
- **National Alliance on Mental Illness (NAMI):** nami.org, 800-950-6264
- **Dissociative Research:** did-research.org

Rape/Sexual Assault Hotlines
- **The National Sexual Assault Hotline:** rainn.org, 800-656-4673
- **Safe Horizons Rape, Sexual Assault, and Incest Hotline:** safehorizons.org, 212-227-3000
- **Take Back the Night Foundation Hotline:** takebackthenight.org, 567-742-8837, Legal support

Self-Harm & Cutting
- helpguide.org, 800-DONT-CUT (366-8288)

Suicide
- **National Suicide Prevention Lifeline:** suicidepreventionlifeline.org, 800-273-8255

Substance Abuse
- **Substance Abuse & Mental Health Services Administration (SAMHSA):** samhsa.gov, 800-662-4357

About the Author

CJ Schaeffer is a certified Biblical Counselor and licensed pastor with Elim Fellowship, active in ministry at her local church. She retired after twenty-five years of service in Children's Ministry and is noted for her generous hospitality and humorous manner of encouragement.

As a writer, she's published many op-ed pieces for her hometown newspaper and created children's missions curriculums, plus devotional material and magazine articles. An accomplished speaker, CJ has shared stories of her own childhood sexual abuse at numerous women and church events, stateside and internationally. She is a passionate advocate for the pro-life agenda and victims of human trafficking.

CJ has lived in seven states and extensively traveled when she resided in Germany. Mission trips have taken her to Russia, Poland, South Africa, and Madagascar. She and her husband currently reside on the East Coast where she holds the titles of Mom and Stepmom to four wonderful adult children and proud Oma to five grandchildren. Her active days include a host of hobbies that add joy to her life such as reading—with cozy mysteries being a favorite genre—word and jigsaw puzzles, cooking, baking, hiking, and traveling especially during the fall foliage season. But her greatest delight is spending time with family, including their sweet cockapoo. *My Life in Pieces* is CJ Schaeffer's first book.

About the Author

If Alice's story has touched your heart in some way, please share this book or purchase one for someone you believe could benefit from her incredible life journey. We all know someone within our sphere of influence who needs help, hope, or the Gospel message.

Additional copies of *My Life in Pieces* are available for purchase at the author's website, www.cj-schaeffer.com or through Amazon. The purchase of this book will help support victims of child abuse.

Planning an in-house or virtual event? Invite CJ Schaeffer, she would love to meet you. She is passionate about *Speaking Hope to the Hearts of the Broken*.

Contact her via email, CJ.Schaeffer@icloud.com to schedule book club chats, book signings, recovery groups, women's events, church events, conference break-out sessions, retreats, or fundraisers. Information can be found on her website, www.cj-schaeffer.com or follow her on Facebook at CJ Schaeffer, Author.